P9-CRR-350

# what next?

## Barbara Moses, Ph.D.

DK PUBLISHING

LONDON, NEW YORK, MUNICH,
MELBOURNE and DELHI

Editor **Don Bastian**
Senior Editor **May Corfield**
Senior Art Editor **Steve Woosnam-Savage**
DTP Designer **Rajen Shah**
Production Controller **Heather Hughes**

Managing Editor **Adèle Hayward**
Managing Art Editor **Karen Self**
Category Publisher **Stephanie Jackson**

First American Edition, 2003

Published in the United States by
DK Publishing, Inc.
375 Hudson Street
New York, New York 10014

03 04 05 06 07 08 10 9 8 7 6 5 4 3 2 1

Text Copyright © 2003 Dr. Barbara Moses

All rights reserved under International and Pan-American
Copyright Conventions. No part of this publication may be
reproduced, stored in any retrieval system, or transmitted
in any form or by any means, electronic, mechanical,
photocopying, recording, or otherwise, without the prior
permission of the copyright owner. Published in
Great Britain by Dorling Kindersley Limited.

A Cataloging-in-Publication record for this book is available
from the Library of Congress

ISBN 0-7894-9355-1

Reproduced by Media Development Printing Ltd, UK
Cover reproduced by Colourscan, Singapore
Printed and bound in Great Britain by Butler & Tanner

See our complete product line at
www.dk.com

# Contents

*"How do I find or create work that is true to my individual nature and makes me feel good about myself—work for which I am uniquely suited?"*

# Introduction

We work for many reasons. Of course, we work for money, but that is not enough for most of us. We also work to be intellectually engaged, to make a difference, to satisfy our needs for connection to others, to refine our craft, to be appreciated for our contribution, to satisfy deeply held personal values. Some of these reasons are more important to us than others.

Each of us has our own story to tell. Each of us is grappling with our own unique career concerns. The new graduate wants to know how to discover what type of work is right for her. The young parent wonders how he can advance in his career and still fulfill parenting responsibilities. The mid-career professional is searching for meaningful work that matches her most important values. The recently fired manager asks, "How can I find and keep work that plays to my special talents?"

Yet, if I had to distill the underlying quest for most of us, it would be this: "How do I find or create work that is true to my individual nature and makes me feel good about myself—work for which I am uniquely suited?"

### The quest for your great work

Work is one of the most intimate expressions of our identity. Bad work crushes us. It destroys our sense of competence and spills over into all areas of our life. Great work, in contrast, inspires us. It makes our souls sing. It allows us to be the best we can be.

Great work provides a sense of purpose and gives our days meaning. It enables us to look after financial needs and still have time for a life; plays to our strengths and provides us the environments we are happiest in; engages us deeply at an emotional and intellectual level. Great work allows us, indeed demands of us, the expression of all our important values, talents, and motivators.

You want great work. That is why you are embarking on this career journey. That is why you are asking yourself one of the most important questions you will ever ask: "What next?"

## What next?

If you are asking this question, you are on the threshold of a new life chapter. The answer to this question will be as individual as you are.

The move you make may be sweeping, such as starting your first real job, making a radical career change, reconfiguring your life in a major way, moving to self-employment after years of working for someone else, or returning to work after a long career break. Then again, the move could be more subtle, such as a shift in your employment status, stretching yourself in a new and unforeseen way, upgrading your skills, taking a lifestyle sabbatical, going back to school, volunteering. Sweeping or subtle, the move you make will have a significant impact on how you feel about your life.

## Two key principles

Underlying this book are two main ideas. The first is: be who you are and express your authentic self in your work. Your work should allow you to express your unique talents and deeply held personal values. It should not require you to wear a mask, or repress important aspects of yourself.

The second principle is: be a career activist. When you are a career activist, you expect—in fact, demand—good work as a right, not a privilege. This means, first, that you have a vision of yourself as worthy of great work, and, second, that you are vigilant in ensuring that your work meets your needs. It also means that you will make the necessary moves to find or create work that plays to your special talents and values.

This book makes it easy for you to follow and apply these principles. As an intelligent person, you need more than canned motivational career advice, such as, "You can be anything you want to be as long as you want it badly enough." You need:

- Information about what makes you unique as an individual.
- A structure for thinking about yourself and the moves you need to make.
- New ideas and inspiring stories and images.

*When you are a career activist, you expect good work as a right, not a privilege.*

*The contemporary work landscape poses many challenges that are both tough and exciting.*

- Information about how you fit with and relate to different work environments.
- Clear advice on what works, why, and how.
- Advice grounded in an understanding of the demands placed on the contemporary worker and the trends that will affect careers.

In my career I have talked to thousands of people of all age groups and from every type of work. I have learned what people struggle with, where they get derailed, and what they need to do to overcome the challenges. In this book, I will show you how to think about and manage life and work issues, as well as provide you with tools to support you throughout your journey, including:

- Diagnostic instruments
- Guided exercises
- Quizzes
- Easy-to-follow samples, models, and worked examples.

I hope that you will think of this book as, in effect, your own personal career counselor and coach.

## Trends that will affect your career

Before you embark on your journey, you need to understand the external landscape that will affect your career and life choices.

The contemporary work landscape poses many challenges that are both tough and exciting. What is tough is that regardless of whether you are self-employed or working for an organization, you are on your own.

You can make no assumptions about employment or income continuity. This means you can never rest on your laurels, and that you must have the mind-set of a temporary worker as you constantly re-earn your right to employment. Work is a constant audition, and you will need to prove and reprove continually that you have the right skills, attitudes, and know-how to be "the best person" for the job.

Your work will be fast and fluid as the teams you are working on constantly reconfigure to meet new challenges. You will need to adapt quickly to master new subject areas, to establish effective working relationships with a rapidly changing cast of players, and to communicate with team members from different disciplines, possibly across large geographical distances without the benefit of face-to-face interaction.

The good news is that even if you cannot make any assumptions about income continuity, you will still have security—the security that comes from being a career activist, the security you create for yourself in knowing your skills are up to date and that you are employable in many work settings. This means not only having the right skills, but also being able to articulate and market them effectively.

Baby-boomer retirements will cause talent shortages in many areas. If you have skills in an in-demand area, organizations will compete to attract and retain your talent. They will offer their unique value proposition based on their culture and enlightened policies toward personal development, wellness, flexible work arrangements, and benefits. Skills shortages are also good news for older workers, who will be courted actively by employers to stay longer in the workplace in some capacity, whether on a part-time or contract basis.

Talent shortages will also put you in the driver's seat. Instead of feeling beholden to your employer, your relationship will be based on mutual exchange—you rent your skills in exchange for learning opportunities and life-friendly work arrangements as well as financial rewards. When your work no longer meets your needs, you will have the confidence to vote with your feet and move on.

Of course, despite the looming talent shortages, there will always be economic fluctuations, as well as sectors and roles in which it is more difficult to find work. This book will show you how to think strategically about your career, in good times or in bad, so that regardless of the economic environment you find yourself in, you can find and engage in the work that is right for you.

*Work is a constant audition, and you will need to prove and re-prove continually that you have the right skills for the job.*

*These experiences along your path will be life-enhancing as well as career-enhancing.*

The best news? You are no longer governed by a strict starting line, such as university graduation, or a finish line, official retirement. Instead, you will have many chapters, each of which meets important needs, whether it be career advancement, education, pursuit of personal passions, time for family, volunteering. You will move in and out of these life domains throughout your career; smart employers—the ones you want to work for —will recognize the value of each of these experiences. These experiences along your path will be life-enhancing as well as career-enhancing and will contribute to a satisfying and rewarding career.

## Managers, human-resources professionals: take note

This book contains fresh ideas and information on attracting, retaining, and coaching the new worker, including developing and rewarding people based on their motivational type, designing work environments and cultures that meet the needs of today's worker, coaching a burned-out or bored staff member, and understanding the skill and attitude requirements for success in different roles and functions. As you complete the exercises, ask yourself, "What are the implications for me as a coach, mentor, people developer, recruiter, and creator of a great organizational culture?"

## Create your own path

Follow the path to great work by going through this book thoughtfully and carefully. Use the Self-Assessment exercises to get a fix on your unique personality traits, motivations, skills, and aspirations. Based on those findings about yourself, use the Portfolio exercises as a creative method to plan, rejuvenate, redesign, or change your career. Begin at the beginning, with the first section, Know yourself. Whatever your career stage or dilemma—starting out, searching for work, dealing with a career crisis, or looking to find more meaning in your work—this is the foundation for answering the question, "What next?" Your self-assessment will be comprehensive along many dimensions, including your motivational type, your core competencies, your underlying career themes, and your most important values.

After that, chart your own course. After all, you have your own unique story, and your own unique needs. In the second section, Find your perfect path, you will assess all the work possibilities. Learn how to think like an organizational psychologist, and about the personality of 10 organizational sectors and numerous functions and roles. Consider different types of work arrangements such as self-employment, telecommuting, and working part-time, and determine which of these is a good match for you. Evaluate other options such as a career change and a portfolio career as the path to finding renewed meaning and purpose.

The section Find great work shows you how to find, design, or create great work by uncovering opportunities, preparing compelling marketing materials, presenting yourself in interviews as the talent the organization needs, and negotiating the best offer.

At some point in your working life, most of you will experience some type of career distress. You may suffer from a low-grade malaise or a full-blown career crisis. You may feel bored or burned out. You may be looking for greater passion. Or perhaps you are struggling to obtain greater balance between your work and personal life. In section 4, Overcome career challenges, I show you how to manage and overcome these difficulties. Different life stages also pose their unique challenges—read the advice for younger and older workers. Learn special strategies for your career stage.

In section 5, you will learn how to boost your career intelligence. Take the quiz to determine your career-activist quotient, and learn how to increase it. Understand how to apply the 12 new strategies for career success in the contemporary workscape.

*Now it is time to start your journey.*

*Chart your own course. After all, you have your own unique story, and your own unique needs.*

# 1 Know yourself

# Who are you

Your work should speak directly and truthfully to your most important values, motivators, and strengths. This is the key to finding, designing, and shaping work that is right for you—work that you love. If you are asking yourself, "What next?" then now is the time to drill down and uncover the answer.

## This chapter shows you how to:

**Look** inside and discover your unique personal constellation of values, aspirations, talents, and life circumstances.

**Ask** the right questions and identify the real issues you are grappling with, foreshadowing future solutions.

**Drill** down and find the answers to the questions you are asking about your career journey.

**Uncover** underlying career themes that have run through your life, from childhood on.

**Recover** excitement of early career themes—the motivations that may still shape your work.

**Follow** the clues from your early work experience to set your future career direction.

*Most of us recognize others' unique characteristics, but do not understand how we are unique.*

# Making the right career decisions

Embark on your career journey by asking yourself the right questions: Who am I? What do I really care about? What are my core strengths? The answers to those questions will get you started. Recognizing your uniqueness is the foundation of making critical work and life decisions.

"What makes you unique?" I often start my career-planning workshops with this question. It startles people. Usually they say, "I don't know" or "I've never really thought about myself in those terms." A few recite singular achievements: "I got good grades in chemistry" or "I won a community award for volunteer work." These are important pieces of information but do not describe who they are.

Most of us recognize others' unique characteristics, but do not understand how we are unique. We do not see our own particular constellation of values, skills, and personality traits. As a result, we make critical decisions about how we want to live and work without thinking about our own very particular needs and desires, about what makes our souls sing. We take the wrong work, or pass up the right work. We choose to continue in unfulfilling work. We chase someone else's dream. We then experience a nagging dissatisfaction, or maybe something worse. We say, "I don't know what to do." "I feel stuck." In other words, we know something is wrong but we do not know why.

### Look inside

When considering a career move, most of us look outside. We search for some great new job or some magic formula that will make our uncertainty go away.

The recent college graduate who is choosing between several options or says she does not have a clue about her professional interests asks, "Should I go into Field A or Field B?" instead of "What are my unique talents? What do I need in a working environment to feel truly engaged?" The mother trying to balance her professional and personal commitments asks, "Should I work part-time?" instead of "What do I want to achieve at this stage in my life? What trade-offs am I prepared to make to get it? What important needs will this fulfill and how?"

The ambitious executive who says he wants to reap the rewards for his own efforts asks, "Should I start my own business?" instead of "What special talents do I have to sell? Do I have reason to believe people will want my services or product? Do I have the temperament and skills for self-employment?"

The questions we need to ask ourselves are much more fundamental, because they go directly to our core. In the next several chapters you will drill down to that core. You will assess your uniqueness by conducting a rigorous self-assessment of your underlying career motivations, your most important values, your special talents, and what you need in a work environment to feel happy and engaged.

# Career counsel

I meet many people who are unhappy professionally. They say they do not like their work, attributing their distress to the technical content of their work.

Often these people, when they go through a meaningful self-assessment, discover that what is really bothering them is something else entirely, such as the pace of their work or a controlling manager. They do not need a career change. They need a minor adjustment to the work they already have. Self-knowledge means being aware not only of what makes you feel good about yourself but also of what makes you unhappy. If you do not know where it hurts, you cannot fix it and you cannot avoid it in the future.

### Assessing your motivation

*Take this time in your life to ask yourself the right questions, uncovering the issues that are unique to you.*

# Career counsel

If you are like most people, in thinking about what you want and need in your professional work life you will identify one or two salient elements. "I want to work with people," you might say. Fine, but what kinds of people do you want to work with? What kinds of work relationships do you want? Do you want to work in a team environment? Do you want opportunities to brainstorm with others but prefer to do the work essentially by yourself? Or maybe you say you want to move out of your comfort zone, without knowing what kind of work would make you feel stretched. Will going someplace new do it? Will putting yourself on the line with a high-stakes project?

## Liberate opportunities

On a personal level, self-assessment answers the questions, "How do I want to be in the world? What will give me a sense of purpose?" On a practical level, self-assessment reveals and liberates opportunities, just as lack of self-knowledge hides and limits them. The more you know about yourself, and the more clearly you can describe your own strengths, preferences, and values, the more options you will begin to see.

## Focus on what you want

Self-assessment also enables you to present yourself to employers in a compelling way. Ask people what they are good at and they typically respond with a cliché such as, "I've got strong communication skills." In translation this could mean:

> "I can quickly establish rapport with people and gain their trust regardless of who they are."

> "I can communicate clearly when I'm presenting to a group of people but I'm awkward in casual interactions."

> "I can work with people who are different from me."

> "I develop strong working relationships with peers, although actually I'm not that good at giving direction to people who report to me."

Most of us define our skills in terms of our job or job title, which limits our career options to that occupation. Consider, for example, the difference between the following two descriptions: "I am a business reporter for the *Acme Post*" vs. "I am a writer with a strong narrative voice, deep knowledge of how business works, the capacity to get to the essence of a story, strong skills in getting people to open up. I currently work for the *Acme Post*." Which description do you think is more compelling?

## Play to your strengths

After completing a self-assessment, rather than celebrate their special talents, many people worry about what they are not good at. Motivational speakers suggest that we can be whatever we want to be if only we want something badly enough and try hard enough. The truth is, we each have our unique portfolio of strengths and aptitudes, as well as areas in which we have less aptitude. Longitudinal psychological studies, which follow people from childhood, have shown that as people age, their personalities do not usually change significantly. The shy child usually becomes the introverted adult, the extroverted child the gregarious adult.

Keep in mind that work is elastic. Being gifted in certain areas can compensate for relative weaknesses in others. If you do have a liability, find ways to minimize the demand for that ability in your work. Many people think they should try to correct their weaknesses. It is true that, with concerted effort, you may be able to develop skills in areas where you have difficulty. A better idea, however, is to play to your strengths, focusing on those strengths and developing your skills in those areas. Are you a good communicator? Become a great communicator. Do you have strong professional skills? Become even more accomplished. You will get more returns on your investment of time and effort.

**Developing your skills**
*Great teachers make ideas perform with their superior communication skills. Smart career moves involve doing work that plays to special talents.*

## Own a portfolio of skills

The key is not to define yourself by your work but to think of yourself as the owner of a self-managed portfolio, a unique group of talents, skills, and competencies that you can use in a wide range of settings. The writer mentioned above could reconfigure her skills in different ways depending on her interests and the other skills in her portfolio. Possible options include:

- Writing a book on a high-profile business scandal.
- Self-employment as a public-relations consultant.
- Speech writing.
- Covering the business beat on television.

The more knowledge of the elements in your portfolio, the more career choices you have.

*The key is not to define yourself by your work but to think of yourself as the owner of a self-managed portfolio.*

**Making time to reflect**

*This is about you, your happiness, and your life satisfaction. Reflect meaningfully. What do you need to feel good about your life?*

# 11 **ways** to maximize your journey

Most of us are so busy simply keeping up with our overcommitted lives that we have lost a sense of what we care about and what we are good at. If we do not step back from the daily frenzy, we will not be able to abstract from our experience what gives us a sense of purpose and makes us feel good about ourselves.

Take this time for yourself. This is about you. Your life may depend on it.

▶ Reflect. Put aside time to complete the exercises in this part of the book. You will get more out of your self-assessment if you complete it over a few sessions rather than doing it all at once. This will give you time to think about what you are learning.

▶ "Divorce" your identity from your profession or job title. Think of yourself as the owner of a self-managed portfolio of skills and attributes that you can apply in many work settings.

▶ Dig down. Get to your core.

▶ Throw away the old scripts. Separate what you think you should want and be, and what others think you should want and be, from who you are and what you really care about. Be honest. This is for your eyes only—unless you want to share it with someone else.

▶ Think big. Open yourself up to new ideas. Be creative. Brainstorm.

▶ Get feedback. If you are not sure about your assessment findings, check them against the perceptions of others who know you well.

▶ Focus on areas most relevant to you and the particular career issues you are grappling with right now.

▶ Revisit your self-assessment as you go along. This is a process. Learning more about yourself in one area will shed new light on other areas. Look for underlying themes and patterns.

▶ Record your learning in the manner best suited to your learning style, whether directly on the pages of this book, in a personal-learning diary, or on a computer and whether pictorially or through charts. Use highlighters to underscore key points and themes.

▶ If you are someone who learns best by talking things through, share your thinking and discoveries with a work partner or partners. Set up regular meetings, and use each other as sounding boards.

▶ Find inspiration from an idea or image that you relate to at a deeper emotional or intellectual level. Place it in a prominent position.

# Uncovering your career themes

As a child, what did you think you wanted to be when you got older? Answering that question may be more revealing than you think, helping you get in touch with your underlying career themes.

Most of us have images of who we want to be in the world. These images are at the core of our identity.

*"I want to make people feel good about themselves."*
*"I want to make a difference in the world."*
*"I want to be famous."*
*"I want to be the best at what I do."*
*"I want to be liked."*
*"I want to be successful."*

We start developing these images in childhood, when they are typically coded as an occupation, such as fireman or ballerina. As children we do not understand the content of the occupation, but it represents something important to us, such as being a hero or an object of adulation. As we age, we may refine these images or reject them in favor of ones that hold more meaning.

Many of us, however, do not refine our images. We continue, sometimes unknowingly, to act on imperatives that are no longer true. Consider the adult whose parents pressured him when he was a child to be the perfect student, perfect athlete, perfect class leader. Today in his work he single-mindedly pursues work that brings success and recognition. However, he is frustrated and feels like a failure. The problem is, he is living to social expectations and not to his own images.

Frustration can also result when we repress or drift away from our childhood images. Perhaps they embarrass us because we think that they make us seem superficial ("I want to be famous") or naive ("I want to change the world"). Often we simply forget them in the melee of daily life.

## Career counsel

About 70 percent of people I have surveyed say it is just an accident that they are doing the work they are doing. When they go through a self-assessment they discover that the work is more or less a good fit—even if it no longer meets their present needs. Instinctively, they had moved toward work that they were good at, and away from work that did not suit them. Other people realize that they are operating from old aspirations no longer true of them. Still others discover that they have drifted away from or lost the image that is fundamental to their life's purpose—their "calling." What is your inner story about who you want to be in the world? When you were 12 years old, what did you see yourself doing later in life? What did that mean to you?

*First jobs, much like first romances, are pivotal experiences that provoke intensely positive or negative emotions.*

When we forget or deliberately deny these images, we feel that something is missing. We have a sense of longing, but we are not sure for what. The result is a nagging malaise or disappointment. However, the images continue to influence our behavior.

### Get in touch with your inner story

Sometimes the influence of our inner stories is positive, sometimes negative. These images may push us toward new and exciting challenges, or they can tie us up in knots. The important thing, though, is to be able to listen to these stories. Then you can see what may be guiding your behavior, and whether the script you are following still makes any sense.

What did you want to be when you grew up? You may have imagined yourself as a lawyer because you wanted to fight for the rights of the little guy. Or as a nurse because you wanted to help people in pain. Getting in touch with these underlying images of yourself can provide important information about what you need from your work and life.

### Learn from early work experiences

My father got me my first job. It was at a stock-brokerage firm. It took me less than two hours to realize I could not spend the rest of the summer chained to a desk, doing something I neither understood nor cared about. I quit and got a job selling postcards at a fairground, instead.

I loved this new work, realizing quickly that it met my need for autonomy—self-knowledge that became fundamental to my later career explorations and decision-making.

### Identify underlying career themes

First jobs, much like first romances, are pivotal experiences that provoke intensely positive or negative emotions. The early career years are when our underlying career themes begin to emerge. If we think about our experiences, we can learn about what interests us. For example:

- managing people vs. being an individual contributor
- developing ideas vs. making things happen

**Early work experiences**

*Young workers should not dismiss what they learned in early jobs. These experiences provide rich information about their likes and dislikes regarding the pace of the work, the amount and nature of people interactions, the kinds of problems they had to solve, and how they were treated.*

Other foundational career themes to explore might be:

- Nurturing others.
- Resolving troubled situations.

Unfortunately, we often forget these career themes just as we lose our images and stories of who we want to be. "I feel flat." "My work does not interest me." "I feel like something is missing." These are frequent presenting complaints that career counselors hear from clients in their 30s, 40s, and beyond. As we get older, we often drift away from our original sources of engagement and reasons for attraction to a particular type of work.

If you feel something is missing but you are not sure what, start to piece together the puzzle. Look at your early work experiences and expectations and initial reasons for being attracted to your particular type of work or profession. Of course, as you will see later when you look at your values, going through natural adult lifestyle changes will change what is important to you.

**Assessing** yourself

**Who are you?**

▶ Learning from early work experiences
*pages 22–23*

▶ Revealing core career themes
*pages 24–25*

## SELF-ASSESSMENT    **Learning from** early work experiences

This exercise is particularly useful if you have little or no "real" work experience or have been out of the workplace for some time. But it can be interesting even for those who are in mid-career.

Think about your early work experiences.
*What did you like?*

........................................................................................................

........................................................................................................

*What did you hate?*

........................................................................................................

........................................................................................................

Here are some things to think about:
*Was the work fast-paced (a lot going on) or slow-paced (not enough going on)?*

........................................................................................................

*Were you bored? Why?*

........................................................................................................

........................................................................................................

*Did you have any say over how you did your work?*
*Did you like that?*

........................................................................................................

*Would you have liked more freedom? Less freedom?*

........................................................................................................

*Did you get feedback from your supervisor? Would you have liked more feedback?*

........................................................................................................

........................................................................................................

*What skills did you use?*

.................................................................................................

.................................................................................................

.................................................................................................

.................................................................................................

.................................................................................................

*How much people interaction was involved? Would you have liked more? Less?*

.................................................................................................

*Did you demonstrate initiative? How?*

.................................................................................................

.................................................................................................

.................................................................................................

.................................................................................................

*Did you demonstrate leadership skills? How?*

.................................................................................................

.................................................................................................

.................................................................................................

.................................................................................................

*What did you learn about yourself from your work experience?*

.................................................................................................

.................................................................................................

.................................................................................................

.................................................................................................

*All work experience, good or bad, simple or complex, matters.*

## SELF-ASSESSMENT  **Revealing core** career themes

This exercise is particularly valuable if you are well into your career and have a sense that something is missing.

Drill down, reflect on your earliest images of work.

*What were your early desires that drew you to your work or profession?*

..................................................................................................
..................................................................................................
..................................................................................................
..................................................................................................
..................................................................................................

*Are those desires still true of you today?*

..................................................................................................

*Does your work allow you to express those desires?*

..................................................................................................

*Can you detect underlying career themes? What are they?*

..................................................................................................
..................................................................................................
..................................................................................................
..................................................................................................
..................................................................................................

*Identify two work experiences (more if you are older) that you really liked.*

..................................................................................................
..................................................................................................
..................................................................................................
..................................................................................................

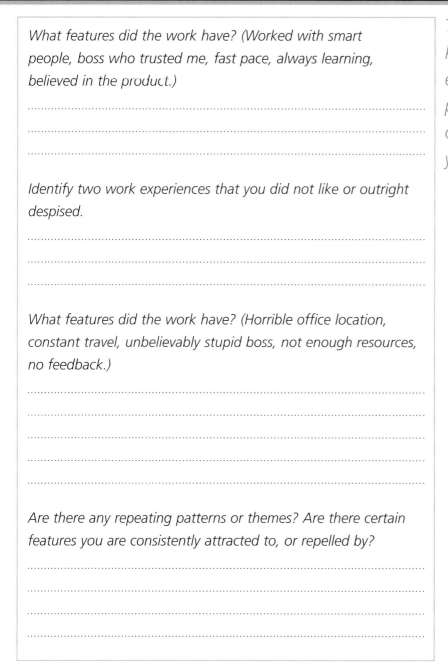

What features did the work have? (Worked with smart people, boss who trusted me, fast pace, always learning, believed in the product.)

..................................................................................

..................................................................................

..................................................................................

Identify two work experiences that you did not like or outright despised.

..................................................................................

..................................................................................

..................................................................................

What features did the work have? (Horrible office location, constant travel, unbelievably stupid boss, not enough resources, no feedback.)

..................................................................................

..................................................................................

..................................................................................

..................................................................................

..................................................................................

Are there any repeating patterns or themes? Are there certain features you are consistently attracted to, or repelled by?

..................................................................................

..................................................................................

..................................................................................

..................................................................................

*The more knowledge of the elements in your portfolio, the more career choices you have.*

# What is your motivational type?

You have a unique constellation of values and motivators that determines your major and minor motivators: what you need in your work and your life to have a sense of purpose and to feel happy and engaged. Knowing what motivates you will give you clear direction in what type of work you should be doing, and what you need to avoid.

## This chapter shows you how to:

**Assess** yourself against eight key motivators and determine your major and minor motivational types.

**Build** on the strengths of your motivational type in environments that support your work style and preferences.

**Identify**, based on your motivational type, the work roles and the environments that you should avoid.

**Know** your most important values and the degree to which they are being satisfied in your work and your life.

**Identify** the persisting conflicts between your motivators and values and make the right trade-offs.

**Determine** what changes you need to make to satisfy your values and to reach your goals.

**Achieving success**

*Ambitious career builders apply as much determination and stamina to their exercise program as they do to their work.*

# Discovering your core motivators

Most of us fit into one or two of eight distinct motivational types. Identifying your major and minor motivational types will help reveal the kind of work that will provide you with the greatest sense of purpose.

*Peter and Jill, both 25, have just received their professional certification as accountants. Both have undergraduate degrees in business from the same prestigious university, and both are working for the same professional-services firm. The similarities end there. Peter is a musician and has his own band. When he applied to his undergraduate program he was torn between studying music or taking a more "practical" course. "No one makes a living from music," his parents argued. "With a professional degree you know you can always get work." Reluctantly, Peter gave in.*

*Today, Peter enjoys his work at the firm, but he remains torn. He is considering going part-time in his work so he has more time to rehearse. He thinks his band has a real chance of making it.*

*Jill, in contrast, has always been ambitious. From the time she was 12, she knew she wanted to be successful. She imagined herself in a big house and in an important career. In college she was captain of the women's field-hockey team and started an entrepreneurial society, matching students' business ideas to venture capital.*

*Although she is not sure what she ultimately wants to do—perhaps become a partner, perhaps shift into industry and move up from there— Jill still has the same long-term vision of success.*

*Peter is a lifestyler. Right now work pays the bills, but the flexibility to pursue his dreams is important to him. Jill is a career builder. Advancement in her field is her key value.*

## Motivational types

Lifestylers and career builders are just two of eight motivational types
I have identified through my research with people of all occupations.
The eight types are:

- Sociability seekers
- Career builders
- Authenticity seekers
- Personal developers
- Autonomy seekers/entrepreneurs
- Novelty seekers
- Stability seekers
- Lifestylers.

Each motivational type possesses a unique constellation of motivators,
values, and challenges. Some will stay stable throughout a person's life,
others will change depending on new values and emerging life
circumstances. There are no "good" or "bad" types. Instead, there
are strengths associated with each one, as well as potential trouble
spots and common conflicts. Your challenge is to find a work
environment that provides the best possible match for you at this
particular stage in your life.

## Matching work with your motivators

You can find most motivational types represented in all work sectors and
all types of work—but not always happily. Below I describe the types of
roles and work environments in which people with a particular
motivational type are often happily employed, to give you a
better sense of each type and the areas that are potentially a
better or worse fit. Few people are purely one type. Typically
they have one key motivator—what I call a major—with one or
two other important driving motivations, their minors.

The following descriptions are idealized and will not describe
you perfectly. Some statements will be truer of you than others
within a given type. As you read, underline statements that are
most true of you. After you read each description, indicate on
the scale the extent to which it is true of you. After you have
gone through all eight types, the exercises will guide you in
thinking further about your motivational type.

*Your challenge
is to find a work
environment that
provides the best
possible match
for you.*

### Thriving on change

*Novelty seekers crave constant
change and challenge in their
work. A job as an overseas tour
guide escorting people for an
adventure vacation company
could fulfill this need.*

*"I'm a people person. I get my energy from being and working with others. Spending too much time by myself makes me restless and lonely."*

## Sociability seekers

If you are a sociability seeker, you love working closely in group environments where there is a lot of banter and social interaction. You want to get to know your colleagues, teammates, or clients personally. You may also enjoy seeing them socially. Your career is important—but working with people you enjoy means even more.

You like belonging to something bigger than yourself and feel a strong sense of loyalty to your co-workers. As a sociability seeker, you are usually attracted to working for larger organizations, but you may choose to work in smaller firms as long as there are enough people to form significant bonds with. You may even have your own business. Whatever the structure of your work, the pleasures of that work flow from relationships with co-workers and clients.

One thing you may find unpleasant is how difficult it is these days to establish a meaningful connection with colleagues. Restructurings are common, and although you may work on teams, they are constantly shifting as people move from project to project.

You are at your best when working with others, getting energy from their ideas, brainstorming. You find it difficult to discipline yourself when you have to work alone. People may describe you as more of a "doer" than a "thinker."

At school you probably found your social life competing with your academic life. You were involved in many student activities. You are more likely to have pursued studies in social sciences, liberal arts, hospitality and tourism, business, or engineering than in the physical or biological sciences, library science, or mathematics—professions with less interaction built right into them.

**To what extent does this describe you?**

| Not at all | | Somewhat | | A lot |
|---|---|---|---|---|
| 1 | 2 | 3 | 4 | 5 |

# Behavioural implications

**Your strengths:**
- Easily and quickly establish relationships with people. Put people at ease.
- Comfortable in unstructured social interactions (before the meeting starts, at conferences with people you do not know).
- Relationship building and sales (although you may have difficulty closing the sale).

**Potential trouble spots:**
- Working alone; having to spend too much time behind closed doors.
- Working with unfriendly people.
- Constantly changing teams without enough time to establish relationships.
- Making the transition from social conversations to task-focused interactions in meetings, on the phone, closing sales.
- Giving negative feedback to or exercising managerial control/authority over an employee with whom you are friendly.
- Feeling hurt when people are abrupt or do not reciprocate your friendliness.
- Properly evaluating the competence of staff because you naturally accept people.
- Deferring to the opinion of the group in order to fit in and be liked.
- Making independent decisions.

**You are most likely to be happily employed in:**
- All work environments, especially professional-advisory services, customer service, hospitality, retail, banking, government, administration, large public and private sector utilities such as hydroelectric, gas, telecoms.
- Services that require a high level of social interaction such as hairdressing (as opposed to massage) or training.
- Customer-service roles.

**You are least likely to be happily employed in:**
- Your own business, especially in work that has little social interaction such as gardening or freelance writing.
- Creative work.
- Information technology including new media.
- Data management/librarian.

**Are you likely to change?**
- Your preference for collegiality will not change much over the course of your career.

## Career builders

Today's career builders to some degree resemble their careerist predecessors who climbed their way, rung by rung, up the corporate ladder. Today, however, rather than moving up in a linear fashion in one company or even one industry, you may leapfrog to another company in another industry. Indeed, your long-term goal may be to start and run your own company. Career builders think strategically about every career move they make. "How will this advance my career?" "Will this look good on my résumé?" "Will it help increase my level and status?" You choose to work on projects with high visibility important to senior management. You want to be recognized for your work.

Some career builders have a clear goal in mind—to become CEO, to become a hotel general manager, to run their own firm—although they may revise that goal as they go along. Others do not have a clear sense of direction. Their guiding principle is that each move will take them higher. Career builders can be very unsentimental. They focus on whether work is résumé-enhancing rather than personally engaging. Hugh, for example, when asked if he liked his new work, said, "I don't care about the product, or what the general manager is like. I'm here to learn what I need—hard-core finance skills—so I can buy a company later on."

But even "macho" career builders can find themselves in an intolerable work situation, as Hugh ultimately did. This can create conflict: Do I plow on and get the great skills while being miserable or do I walk away?

At school you are more likely to have pursued a degree in career-oriented disciplines, such as business, engineering, or law, than in the arts or social sciences. You probably played a leadership role in high-profile societies and activities.

*"I'll be honest with you. I'm ambitious. Every step should take me one step higher—to a bigger responsibility with more prestige and money."*

**To what extent does this describe you?**

| Not at all | | Somewhat | | A lot |
|---|---|---|---|---|
| 1 | 2 | 3 | 4 | 5 |

# **Behavioural** implications

### Your strengths:
- Strong achievement orientation.
- Will take qualified risks for the right payoff, such as learning a skill that will take you to the next level; will enter into an uncomfortable situation if work is high profile.
- Can discriminate between work that is strategically important and work that is not, and direct energy accordingly.
- Strong leadership skills.
- Good at self-marketing and articulating accomplishments.
- Politically skilled; careful to be seen in a positive light.

### Potential trouble spots:
- Spending enough time in a role to consolidate skills.
- Being so concerned about money and recognition that not enough attention is paid to developing skills that will assure long-term success.
- Being overly engaged in impression management, focusing only on work that is visible to senior management.
- Sharing the credit with others in a teamwork environment.
- Working on something only if it will look good on your résumé.
- If you are also a lifestyler, feeling conflict between putting in long work hours to get ahead and having time for meeting personal needs.
- Making work unnecessarily complex to satisfy your desire for a broad arena to play in (common mistake of fired executives who set up own businesses).
- If you lose your work, maintaining a sense of self-worth.

### You are most likely to be happily employed in:
- All work environments, including global organizations, professional-advisory services, large public-sector organizations, manufacturing and operations, telecom firms that provide significant career-development opportunities.
- Your own business; building a company from the ground up.

### You are least likely to be happily employed in:
- A low-profile, nonprofit organization.
- Service occupations such as nursing, social work, or resources.
- Contract work, because of its anonymity.

### Are you likely to change?
- Your preference for career building may shift as your lifestyle circumstances change or you attain your original goals. Your life priorities may also shift due to normal adult growth, or through a life-defining event such as job loss or divorce.

*"I need to be working in a product line or service I believe in. The work I do must reflect who I am and what I care about. I need to be able to express myself."*

## Authenticity seekers

If you are an authenticity seeker, you refuse to "hang up your personality" at the corporate door. You will not sacrifice your own personal expressiveness to play a corporate role or repress your personal values in favor of what is good for the team or the organization.

Authenticity seekers fall into two groups. Some are motivated by a desire to work for a particular cause, such as the environment. Mid-career changers who move to the nonprofit sector because it is in sync with personal values often fall into this category. Others are motivated primarily by a need for self-expression. They seek work that allows them to be themselves, that is consistent with their personal style, that "feels right." They use the word "fit" frequently to describe their happiness in their work.

Authenticity seekers need to identify with the product or service because it is important or meets their aesthetic needs. Creative or young authenticity seekers, for example, are more likely to be drawn to a company operating out of a loft in an older downtown area than to one in an industrial park. Most authenticity seekers have difficulty with office politics and heavily mandated policies or procedures. At school you may have been involved in arts-related extracurricular activities (film society, a performance art) or you may have been an activist. Perhaps you played a role in student politics, the daily newspaper, or community outreach.

You may have studied anything from fashion to languages to the social or physical sciences. You might have been described as "artsy." You probably did not study in an applied professional program such as dentistry, engineering, or business. One notable exception to this rule is law. I have met many authenticity-seeking lawyers who are unhappy with having to put aside their personal values in their work. If you are an authenticity seeker, you are part of a small percentage of the workforce.

**To what extent does this describe you?**

| Not at all | | Somewhat | | A lot |
|---|---|---|---|---|
| 1 | 2 | 3 | 4 | 5 |

# Behavioural implications

## Your strengths:
- Self-awareness; knowledge of what is important to you.
- Strong sense of integrity.
- Passionate about what you believe in.
- Consistent, not changing personality from situation to situation.
- Prepared to tackle difficult issues that support values and take unpopular stands.
- Self-expressive.

## Potential trouble spots:
- Being inflexible or intolerant; unable to blend in because of too strong a personality.
- Making decisions based on first impressions of what the environment looks like or what people say; dismissing people because their values are different.
- Turning down work that is "inauthentic" early in your career and therefore not acquiring important skills that would help you end up where you want to be.
- Clashing with people who have different values.
- Focusing on one issue to the point that you fail to recognize the impact of your actions on others; being seen as unfeeling or uncaring.
- If you are also a career builder, finding work that combines your needs to express important values and to be in a high-status role.

## You are most likely to be happily employed in:
- Creative environments, media, and cultural organizations.
- Entrepreneurial environments.
- Self-employed environments.
- NGOs and community-based organizations.
- The arts.
- Healthcare.
- Advocacy roles, whether as a lawyer, healthcare professional, or scientist.

## You are least likely to be happily employed in:
- A larger multinational company; an engineering/operations environment.

## Are you likely to change?
- If you have started out as an authenticity seeker you probably will not change, although the strength of your preference may be modified by financial circumstances or a disillusioning work experience. On the other hand, you may have become an authenticity seeker as you reevaluated your life priorities at mid-career.

*"In order to be happy, I need to be learning, I need to be stretched. I ask myself routinely, 'What have I learned in the last little while? What can I expect to learn in the next little while?'"*

## Personal developers

You evaluate your work in terms of whether you are honing skills and acquiring new ones. You become restless doing the same thing over and over again. Once you have mastered a challenge, you are eager to move on.

Although you are not necessarily a risk taker by nature, you are prepared to take risks if the result will enhance your skills portfolio by exposing you to new technology or to people you can learn from. You are always looking for ways to upgrade credentials. You may be very ambitious to advance in your career and become a player in your profession. Or you may be happy to hone your professional skills without accompanying status. Your identification is to profession and work rather than employer. It is important that your professional competence is respected. You find nothing quite as dispiriting as finding yourself with inadequate resources—financial or staff—to complete work to your standards.

In today's bottom-line-obsessed organizations, you may experience a dilemma: doing work to personally held standards within constraints imposed by business needs. You often feel you do not have enough time to complete work to professional standards, take on activities that will stretch you, and still have time for a life. Burnout is common. Another common dilemma is turning down an intriguing professional assignment.

Educationally, you may have studied anything from liberal arts to social sciences, law, and accounting. You may have taken extra or advanced courses because they were challenging. You likely were active in extracurricular activities. You are part of a group that accounts for a large percentage of the managerial and professional population, including 20-something contract workers, frequent job changers, research scientists, educators and enablers, and independent consultants.

**To what extent does this describe you?**

| Not at all | | Somewhat | | A lot |
|---|---|---|---|---|
| 1 | 2 | 3 | 4 | 5 |

# **Behavioural** implications

**Your strengths:**
- Strong achievement orientation.
- Self-managing.
- Continuous learner; curious about content related to your area of expertise.
- Risk taker—willing to move into new professional territory if it is challenging.
- Set high professional standards for yourself; you will go beyond what is expected to satisfy personal standards of excellence.
- High level of engagement when doing challenging work.
- Integrity—you will lobby for the right way to do something.

**Potential trouble spots:**
- Becoming bored when not learning or being stretched.
- Becoming impatient with people who are not smart, highly skilled, or competent; you may be intolerant.
- Balancing work and personal and family commitments; becoming burned out.
- Not knowing when to give up on a challenge, persisting against all odds.
- Making compromises; recognizing that what is important to you may not be to an employer or client satisfied with what you regard as second best.
- Spreading yourself too thin and not accomplishing anything to your standards.
- Lacking interest in areas outside your own, leading to narrowness.

**You are most likely to be happily employed in:**
- Sectors of the economy within the managerial or professional ranks (teacher, lawyer, doctor, accountant, human-resources specialist, trainer).
- Organizations where change is a constant.
- Organizations in which your area of expertise is valued, where resources to help you carry out your work are available.
- An organization where there are significant developmental opportunities (new assignments, lateral moves, promotions up a professional ladder, training).
- Any role in which craft or skill is important, such as that of chef, gardener, artist.
- Work where you act as an independent.

**You are least likely to be happily employed in:**
- Custodial and service-sector work, or supervising low-skilled workers.
- Customer-service roles.

**Are you likely to change?**
- Most personal developers do not change in their desire to develop themselves; once they have attained their goals, they may shift to a new field.

*Once you have mastered a challenge you are eager to move on.*

## Autonomy seekers

You want to own or build your work, whether in an organization or your own business. If you are working for someone else, you need to have the psychological experience of "owning" your work as if you were self-employed. You are impatient with rules and uncomfortable with authority. You do not derive identity from the organization. Chances are that people describe you as "a maverick" or "not a good team player."

Some autonomy seekers wish to pursue their own vision, unfettered by "how things should be done." They hold strong personal values and are unwilling to compromise the integrity of their work. It is not that they want to think outside the box—they do not even see the box. Others are motivated not so much by a creative vision as by an almost visceral reaction to being told what to do—think John Wayne. While they may not be visionaries, they take initiative, make things happen, and buck the bureaucracy. Autonomy seekers are often outsiders who do not quite understand the nuances and unspoken expectations of organizational life.

If you work in an organization you have little patience with endless meetings and office politicking. If someone wants to get you really angry all they have to say is, "You can't do that. It's not in the policy manual." You do not like to be told what you can and cannot do. Managing you is a challenge—you frequently would be described as someone who cannot take direction.

You want to be accountable for your successes and failures. You prefer a compensation package weighted toward bonuses and commission. You may not like team environments where others can interfere with your work. As a student you might have been an activist or played a leadership role in creating clubs. You were not a joiner in rah-rah student activities.

*"I need to take charge of what I do, when I do it, and how I do it. I need to own my work."*

**To what extent does this describe you?**

| Not at all | | Somewhat | | A lot |
|---|---|---|---|---|
| 1 | 2 | 3 | 4 | 5 |

## **Behavioural** implications

### Your strengths:
- Comfortable taking risks, thrive on ambiguity.
- Creative independent thinker, challenging the way the things have been done.
- Comfortable with fluid, unstructured, or entrepreneurial environments.
- Highly engaged; will "go the limit," because you own your work.
- Often highly innovative—great at developing ideas and brainstorming solutions outside the way things have always been done.

### Potential trouble spots:
- Taking direction, showing flexibility.
- Fitting into team environments, especially ones with a lot of politics.
- Tolerating things that interfere with getting the work done.
- Missing out on important information because of disdain for office politics.
- Ruffling feathers by failing to pick up on subtle nuances of "how things are done."
- If you are also a sociability seeker, balancing your desire to "do your own thing" with fitting in with the group or team.
- Being quick to reject other people's ideas and "the way it has always been done."

### You are most likely to be happily employed in:
- Any environment where you have the opportunity to feel ownership of your work by virtue of the nature of the work or the boss's management style.
- Project and entrepreneurial environments.
- Smaller organizations or independent work units in larger organizations (e.g., an R&D unit) that provide greater freedom and are less encumbered by bureaucracy.
- Managerial roles in which you have significant control over your operation.
- Professional or individual-contributor roles.
- Roles with significant autonomy such as sales roles, teaching, or high-end chefs.
- Your own business.
- Contract stints as a hired gun or turnaround artist.

### You are least likely to be happily employed in:
- Large bureaucratic organizations, especially at head office.
- Policy development roles (who needs policies?).
- Service/custodial roles or managerial roles if expected to provide close supervision.
- Customer-service roles.
- Working with micromanaging bosses or clients.

### Are you likely to change?
- You are not likely to change over the course of your career.

*"I thrive on change. I get bored if I'm working with the same people or doing the same thing for a long period of time."*

## Novelty seekers

If you are a novelty seeker you are constantly on the move, from project to project and industry to industry. Indeed, in the course of your life you may have several radically different careers. How you work will often change, too, as you shuttle between various configurations of full-time work, contract work, and running your own business.

Some novelty seekers constantly change not only where they work but also the professional content of their work. Others will stick with the same content but cannot stay in one position or place for long. Norman is typical of many novelty seekers. "When I was a director of systems," he says, "I got bored. Now I go from contract to contract as a project manager. It's stimulating because with each new contract I have the challenge of starting something new."

A novelty seeker may end up with a résumé that looks like that of a personal developer. But the motivation is different. Novelty seekers need change for its own sake. If you are a novelty seeker, you may also be ambitious for recognition and financial rewards, but they are not enough to induce you to stay once you become bored.

"I get excited about change," says Miranda, an inveterate job hopper. "When I was looking for a new job, I was also breaking up with my boyfriend. My friends said, 'You've got so many stressors going on in your life, selling your condo, new boyfriend, and you want to change your work as well?'"

Because novelty seekers are fairly good at everything, they find it difficult to select one field over another. You may have studied anything in school— in fact you may have studied everything, moving back and forth between different majors.

**To what extent does this describe you?**

| Not at all | | Somewhat | | A lot |
|---|---|---|---|---|
| 1 | 2 | 3 | 4 | 5 |

## **Behavioural** implications

**Your strengths:**
- Achievement-oriented.
- Able to deal with ambiguity and free-flowing environments.
- Prepared to take risks.
- Can hit the ground running in unfamiliar territory.
- Continuous learner—curious about the unfamiliar.
- Knowing a little bit about everything.
- Highly energetic (at least until enthusiasm wanes).

**Potential trouble spots:**
- Becoming easily bored; having a short attention span.
- Consolidating skills or making a meaningful contribution because you spend too little time in a position.
- Being too much of a generalist—experiencing yourself as "content-free," with no allegiance to any particular field of expertise.
- Leaving messes behind when you move on.
- Being too eager to jump ship and missing new challenges.
- Being impatient with people, irritated by having to explain things you already know.
- Making career decisions—everything sounds interesting.
- Committing to a particular field.

**You are most likely to be happily employed in:**
- Start-ups.
- Environments with new content and new challenges to be mastered.
- Generalist roles, perhaps in a large organization willing to develop people by moving them into new functions; large government organizations; global organizations (marketing and sales, pharmaceuticals, banks) that provide diverse opportunities, particularly for top performers.
- Venture-capital or deal-making roles.
- Your own business, in particular as a contract worker or independent consultant.
- Professional-services firms.
- Project management.

**You are least likely to be happily employed in:**
- Any given assignment for a long period of time.

**Are you likely to change?**
- You are not likely to change in your underlying preference for change.

*In the course of your life, you may have several radically different careers.*

*"I like structure. Having predictability and stability in my life is important to me."*

## Stability seekers

You enjoy seeing the same people regularly and following established routines. Fluid environments that lack direction and discipline can be a challenge. Although you may like to explore new things, when it actually comes down to doing something new, you assess all the risks and benefits. No one would describe you as a risk taker. Surprises in your work routine can be stressful, as can starting new work.

You identify with organizational life and its values, norms, and standards. You are comfortable taking direction from others and do not second-guess the rights of your manager or organization to set out clearly defined standards and expectations. You are the classic "organizational man" (or woman). Christine, an accountant, quit her work at a large firm to spend more time with her children. She quickly discovered, however, that she missed the sense of belonging to a team.

You probably prefer to work for an organization as opposed to being self-employed—and preferably for the same organization for as long as possible. But in today's work world, such a stable form of work is unusual, and stability seekers have had to make their accommodations. If you are a self-employed individual working on contract for a large organization, you may make the work feel like a more traditional job and identify with your employer as if you were a permanent employee.

You have difficulty, however, adapting to a new work world in which you are forced to switch loyalties from your employer to yourself, viewing yourself as a self-managing free agent. You are less equipped to deal with uncertainty—a real challenge in an era in which job security is rare. This is a dilemma for a significant number of people who would like to take advantage of reduced workweeks or sabbaticals but worry about whether their job will be guaranteed.

**To what extent does this describe you?**

| Not at all | | Somewhat | | A lot |
| --- | --- | --- | --- | --- |
| 1 | 2 | 3 | 4 | 5 |

# **Behavioural** implications

**Your strengths:**
- Reliable, loyal, putting company needs first.
- Good team player (as long as team is stable); low ego needs (unless you are also a career builder).
- Organized and efficient, a good planner.
- Dependable; will carry work through and honor commitments.
- Backbone of organizations.

**Potential trouble spots:**
- Switching gears midstream; working in free-flowing environments.
- Dealing with ambiguity—may try to resolve it too quickly.
- Solving problems on your own.
- Showing flexibility.
- Accepting interesting work because it is new, involves change, or is risky.
- If you are also a career builder or personal developer, balancing your need for stability with the need to stretch yourself or get ahead in your career.
- If you are also a lifestyler looking for reduced work hours, balancing your need for personal-development time with your need for the security of a guaranteed job.

**You are most likely to be happily employed in:**
- Positions and organizations with a clear structure; large organizations such as banks, oil companies, telecoms, and the public services.
- Work that is not affected by downturns in the economy, such as education; childcare; medicine; manufacturers of personal-care staples.

**You are least likely to be happily employed in:**
- Entrepreneurial environments.
- Creative environments; sales roles.
- High-turnover, less-stable, frequently restructuring environments such as marketing and sales; deal-making/venture capital, entrepreneurial organizations; and businesses in which people can have a short shelf life, such as dot-coms and biotechnology.
- Your own business if it involves high risk.

**Are you likely to change?**
- Preference for stability may be a reflection of an underlying personality preference, or may be related to your current life circumstances. Although today fewer people indicate stability as their most important motivator, a larger number indicate it is their second most important.

*Preference for stability may be a reflection of an underlying personality preference, or may be related to your current life circumstances.*

*"I work to live, not live to work. I want to enjoy my work, but I also want the flexibility to pursue my life outside work."*

## Lifestylers

There are many varieties of lifestyler. You could be a young resort worker who wants to spend time in leisure pursuits, or a 30-something parent determined to balance work with family life. You could be a mid-career professional with eldercare responsibilities or someone at any age with strong interests beyond work, whether writing a novel or raising cattle. Maintaining reasonable control over work demands in order to honor personal commitments is critical to your life satisfaction.

Office location and length of commute are similarly important. You may be reluctant to accept a geographical transfer even if it means substantial career or financial rewards. Then again, you may leap at the chance to move to the right place—the small town with a 10-minute commute.

The common denominator: while you care about your work, in the final analysis you put personal life before work. If you do not, you suffer terribly. You are anxious about not being able to fulfill important personal commitments. You have a nagging feeling that you are not doing anything right—either in your work or personally. You are constantly exhausted from all the juggling.

Many people say that lifestyle is most important to them, that work is not the centerpiece of their identity. But when actually forced to make a choice between expressing themselves in the work arena or freeing up their time, they choose the work option. They are not true lifestylers.

To be happy, lifestylers need to be prepared to make the tough choices: to leave work at the office, demand flexibility in scheduling, and do whatever else is required to fulfill personal commitments. A significant number of people of all ages describe lifestyle as their first or second most important motivator.

**To what extent does this describe you?**

| Not at all | | Somewhat | | A lot |
|---|---|---|---|---|
| 1 | 2 | 3 | 4 | 5 |

# Behavioural implications

## Your strengths:
- Clear vision of priorities and a commitment to satisfying them.
- Multidimensionality, with a sense of identity coming from many sources.
- Self-motivated, self-managing, self-disciplined.
- Satisfaction with your work and personal life, taking pride in achieving that satisfaction in spite of external pressures.
- Capable of making tough decisions.

## Potential trouble spots:
- Balancing your work and personal life, especially if you are a career builder, personal developer, or authenticity seeker (when you believe you are doing important work, it is hard to leave the office at 5 p.m.).
- Annoying team members left to pick up the slack when you leave work or will not compromise your work schedule.
- Coming across to management as not being a team player, as being unrealistic in your expectations about work demands.
- Committing fully to your work; being rigid about changing work schedules.

## You are most likely to be happily employed in:
- Organizations in which the employer is sensitive to work–life issues. These environments are typically talent-sensitive with large numbers of in-demand knowledge workers who will "vote with their feet" if their needs for work–life balance are not met.
- Free-flowing offices—you won't find me easily; I'm working part-time, telecommuting, etc.
- Your own business as an independent contractor with control over schedules.

## You are least likely to be happily employed in:
- Deal-making environments such as investment banking, brokerages.
- Engineering/Operations.
- Some professional advisory firms in which you end up running an office on an airplane, working 24/7.

## Are you likely to change?
- Your preferences may change as a result of changing life circumstances and personal goals and priorities.

## Assessing yourself

### What is your motivational type?

▶ Your key motivators
*pages 46–47*

▶ Identifying potential conflicts
*page 49*

▶ Identifying your personal values
*pages 52–53*

▶ Completing the values assessor
*page 54*

▶ Summarizing your values
*page 55*

**PORTFOLIO**    **Your key** motivators

Enter your score at the end of the motivational types. Your highest score is your major; your next highest is your minor. If you have any ties, read the descriptions again. Which is truer of you?

| Motivational type | Score | Motivational type | Score |
|---|---|---|---|
| Sociability seeker | ☐ | Autonomy seeker | ☐ |
| Career builder | ☐ | Novelty seeker | ☐ |
| Authenticity seeker | ☐ | Stability seeker | ☐ |
| Personal developer | ☐ | Lifestyler | ☐ |

*What is the highest score? This is your major motivator.*
*Major*..................................................................................................

*What are the next highest scores? These are your minors.*
*Minor*..................................................................................................
*Minor (second)* ....................................................................................

### Implications of my motivational types

Read and select the points relevant to your interests and work situation.

Implications of my major motivator

*Roles and environments I am happiest in:*

............................................................................................................
............................................................................................................

*Roles and environments I should avoid:*

............................................................................................................
............................................................................................................

*My strengths are:*

............................................................................................................

Implications of my minor motivator(s)

*Roles and environments I am happiest in:*

..........................................................................................................

..........................................................................................................

..........................................................................................................

..........................................................................................................

*Roles and environments I should avoid:*

..........................................................................................................

..........................................................................................................

..........................................................................................................

..........................................................................................................

## Applying the information

*Does your current work support your motivational types?*

..........................................................................................................

*How or how not?*

(If you are currently unemployed, think of your most recent work to get an insight into what you need and what you should avoid.)

..........................................................................................................

..........................................................................................................

..........................................................................................................

*What would you need to change to make it a better match?*

Consider the role(s) you play, your work environment and organizational culture, and your boss's management style.

..........................................................................................................

..........................................................................................................

*There are strengths associated with each motivational type, as well as potential trouble spots and common conflicts.*

### Running a business

*Lifestylers like autonomy and are well suited to running a business on their own. However, they also like interacting with people on the projects they manage.*

---

**Assessing** yourself

**What is your motivational type?**

▶ Your key motivators
*pages 46–47*

▶ Identifying potential conflicts
*page 49*

▶ Identifying your personal values
*pages 52–53*

▶ Completing the values assessor
*page 54*

▶ Summarizing your values
*page 55*

---

## Manage conflicts between motivators

Ideally, your work will satisfy both your major and minor motivators. Commonly, however, our motivators may conflict. Consider, for example, the following common dilemmas.

> *"I want to get ahead (career builder) and I want to be available for my kids during the day (lifestyler)."*
> *"I am easily bored (novelty seeker) and I want financial security (stability seeker)."*
> *"I want to run my own show (autonomy seeker) and I want to be part of a team (sociability seeker)."*

Are there any trouble spots or conflicts between your key motivators? Be creative in thinking through your options. Can you design your work to satisfy your needs? An ambitious lifestyler parent, for instance, might pitch his boss on a high-profile assignment that can be completed largely at home.

Sometimes you will have to make trade-offs: for example, trading security in favor of challenging, changing work. But before you can make the trade-offs, you need to know what it is you are trading off. A trade-off is not a permanent state of affairs. It is making an informed decision to satisfy one need over another for a given period of time. (For more on Making trade-offs, *see page 159*).

Review your major and minor motivators. What conflicts, if any, exist? How can you manage these conflicts?

Consider:

- Your career stage. If starting out or moving on to a new career track, you may need to make greater compromises to satisfy your career needs longer-term.
- Your well-being. What is the emotional toll of not meeting important needs?
- Meeting needs sequentially in relation to life chapters.

**PORTFOLIO** | **Identifying** potential conflicts

Review your major and minor motivators. What are the conflicts?

Major motivators

*My key needs/aspirations are:*

..........................................................................................................
..........................................................................................................
..........................................................................................................
..........................................................................................................

*I can manage/overcome these trouble spots by (brainstorm):*

..........................................................................................................
..........................................................................................................
..........................................................................................................
..........................................................................................................
..........................................................................................................

Minor motivators

*My key needs/aspirations are:*

..........................................................................................................
..........................................................................................................
..........................................................................................................
..........................................................................................................
..........................................................................................................

*I can manage these conflicts by (brainstorm):*

..........................................................................................................
..........................................................................................................
..........................................................................................................
..........................................................................................................

*When our work supports our most important values, each day has a heightened sense of meaning.*

# Uncovering your key values

What values are central to giving your life meaning? How well are you currently meeting those values in your work and personal life? How well does your work meet your most important values?

Our values are what we care about most. They give direction to our work and lives. When our work supports our most important values, each day has a heightened sense of meaning.

What do you really care about? It pays to reflect carefully on what is really important to you. You may discover that what you think is important and what really is important are two very different things.

Young people, for example, often say that their number-one value is money. After they go through a meaningful values assessment, such as the one you are going to do now, they typically discover that other things are equally or more important, whether having the opportunity to work in an environment where they can learn, having time for friends and family, or contributing to something they believe in.

**Meaningful work**
*By working out your key values you can find out what is important to you. You may discover that a job helping to protect the environment has the most meaning for you.*

## Values change

Our priorities change over time, reflecting new life stages and experiences, such as establishing a relationship, rearing a child, or dealing with the death of a loved one. Unless we stop to reexamine our values from time to time, we may fail to catch up with the ways in which we and our world have changed.

We frequently make important decisions based on old scripts, force-feeding values that no longer make sense in terms of current psychological and life realities. Often, for example, mid-career individuals turn down exciting opportunities because they are too risky financially. They do not stop to think that maybe they do not have the same need for financial prudence now that their children have grown up.

Peter, for example, a pilot, dreamed of setting up an HR department for a small start-up airline. At the age of 40, he was offered this kind of opportunity but turned it down because it was too risky. Several years later, he was offered a similar opportunity, which he also turned down, for the very same reason. However, with grown-up kids at this life point, he could afford to take a risk. It was only when he went through the following exercise that he realized he was making critical decisions based on old scripts.

## Know what is most important

Most of us have many important values. When I ask people to describe their most important values they typically provide a laundry list of images of the good life, such as "time to spend with my family," "challenging work," "good income," "time for hobbies," and so on. Of course these are all desirable. But the truth of the matter is that some values are more important to you than others.

**Time for family**
*Many people today identify "being with family" as one of their most important values.*

**Assessing** yourself

**What is your motivational type?**

▶ Your key motivators
*pages 46–47*

▶ Identifying potential conflicts
*page 49*

▶ Identifying your personal values
*pages 52–53*

▶ Completing the values assessor
*page 54*

▶ Summarizing your values
*page 55*

### ● SELF-ASSESSMENT    Identifying your personal values

Read the values listed below. Evaluate each value in terms of how important it is to you. Try to assign roughly one-third of the values to each category.

| Value | Value description | High | Med | Low |
|---|---|---|---|---|
| **Achievement** | To accomplish important things | ☐ | ☐ | ☐ |
| **Advancement** | To reach the top of an organization or profession | ☐ | ☐ | ☐ |
| **Adventure** | To explore new frontiers and discover new things; to find excitement; to take risks | ☐ | ☐ | ☐ |
| **Affiliation** | To be accepted and liked; to work closely with others | ☐ | ☐ | ☐ |
| **Aesthetics** | To gain inspiration/enjoyment from art, music, etc. | ☐ | ☐ | ☐ |
| **Autonomy/Freedom** | To act on personal priorities and time schedule; to be free of organizational rules and norms | ☐ | ☐ | ☐ |
| **Challenge** | To be involved in interesting, challenging work | ☐ | ☐ | ☐ |
| **Community** | To belong; to participate actively in a community; to support community goals | ☐ | ☐ | ☐ |
| **Creativity** | To be creative; to express yourself | ☐ | ☐ | ☐ |
| **Expertise** | To be respected for your competence; to become a known and respected authority; to achieve excellence | ☐ | ☐ | ☐ |
| **Family** | To spend time with your family; to have strong family relationships; to help in the development of children | ☐ | ☐ | ☐ |
| **Friendship/ Relationships** | To maintain strong friendships; to look after your friends; to have meaningful relationships with others | ☐ | ☐ | ☐ |
| **Fun** | To have fun; to enjoy your life and your work | ☐ | ☐ | ☐ |
| **Growth** | To develop to your full potential professionally and personally | ☐ | ☐ | ☐ |

| | | | | |
|---|---|---|---|---|
| **Happiness** | To be happy; to make others happy | ☐ | ☐ | ☐ |
| **Health/Wellness** | To be physically and psychologically healthy | ☐ | ☐ | ☐ |
| **Home/Retreat** | To have a comfortable and/or beautiful home, retreat, or cottage | ☐ | ☐ | ☐ |
| **Integrity** | To act in terms of your convictions; to be honest; to stand up for your beliefs | ☐ | ☐ | ☐ |
| **Leadership** | To communicate a vision to other people and motivate them to implement it | ☐ | ☐ | ☐ |
| **Learning** | To be constantly learning and developing | ☐ | ☐ | ☐ |
| **Location** | To live where you want to live | ☐ | ☐ | ☐ |
| **Making a difference** | To make a difference in the world; to have an impact on people's lives | ☐ | ☐ | ☐ |
| **Money** | To be financially successful | ☐ | ☐ | ☐ |
| **Passion** | To care deeply about something; to be passionate | ☐ | ☐ | ☐ |
| **Recognition/Status** | To have status; to earn the respect and recognition of others | ☐ | ☐ | ☐ |
| **Recreation** | To pursue hobbies, sports, or personal interests | ☐ | ☐ | ☐ |
| **Security** | To achieve a secure and stable work and financial situation | ☐ | ☐ | ☐ |
| **Self-expression** | To be yourself, and to behave in a way consistent with your ideas and values, not repressing important parts of your personality | ☐ | ☐ | ☐ |
| **Service** | To help other people; to make a contribution to the well-being of others; to help improve society | ☐ | ☐ | ☐ |
| **Spirituality** | To achieve inner harmony; to be at peace with yourself; to live by your religious beliefs | ☐ | ☐ | ☐ |
| **Structure** | To live a well-ordered life | ☐ | ☐ | ☐ |

*Our priorities change over time, reflecting new life stages and experiences.*

**SELF-ASSESSMENT    Completing** the values assessor

Copy the values identified as being of high importance in the first column. Now comes the hard work: determining what is really, truly most important to you. Rank your values, from 1 to 10, in the second column. No ties, please. In column 3, indicate the degree to which that value is being satisfied in your work. In column 4, indicate the degree to which that value is being satisfied in your personal life.

## Scale
**0 = not at all well, 5 = reasonably well, 10 = extremely well**
Use other numbers between 0 and 10 as appropriate.

| Your values | Rank your values in order of importance | How well am I meeting this value at work? | How well am I meeting this value in my personal life? |
|---|---|---|---|
|  |  |  |  |
|  |  |  |  |
|  |  |  |  |
|  |  |  |  |
|  |  |  |  |
|  |  |  |  |
|  |  |  |  |
|  |  |  |  |
|  |  |  |  |
|  |  |  |  |

**PORTFOLIO**

# **Summarizing** your values

List below your most important values:

*My values that are currently being satisfied in my work:*

.........................................................................................................

.........................................................................................................

*My values that are currently being satisfied in my personal life:*

.........................................................................................................

.........................................................................................................

*My values that are not being satisfied at work:*

.........................................................................................................

.........................................................................................................

*My values that are not being satisfied in my personal life:*

.........................................................................................................

.........................................................................................................

*Ways I can better meet my values in my work (brainstorm):*

.........................................................................................................

.........................................................................................................

.........................................................................................................

*Ways I can better meet my values in my personal life (brainstorm):*

.........................................................................................................

.........................................................................................................

.........................................................................................................

.........................................................................................................

# What are your career assets?

The journey you are about to embark on will show you how to identify your accomplishments and the unique set of personal competencies that underlie them. It will demonstrate your skills, knowledge, and interests that make up your career assets when you are looking for work, reconfiguring your career, or changing careers.

## This chapter shows you how to:

**Identify** and describe the roles and accomplishments that have given you the most satisfaction.

**Discover** your core competencies—your unique strengths—that lie beneath your work and life accomplishments.

**Build** on your core competencies for career moves that play to your strengths and developmental needs.

**Determine** whether you are happier as a specialist or generalist, and as an individual contributor or manager.

**Conduct** an inventory of your key skills and knowledge— the foundation of pitching yourself for great work.

**Match** your technical and professional skills and personal interests with work that is made for you.

## Case study

Carrie, an unemployed 29-year-old, worked on several short contracts in various industries after receiving her biology degree. "My interests are all over the map, and I have no particular skills," she said.

Carrie listed her achievements as winning a college scholarship, convincing a knowledgeable gardener to install a much-publicized wildflower garden, and setting up a pilot program for implementing insecticide-free parks. After analyzing her accomplishments, she discovered her underlying competencies to be an ability to innovate, resilience, the ability to influence others, a knack for sniffing out opportunities, and an ability to work by herself.

# Assessing your accomplishments

What accomplishments in your work and personal life have given you the most satisfaction? What most engages you? The answers to these questions will reveal the core competencies that underlie your talents.

Ask people today to describe their accomplishments and many of them can only think of what they have not done—the 10 things still not crossed off on their to-do list. It is telling, therefore, that when pressed to reflect more seriously, they can usually generate several.

Most of us are accomplishing much more than we realize. We are just too busy to recognize our achievements. No sooner do we finish something than something else is thrown at us. The result is that there is no down time between tasks to think about what we are achieving.

This is tragic. If we do not have a sense of accomplishment, how are we going to feel good about ourselves? If we do not feel good about ourselves, how are we going to make effective career choices?

I love watching people complete the following accomplishments workout exercise because the information it yields is so powerful and rich. People experience a rise in their self-esteem when they discover that they have in fact been making meaningful contributions.

After identifying their accomplishments, they say, "I really do have some talents that uniquely define my strengths," or "I never really thought about these skills—I just took them for granted."

Some people find listing their accomplishments difficult. They diminish or disown even very significant accomplishments, saying, "It wasn't anything special," or "Anyone could have done it." Do not let modesty interfere with completing this exercise. If you cannot boast to a book,

## Examples of common accomplishments

Use these common types of accomplishments from work and personal life to stimulate thinking about your own accomplishments.

**Early-career individuals:**
- In college, created a special-interest group/event. Became an annual event.
- Paid off my student loans. (This is a frequent comment.)
- Won an award for student journalism/public speaking/athletics, etc.
- Planned my wedding—with lots of different people to please—while working full-time.
- Started and ran my own painting business during college.
- Got a job teaching English in Japan, where I did not know anyone; backpacked my way through the Far East.
- Developed/invented/designed a website that linked a community of . . .
- Sold myself for a job for which I was not really qualified by demonstrating my eagerness and capacity to learn.

**Mid-career individuals:**
- Made a significant career change involving major risks.
- Ended a long-term relationship.
- Started and stuck to a fitness program.
- Took an unpopular position with management. Stood up to my boss. Put my work at risk.
- Created a new strategy to increase sales, which resulted in . . .
- Built a high-functioning department from scratch.
- Created a new role at work that addressed an important issue.

**Late-career individuals:**
- Made a successful career transition from . . . to . . .
- Mentored several junior workers who ended up in senior management.
- Played a significant leadership role in . . . Developed important strategic alliances.
- Went out on my own after a career of always working for the same company.
- Made myself a priority, taking time for friends, contemplation, learning, fitness, looking after myself, instead of always looking after everyone else's needs.
- Made a successful transition from . . . to . . . under stressful conditions.

*If we do not have a sense of accomplishment, how are we going to feel good about ourselves?*

## Sources of satisfaction

*Achievements outside work provide important clues to your skills, interests, and sources of satisfaction.*

how are you going to sell yourself in interviews or talk to your boss about why you deserve a raise?

### Focus on personal satisfaction

Use personal satisfaction as your criterion in selecting your accomplishments, not their prestige or what others might have thought about them. For instance, if it was more satisfying to you, select losing 15 pounds and sticking to a fitness regimen over a work achievement, even if the latter earned high praise.

It is not enough simply to be competent and effective. You also have to be able to talk about what you do best and the results you have achieved. You need to be able to describe the underlying skills that characterize your achievements over the years. This is particularly crucial information if you are planning a work search. Your achievements will be the building blocks of your résumé and the foundation of how you describe yourself in interviews.

You will see that these core competencies provide critical information about the types of work and work roles to pursue and those to avoid.

**SELF-ASSESSMENT** **Preparing for the** accomplishments workout

In the exercise that follows, you will generate 10 accomplishments. After studying the Sample accomplishments workout (*see below*), use these additional tools: your Skills workout (*pages 74–77*), to describe the skills you used, and the Examples of common accomplishments (*page 59*), to stimulate your own thinking.

## Sample accomplishments workout

| Accomplishments | Skills and competencies used | Why satisfying? |
|---|---|---|
| Started up and led a fundraising program for a medical charity. Raised over $100,000—was told this would be a model for other fundraisers. | Creativity, enterprise<br><br>Problem-solving (coming up with new ways of doing things).<br><br>Political savviness: "worked the network"<br><br>Communication<br><br>Schmoozing! | Made a contribution to something I really believed in.<br><br>Got a lot of recognition being a star for a day! (loved being on TV)<br><br>Stretched myself in new ways, proving to myself I could pull it off—that when I want to I can be pretty enterprising and creative. |
| Pioneered a new product line for the company that increased profits by 25 percent in first year and significantly reduced returns. | Change agent<br><br>Leadership: created and led a highly motivated team (where talent rather than age or position counted).<br><br>Marketing know-how<br><br>Enterprise<br><br>Connecting with customers: we really heard what they were telling us. | Worked well with a team.<br><br>Cast a vision and then made it happen.<br><br>Forced myself to move outside my comfort zone.<br><br>Showed the company that there is an organic, nonbureaucratic way of working that gets results.<br><br>Invented something new rather than doing what we have always done. |

## SELF-ASSESSMENT   **Accomplishments** workout

In thinking about your accomplishments, consider both recent ones as well as some from earlier years. Draw from work, educational, personal, community, or volunteer activities.

| Accomplishments | Skills and competencies used | Why satisfying? |
|---|---|---|
|  |  |  |
|  |  |  |
|  |  |  |
|  |  |  |
|  |  |  |

| Accomplishments | Skills and competencies used | Why satisfying? |
|---|---|---|
|  |  |  |
|  |  |  |
|  |  |  |
|  |  |  |
|  |  |  |

*Your achievements will be the building blocks of your résumé and the foundation of how you describe yourself in interviews.*

**SELF-ASSESSMENT    Core competencies workout**

Go back to the Accomplishments workout on pages 62–63 and number each one. Then, in the chart that follows, check off the characteristics that apply to each accomplishment.

| Characteristics | 1 | 2 | 3 | 4 | 5 | 6 | 7 | 8 | 9 | 10 |
|---|---|---|---|---|---|---|---|---|---|---|
| **Interpersonal skills** | | | | | | | | | | |
| ● Influencing/persuading | ☐ | ☐ | ☐ | ☐ | ☐ | ☐ | ☐ | ☐ | ☐ | ☐ |
| ● Networking | ☐ | ☐ | ☐ | ☐ | ☐ | ☐ | ☐ | ☐ | ☐ | ☐ |
| ● Relating to diverse people | ☐ | ☐ | ☐ | ☐ | ☐ | ☐ | ☐ | ☐ | ☐ | ☐ |
| ● Negotiating | ☐ | ☐ | ☐ | ☐ | ☐ | ☐ | ☐ | ☐ | ☐ | ☐ |
| ● Collaborating | ☐ | ☐ | ☐ | ☐ | ☐ | ☐ | ☐ | ☐ | ☐ | ☐ |
| ● Team-building | ☐ | ☐ | ☐ | ☐ | ☐ | ☐ | ☐ | ☐ | ☐ | ☐ |
| ● Contributing to team | ☐ | ☐ | ☐ | ☐ | ☐ | ☐ | ☐ | ☐ | ☐ | ☐ |
| ● Mentoring | ☐ | ☐ | ☐ | ☐ | ☐ | ☐ | ☐ | ☐ | ☐ | ☐ |
| **Leading/managing** | | | | | | | | | | |
| ● Strategic thinking | ☐ | ☐ | ☐ | ☐ | ☐ | ☐ | ☐ | ☐ | ☐ | ☐ |
| ● Developing and communicating a compelling vision | ☐ | ☐ | ☐ | ☐ | ☐ | ☐ | ☐ | ☐ | ☐ | ☐ |
| ● Inspiring/motivating others | ☐ | ☐ | ☐ | ☐ | ☐ | ☐ | ☐ | ☐ | ☐ | ☐ |
| ● Coordinating/organizing | ☐ | ☐ | ☐ | ☐ | ☐ | ☐ | ☐ | ☐ | ☐ | ☐ |
| ● Managing projects | ☐ | ☐ | ☐ | ☐ | ☐ | ☐ | ☐ | ☐ | ☐ | ☐ |
| ● Planning | ☐ | ☐ | ☐ | ☐ | ☐ | ☐ | ☐ | ☐ | ☐ | ☐ |
| ● Developing others | ☐ | ☐ | ☐ | ☐ | ☐ | ☐ | ☐ | ☐ | ☐ | ☐ |
| ● Coaching and counseling | ☐ | ☐ | ☐ | ☐ | ☐ | ☐ | ☐ | ☐ | ☐ | ☐ |
| **Learning** | | | | | | | | | | |
| ● Staying current | ☐ | ☐ | ☐ | ☐ | ☐ | ☐ | ☐ | ☐ | ☐ | ☐ |
| ● Developing new skills/knowledge | ☐ | ☐ | ☐ | ☐ | ☐ | ☐ | ☐ | ☐ | ☐ | ☐ |

Accomplishment No.

- Going beyond comfort zone
- Continuing education

**Professional expertise**
- Learning and developing
- Being on leading edge
- Being seen as expert in field
- Being consulted by others in field

**Change management**
- Being a change agent
- Dealing with uncertainty
- Identifying opportunities

**Self-management/personal**
- Concerted focus to reach goal
- Self-confidence
- Taking significant risks
- Setting high standards for myself and others
- Self-reliance and independence
- Working alone
- High level of flexibility
- Resilience/overcoming obstacles
- High energy/stamina
- Resourceful/enterprising
- Showing initiative
- Maintaining self-control
- Effectively managing stress

*Core competencies provide critical information about the types of work and work roles to pursue.*

**SELF-ASSESSMENT**   **Core** competencies workout cont'd

| Characteristics | Accomplishment No. | | | | | | | | | |
|---|---|---|---|---|---|---|---|---|---|---|
| | 1 | 2 | 3 | 4 | 5 | 6 | 7 | 8 | 9 | 10 |

**Customer/client relations**

- Establishing effective customer/client relationships
- Making a real difference to customer/client
- Anticipating needs
- Creating long-term relationships
- Providing advice/expertise

**Thinking (decision-making/judgment)**

- Strategic/conceptual/ analytical thinking
- Seeing the big picture
- Creative thinking
- Planning
- Solving problems
- Exercising judgment
- Making decisions

**Marketing/selling/persuading**

- Influencing/persuading
- Identifying opportunities
- Opportunity-seeking
- Developing new products to meet emerging needs
- Selling idea/product
- Marketing/promoting myself
- Building relationships

**Involved/receiving recognition**
- Financial rewards
- Others hearing about it
- High visibility
- Becoming known as authority

**Operational effectiveness**
- Improving processes
- Maximizing resources
- Implementing programs/processes
- Working across business lines
- Cost savings

*Most of us are accomplishing much more than we realize.*

## Identifying key competencies

Review your completed core competencies workout. Where do your check marks lie? Using colored markers:
(1) Highlight in one color the words where you have the most check marks.
(2) Highlight in a second color the words where you have some check marks.
(3) Highlight in a third color the words with no check marks.

| Characteristics | 1 | 2 | 3 | 4 | 5 | 6 | 7 | 8 | 9 | 10 |
|---|---|---|---|---|---|---|---|---|---|---|
| **Interpersonal skills** | | | | | | | | | | |
| Influencing/persuading | | | ✔ | | | | | | | |
| Networking | | ✔ | | | | | | | | |
| Relating to diverse people | | ✔ | | ✔ | | ✔ | | | ✔ | |
| Negotiating | ✔ | | | | | | | | | |
| Collaborating | ✔ | | | ✔ | | | | | ✔ | |
| Team-building | ✔ | ✔ | ✔ | ✔ | | ✔ | ✔ | ✔ | | |
| Contributing to team | ✔ | ✔ | | | | ✔ | | | | |
| Mentoring | | | | | | | | | | |

**SELF-ASSESSMENT    Core** competencies workout cont'd

### Analyzing your core competencies

Your profile of checks marks shows you where your greatest interests and strengths are—your core competencies. Frequently occurring checks indicate a core competency—an attribute you have used in a range of situations. These are central talents that you use over and over again regardless of the situation.

When I ask people to take a moment and think about their profile of check marks most of them say, "This describes me." Occasionally, however, someone asks, "Doesn't this profile simply reflect the accomplishments I've selected?" This is rarely the case: over 95 percent of the people I have worked with end up with a similar profile when asked to generate 10 more accomplishments. This has significant implications.

First, you will be happiest and most effective in work that uses those competencies. These are your special talents describing what you do best. Second, you will receive the most value in your learning and self-development by building on your underlying strengths and aptitudes—becoming better at what you are already good at. Identify learning opportunities for improving your skills in these areas further.

### Analyzing your developing competencies

Do you have lots of check marks in some areas, and only three or four in other areas? The latter may suggest that you are at a point in your life where you are changing direction; the areas with fewer check marks often show a competency or interest you are moving into developing. Is this true of you? If so, find ways to develop yourself further in these areas; consider how you can incorporate them into your work.

What about areas where you do not have any check marks? Your basic talents and interests probably do not lie in these areas. Try to avoid situations that demand these skills, unless you need them in your current work assignment or to achieve longer-term goals. If the missing skills are critical to your success, develop a plan to improve in these areas.

## Specialist or generalist?

If you have a lot of check marks in a lot of places, you probably are a generalist: you apply a broad range of skills in achieving your goals.

If your check marks are clustered in certain areas—for example, Learning and Change Management—and less in others, such as Leading/Managing, you are probably more of a specialist: someone who uses a narrower range of skills in a more focused way.

Do you want to grow and develop within your specialty? Or do you prefer to broaden rather than deepen your skills and knowledge?

What do you like to think about? Problems associated with your technical specialty? Would you be unhappy making a career shift into a new area?

## Individual contributor or manager?

"I love to inspire my people, to get the best out of them. I like dealing with the problems you get as a manager. I want to be the decision-maker changing how we do business." This comment is typical of people who love to manage.

Contrast this with a comment by a woman who has chosen an individual-contributor role: "To be honest—and I know this isn't something you are supposed to say if you want to get ahead—I really don't like the hassles of dealing with other people's personalities and needs. I just want to do my thing and not have to deal with management headaches. I like using my professional skills at a high level to serve my clients the best I can."

Which of these two quotes do you identify with more?

Your answer is important in making effective career decisions. It is related to the specialist/generalist question but is not the same thing. Although most senior managers see themselves as generalists, and most individual contributors see themselves as specialists, there are generalists who prefer to play an individual-contributor role, and there are managers who enjoy supervising specialists while carrying out specialist work themselves.

## Career counsel

Specialist or generalist?
Some people are clearly more interested in specializing in a narrow aspect of their work, whether within psychology, marketing, or information technology. They enjoy thinking deeply about the problems associated with their technical specialty. Others prefer to play a generalist role in a broader arena within or outside their profession.

### Assessing yourself

**What are your career assets?**

▶ Preparing for the accomplishments workout
*page 61*

▶ Accomplishments workout
*pages 62–63*

▶ Core competencies workout
*pages 64–68*

▶ Summary of key competencies
*pages 70–71*

▶ Skills workout
*pages 74–77*

▶ Summary of skills, knowledge, and interests
*pages 78–79*

▶ Summing up your portfolio
*pages 82–85*

**PORTFOLIO**     **Summary of** key competencies

Now, having reviewed your chart on pages 64–67, fill in the following:

*I excel in/have special aptitude for:*

(Competencies where you have the most check marks)

.................................................................................................................................................

.................................................................................................................................................

.................................................................................................................................................

.................................................................................................................................................

.................................................................................................................................................

.................................................................................................................................................

.................................................................................................................................................

.................................................................................................................................................

.................................................................................................................................................

.................................................................................................................................................

.................................................................................................................................................

.................................................................................................................................................

.................................................................................................................................................

*Areas of lesser strength:*

(Competencies where you have the fewest check marks)

.................................................................................................................................................

.................................................................................................................................................

.................................................................................................................................................

.................................................................................................................................................

.................................................................................................................................................

.................................................................................................................................................

.................................................................................................................................................

.................................................................................................................................................

.................................................................................................................................................

.................................................................................................................................................

.................................................................................................................................................

*Skills and/or knowledge in which I am already strong that I want to develop further/build on:*

(Competencies where you have some or many check marks)

..........................................................................................................

..........................................................................................................

..........................................................................................................

..........................................................................................................

..........................................................................................................

..........................................................................................................

..........................................................................................................

..........................................................................................................

*Areas of lesser strength that I want to improve/learn more about:*

(Competencies where you have a few check marks)

..........................................................................................................

..........................................................................................................

..........................................................................................................

..........................................................................................................

..........................................................................................................

..........................................................................................................

..........................................................................................................

..........................................................................................................

*Other important attributes:*

..........................................................................................................

..........................................................................................................

..........................................................................................................

..........................................................................................................

*People experience a rise in their self-esteem when they discover that they have been making meaningful contributions.*

*"If I hear one more person say 'I'm good with people,' I'll scream."*

# Determining your key skills, knowledge, and interests

What skills do you have that you most enjoy using? In what areas do you have a depth of knowledge? Can you clearly describe your key skill and knowledge assets?

"We have people who are really talented but keep being passed over for promotions. They think their accomplishments should speak for themselves, but they do not. They cannot even describe their skills. If I hear one more person say 'I'm good with people,' I'll scream."

This comment is typical of many HR directors lamenting staff's inability to describe their aptitudes. Now that you have identified your accomplishments and your core competencies, you are going to drill down into a deeper examination of all your skills and knowledge.

As we have already seen, many people sell themselves short because they are not aware of the full range of their skills and knowledge or else they "don't have the words" to describe what they are really good at.

## Completing the skills workout

In the exercise you are about to complete, you will assess your transferable skills. These are skills you can apply to a broad range of work situations and settings. Consider, for example, interpersonal skills such as building teams, resolving conflicts, and networking.

You will then complete your talent analysis by identifying both your technical skills and knowledge, and your personal interests.

Keep in mind that the most effective career moves are to work situations that involve the exercise of professional skills and knowledge that are most personally challenging to you. They also involve the situations that speak to your most deeply held personal interests.

## Technical skills and personal interests

In completing this exercise, use the following to help you identify your technical skills and personal interests. Technical skills and knowledge are acquired through education, work or volunteer experience, and personal interests. Examples include:

- Knowledge of the hospitality/healthcare/volunteer sector.
- Understanding of the impact of government legislation on pension planning.
- Ability to design management-development programs consistent with adult-learning principles.
- Skills in editing scientific materials for mass readership.
- Knowledge of garden design.
- Ability to design a survey.
- Specialized knowledge of the application of principles of xyz to abc; fashion design/trends.
- Understanding how to liaise with governments and private organizations to build social housing.

Some questions will help you to be specific about your personal interests:

- What nonfiction do you like to read (home decor or the juvenile justice system)?
- What do you like to do in your spare time? garden? shop? snowboard? give relationship advice?
- What would you like to volunteer for?
- What magazines, books, specialty TV shows, internet sites do you follow?
- If you were to take a course, just for the fun of it, what would you study?
- If you won the lottery and could do anything, how would you spend your time?

Examples: home renovation/decoration; children's wellness; cooking; juvenile justice; art and culture (be specific); yoga; literature (what kind); business; politics; bird watching; history; adventure travel.

# Career counsel

If you are having difficulty identifying your skills, knowledge, and interests, consider the following: When people come to you for advice, on what issues do they consult you (e.g., advice on kids, how to deal with a tricky situation at work)? On what do your friends compliment you? How would people who know you well describe your strengths?

## Assessing yourself

### What are your career assets?

▶ Preparing for the accomplishments workout
*page 61*

▶ Accomplishments workout
*pages 62–63*

▶ Core competencies workout
*pages 64–68*

▶ Summary of key competencies
*pages 70–71*

▶ Skills workout
*pages 74–77*

▶ Summary of skills, knowledge, and interests
*pages 78–79*

▶ Summing up your portfolio
*pages 82–85*

### SELF-ASSESSMENT    **Skills** workout

The following exercise will help you discover and articulate the full range of your skills. This exercise will be particularly helpful if you are: starting out or returning to the workforce after several years; considering making a career change; embarking on a job search; interested in identifying areas for development; or having difficulty articulating what you are really good at.

In evaluating each skill, recall a situation in which you demonstrated the skill, whether at work, in education, or in any other area of your life. If you are not sure whether you have a skill, think about how others would describe you. Read each skill listed and rate your enjoyment and feelings of satisfaction in using the skill as:

**V=Very High  H=High  M=Medium  L=Low**

Rate your degree of skill using the same scale:

| Skill | Enjoyment | Degree of skill |
|---|---|---|
| **Interpersonal** | | |
| ● Gaining trust and respect of others/building relationships | ☐ | ☐ |
| ● Relating to diverse people | ☐ | ☐ |
| ● Being sensitive to people's needs and feelings/empathy | ☐ | ☐ |
| ● Building teams | ☐ | ☐ |
| ● Contributing effectively to teams | ☐ | ☐ |
| ● Mediating/resolving conflicts/building consensus | ☐ | ☐ |
| ● Networking/building relationships | ☐ | ☐ |
| **Communication** | | |
| ● Listening effectively | ☐ | ☐ |
| ● Writing concisely and persuasively | ☐ | ☐ |
| ● Speaking persuasively | ☐ | ☐ |
| ● Translating complex ideas into everyday language | ☐ | ☐ |
| ● Giving helpful, constructive feedback | ☐ | ☐ |
| ● Making effective presentations | ☐ | ☐ |
| ● Having compelling sales approach/presentation | ☐ | ☐ |
| **Leading/managing** | | |
| ● Developing and communicating a compelling vision | ☐ | ☐ |
| ● Inspiring/motivating others | ☐ | ☐ |

- Gaining trust of others ☐ ☐
- Giving direction ☐ ☐
- Thinking strategically ☐ ☐
- Coordinating/organizing others ☐ ☐
- Managing projects ☐ ☐
- Planning ☐ ☐
- Communicating persuasively ☐ ☐
- Gaining cooperation of people you have no direct control of ☐ ☐

### Developing/coaching
- Counseling, advising ☐ ☐
- Coaching, training, and teaching new skills and competencies ☐ ☐
- Motivating others to achieve their goals ☐ ☐
- Giving helpful, constructive feedback ☐ ☐
- Mentoring ☐ ☐

### Planning and organizing
- Prioritizing tasks and assignments ☐ ☐
- Delegating effectively to make best use of others' skills ☐ ☐
- Integrating efforts of others ☐ ☐
- Thinking ahead and contingency planning ☐ ☐

### Time management
- Prioritizing to best meet customers'/organization's needs ☐ ☐
- Establishing achievable goals and objectives ☐ ☐
- Working effectively under pressure/demanding deadlines ☐ ☐
- Balancing work and personal life ☐ ☐

*People sell themselves short because they are not aware of the full range of their skills.*

**SELF-ASSESSMENT**  **Skills** workout cont'd

| Skill | Enjoyment | Degree of skill |
|---|---|---|
| **Learning and professional expertise** | | |
| ● Staying current | ☐ | ☐ |
| ● Developing new skills and knowledge to remain leading-edge | ☐ | ☐ |
| ● Expert in field | ☐ | ☐ |
| **Thinking** | | |
| ● Seeing the "big picture" | ☐ | ☐ |
| ● Conceptualizing ideas, models, relationships | ☐ | ☐ |
| ● Thinking strategically | ☐ | ☐ |
| ● Integrating and synthesizing information from different sources | ☐ | ☐ |
| ● Forward-thinking—anticipating future needs and requirements | ☐ | ☐ |
| ● Establishing achievable objectives | ☐ | ☐ |
| ● Creative/imaginative thinking | ☐ | ☐ |
| ● Understanding relationships between different events and ideas | ☐ | ☐ |
| **Problem-solving/decision-making** | | |
| ● Identifying and diagnosing a problem to get at root | ☐ | ☐ |
| ● Developing innovative, effective solutions to complex problems | ☐ | ☐ |
| ● Initiating projects, interventions, programs | ☐ | ☐ |
| ● Making decisions and following through | ☐ | ☐ |
| ● Taking personal responsibility for decisions | ☐ | ☐ |
| ● Dealing with ambiguity | ☐ | ☐ |
| **Researching/analyzing** | | |
| ● Gathering information; doing research | ☐ | ☐ |
| ● Attending to small details | ☐ | ☐ |
| ● Interpreting underlying themes from complex information | ☐ | ☐ |

**Cost sensitivity**
- Preparing budgets, computing costs, etc. □ □
- Establishing cost controls □ □
- Managing activities to stay within budget □ □
- Increasing profitability by reducing overhead □ □

**Innovation/business development**
- Identifying and capitalizing on opportunities □ □
- Developing new products to meet emerging needs □ □
- Actively seeking new opportunities □ □
- Generating income □ □

**Customer/client service**
- Strong customer/client-service focus □ □
- Making a real difference to customer/client (high impact) □ □
- Building and maintaining relationships □ □
- Being seen as a business partner □ □

**Technical skills and knowledge (list)**
- 
- 
- 
- 

**Personal interests (list)**
- 
- 
-

**PORTFOLIO**         **Summary of** skills, knowledge, and interests

**Strongest skills and knowledge**

*I am skilled at:*

..................................................................................................................

..................................................................................................................

..................................................................................................................

..................................................................................................................

..................................................................................................................

*I have specialized knowledge and interests in:*

..................................................................................................................

..................................................................................................................

..................................................................................................................

..................................................................................................................

..................................................................................................................

**Areas for development**

*Skills I really enjoy using (H or V in Column 1) but am not so good at (M or L in Column 2):*

..................................................................................................................

..................................................................................................................

..................................................................................................................

..................................................................................................................

*Technical skills, knowledge, and interests that I enjoy but am not expert in (M or L in Column 2):*

..................................................................................................................

..................................................................................................................

..................................................................................................................

*I may be able to improve these skills, knowledge, and interest areas by (brainstorm):*

...........................................................................................

...........................................................................................

...........................................................................................

...........................................................................................

...........................................................................................

...........................................................................................

...........................................................................................

...........................................................................................

...........................................................................................

...........................................................................................

*The skill areas in which I am strongest are:*

Look at the category headings (e.g., Communication, Problem-solving, Leading) under which most of your strongest skills fall, along with your deepest sense of satisfaction. Using these skills represents your greatest opportunity for optimizing career satisfaction and effectiveness.

...........................................................................................

...........................................................................................

...........................................................................................

...........................................................................................

...........................................................................................

...........................................................................................

...........................................................................................

...........................................................................................

...........................................................................................

*If you were to take a course just for the fun of it, what would you study?*

*If people err in their self-assessment, it is usually on the side of being too hard on themselves.*

**Sources of insight**
*Colleagues and friends can provide valuable insights into your strengths and trouble spots. Pay particular attention to comments you hear more than once—even if you do not like them.*

## Get feedback

Have you evaluated your career assets accurately? How do others see you? If people err in their self-assessment, it is usually on the side of being too hard on themselves. Yes, it is true that most of us have blind spots, and that others can point to trouble spots we may be unaware of. More often, however, they will identify skills, assets, and personal characteristics we have overlooked or significantly underestimated.

Check your results by speaking to people whose opinion you value (even those who are not your greatest fans). As long as they know how you tend to react to different situations, they can provide important insights. Consider asking past and current managers and team members, friends, clients, people you manage.

Questions you can ask include:

- What do you see as my major strengths? Trouble spots?
- If you had a problem, what would you consult me for advice on?
- Under what circumstances do you think I do my best work? When have you seen me "shine"?
- Under what circumstances do I seem to you to have most difficulty?
- If someone was not a fan of mine, what would they say about me?
- How can I improve how I am perceived by others?

Probe for information in such areas as: interpersonal skills; decision-making style; judgment; communication (written and oral) skills; ease in social interaction; kinds of people you interact with most and least effectively; personality characteristics; ability to plan, organize, follow through.

Be open to their feedback. If you do not like something they said, do not attack them—you asked for their feedback. If you do not understand something, probe for clarification and examples of the behavior. Pay special attention to comments you hear from several people.

**Assessing** yourself

**What are your career assets?**

▶ Preparing for the accomplishments workout
*page 61*

▶ Accomplishments workout
*pages 62–63*

▶ Core competencies workout
*pages 64–68*

▶ Summary of key competencies
*pages 70–71*

▶ Skills workout
*pages 74–77*

▶ Summary of skills, knowledge, and interests
*pages 78–79*

▶ Summing up your portfolio
*pages 82–85*

# **Summing up** your portfolio

Your analysis of your career portfolio is nearly complete: you have looked at your accomplishments, your core competencies, and your skills, knowledge, and interests. Now it is time to put this information together.

As you are writing, reflect on what you are saying about yourself. Even better, say it out loud.

*My underlying career images and themes are: (see Revealing core career themes, pages 24–25)*

......................................................................................................

......................................................................................................

......................................................................................................

......................................................................................................

*My key career motivators are: (see Your key motivators, pages 46–47)*

*Major*

......................................................................................................

*Minor(s)*

......................................................................................................

......................................................................................................

*My most important values are: (see Identifying your personal values, pages 52–54)*

......................................................................................................

......................................................................................................

......................................................................................................

......................................................................................................

*Based on this, I should avoid work that:*

......................................................................................................

......................................................................................................

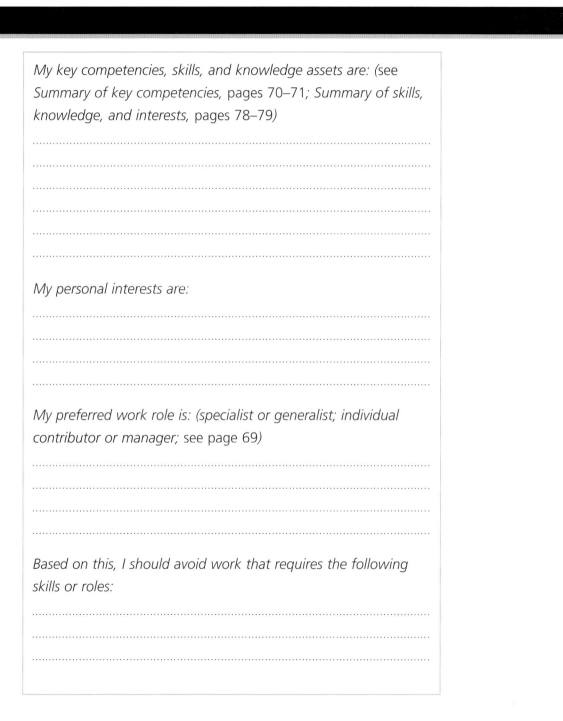

*My key competencies, skills, and knowledge assets are: (see Summary of key competencies, pages 70–71; Summary of skills, knowledge, and interests, pages 78–79)*

........................................................................................................

........................................................................................................

........................................................................................................

........................................................................................................

........................................................................................................

........................................................................................................

*My personal interests are:*

........................................................................................................

........................................................................................................

........................................................................................................

........................................................................................................

*My preferred work role is: (specialist or generalist; individual contributor or manager; see page 69)*

........................................................................................................

........................................................................................................

........................................................................................................

........................................................................................................

*Based on this, I should avoid work that requires the following skills or roles:*

........................................................................................................

........................................................................................................

........................................................................................................

PORTFOLIO　　　**Summing up** your portfolio cont'd

In thinking about your ideal work, do not worry about being overly realistic. This is private and a fantasy. If you can think of more than one ideal assignment, list them, too. (If you cannot think of anything, try answering the following question: "If I could be anything I wanted—with money no object—what would I be?")

*My ideal work (role, position, assignment) would be:*

..................................................................................................................

..................................................................................................................

..................................................................................................................

*What skills and competencies would you be using?*

..................................................................................................................

..................................................................................................................

..................................................................................................................

*What kinds of people would you be interacting with?*

..................................................................................................................

..................................................................................................................

..................................................................................................................

*What would be the special features of your working environment?*

..................................................................................................................

..................................................................................................................

..................................................................................................................

*What kind of roles or functions would you be playing?*

..................................................................................................................

..................................................................................................................

..................................................................................................................

*What kinds of problems would you be solving? What kinds of issues would you be thinking about?*

.......................................................................................

.......................................................................................

*Which of your important values would you be satisfying?*

.......................................................................................

.......................................................................................

.......................................................................................

*If you are currently employed, how well does your current work match your ideal work in terms of:*

| Work ideals | 1<br>Poor | 2 | 3<br>Somewhat | 4 | 5<br>Great |
|---|---|---|---|---|---|
| ● career motivators satisfied | ☐ | ☐ | ☐ | ☐ | ☐ |
| ● skills and competencies used | ☐ | ☐ | ☐ | ☐ | ☐ |
| ● kinds of people working with | ☐ | ☐ | ☐ | ☐ | ☐ |
| ● features of work environment | ☐ | ☐ | ☐ | ☐ | ☐ |
| ● roles or functions | ☐ | ☐ | ☐ | ☐ | ☐ |
| ● values being fulfilled | ☐ | ☐ | ☐ | ☐ | ☐ |

*What conflicts exist in your career motivators and values?*
*(Identifying potential conflicts; see page 49)*

.......................................................................................

.......................................................................................

.......................................................................................

*What trade-offs might you need to make?*

.......................................................................................

.......................................................................................

*Self-knowledge means being aware not only of what makes you feel good about yourself, but also what makes you unhappy.*

# 2 Find your perfect path

# Finding the right work match

Now it is time for you to look outside yourself. Which of 10 work sectors best fits your unique constellation of motivators, values, core competencies, and special knowledge? What constitutes a great organization for you? What kind of boss are you looking for?

## This chapter shows you how to:

**Decode** the culture of an organization and determine the types of work you should avoid or embrace.

**Put on** an organizational psychologist's hat and find the workplace "personality" that matches your temperament.

**Identify** your best cultural fit in 10 organizational sectors and numerous roles.

**Determine** where you would be happier—working in a large or small organization.

**Determine** which of 12 potential organizational rewards and benefits you need from a great employer.

**Understand** the management style you need in a boss to feel good about your work and yourself.

**Culture matters**

*The culture of the workplace—location, type of staff, management style—is as important as the content of the work.*

# Decoding organizational culture

It is not just what you do, it is also where you do it that determines a great work match. Understanding the culture of the different work sectors will show you where you should work—your best cultural fit given your needs, core values, and special skills. Knowing "what it feels like" to work in a particular environment is key.

If I asked you to describe a friend of yours, you might talk about their personality using such adjectives as warm, smart, dynamic, fun. Organizations have personalities, too: sluggish or dynamic, friendly or cool, relaxed or time-urgent. When people are thinking about whether they would like a particular type of work, they focus primarily on its technical content. However, equally important is where the work is done. The same work done for two different employers will have its own distinct feel because the work is determined by the personality of the organization and the character of its staff. These, in turn, will be influenced by many factors, including:

- The location of the business along with the look of the building and the design of its workspaces.
- The kinds of staff, including the dominant occupations and education of the key players, along with their age range and cultural diversity.
- The management style and history of the organization.
- The organization's size.
- The timelines set for success, risks associated with failure, and consequences of making a mistake.

## Think like an organizational psychologist

What is true of different companies within a sector is even truer of companies from different sectors. For a moment put on an organizational psychologist's hat and consider the very different personalities of two companies. One is a firm that processes payrolls at a few cents per transaction, but with millions of transactions. It used to be owned by a bank but several years ago was sold off to an international human-resources firm. Other than the company name, nothing much changed, including the management. Profitability ebbs and flows in response to the economy, internal efficiencies, and the ability of the firm to attract and retain high-value clients.

The other is a mid-sized TV production company making series and documentaries. The company was started 10 years ago by two network producers who were tired of in-house politics and compromising their work for advertisers. It was touch and go for a while, but now the company is on a relatively sound footing. Nothing is ever certain, however: investors are sought, deals are made, and deals are broken; the company will not know until the ratings come in three years later whether their investment in a production has paid off.

## Consider "feel"

Can you imagine how these companies might have a very different "feel"? Do you think the nature of the problems you would be solving would be different in the two firms? If you were a manager, would you use the same management style in both companies?

An organizational psychologist would think about these organizations and understand the nature of their work environments as follows. Most of the people in the payroll-processing firm are high-school grads; some of them are college-educated. This is not high-level knowledge work. Because profitability is dependent on internal efficiencies, there are clearly defined procedures with little room for initiative. Most of the managers are in their late 40s and 50s; many worked their way up. They are nice enough to be around socially, but at work they tend to be micromanagers.

As these managers approach retirement, new blood is being brought in. The new managers are younger and better educated than the old guard. They have been exposed socially and through their education to ideas of

*The same work done for two different companies will have its own distinct feel.*

*Panic is common—
the project is not
on schedule, it
is over budget,
it is garbage.*

empowerment and egalitarian work relationships. This leads to a clash of cultures and much jostling for power in the company.

The older ones say, "This is the way we've always done it. If it's not broke, don't fix it." Some of the younger managers are frustrated, thinking, "You would not have gotten this job today with your skills and qualifications." The older managers have worked together for a long time and enjoy collegial relationships. They feel they are one big family. They see each other socially and know their colleagues' kids.

As always happens in families, the company is not without its share of petty rivalries and tensions. ("I should have gotten that promotion, I've got more experience.")

People do not worry much about their jobs; they are pretty safe unless the economy sours. The work is routine. The atmosphere is pleasant, calm, and collected. People leave at 5 p.m. Many stability seekers and lifestylers work there.

In contrast, most of the people working for the TV production company are young and well educated. Many are contract employees. They do not know if they will be around beyond the project, though they would like to be. This means they are looking out for themselves: while they are working on one project, they are networking and looking for the next one. Because the work is uncertain and competitive, some backstabbing is inevitable.

This is a high-energy, hit-the-ground-running work environment; incompetence is not tolerated. Things go wrong all the time, and the consequences are serious. With so many egos involved, both internally and externally, and with so much money on the line, tempers often flare.

Panic is common—the project is not on schedule, it is over budget, it is garbage. This often leads to long work hours. Management is not very disciplined, and sometimes they "lose it" under the pressure. After all, senior management consists of people who have their own money on the line. And remember how they got started—they are professional people first, managers second.

People "hang out" together—going for drinks after work, for example—but relationships are constantly shifting. And there are some people who can never be trusted. Big egos mean junior staff have to be careful not to ruffle feathers—this is a great opportunity to get their foot in the door in a very competitive business. Sometimes this means dealing with temper tantrums when senior producers go into panic mode. The production company employs creative types: authenticity seekers, personal developers, and autonomy seekers. They are independent and challenge-seeking.

## Two organizational cultures

| Characteristics | Payroll company | TV production company |
|---|---|---|
| **Types of workers** | Lifestylers<br>Stability seekers | Personal developers<br>Authenticity seekers<br>Autonomy seekers |
| **Employment relationship** | Full-time | Many contractors |
| **Education** | Low to moderate | High |
| **Skill/Knowledge** | Low to medium | High |
| **Expandability** | More difficult to fire but lower skills make it easier to replace | High talent, but easy to fire because on contract |
| **Timelines** | Short | Up to three years |
| **Predictability** | Routine work | Lots of things can go wrong |
| **Investment** | Low | Moderate |
| **Emotional tone** | Calm | Frantic sometimes |

## Case study

Karen liked the consulting role she was playing in a warm, collegial human-resources department in a large bank. Her competence was respected, she had the ear of the CEO, and she was applying professional skills at a high level. But she felt she could not turn down the opportunity when she was headhunted for the top HR role with an oil refinery, with a significant increase in base pay and great stock options. Six months later she was out on the street by mutual agreement. The oil company said she was too soft, could not make the tough decisions, was too concerned about people's feelings. She said they were brutal. It was not her professional skills that were the problem, it was the work environment of the business sector.

# Finding your fit in the 10 industry sectors

**Each organizational sector has its own personality. Where do you see yourself?**

In the following pages you will get to know the dominant cultural characteristics of the 10 work sectors. The descriptions are a guideline only. Factors such as size, management philosophy and style of the CEO, and how entrepreneurial the organization is will significantly influence its personality. Use this information to:

- Learn more about yourself. What words/descriptors appeal to you? What turns you off?
- Learn more about the working environment of different industries. What is the best match for you given your self-assessment? Ask yourself, "Would I fit in here?" If you are currently employed but are unhappy, it may not be the work you are doing but where you are doing the work.
- Learn about different roles, functions, and departments within an industry sector. Many key organizational functions, such as marketing and sales, engineering, human resources, finance and administration, are described below.
- Get deeper insights into how different work combinations would look. For example, if you are interested in human resources, check out the Educators/Helpers sector. Then look at the other sectors to see what it might "feel like" to work as an HR professional in those sectors. Although to some degree HR departments have their own personality, that personality will be shaped by the culture of the industry. The result is a hybrid.

Read the descriptions for each work sector carefully. Circle the descriptions that you find most attractive and underline the ones that are least attractive.

## Marketing and sales

**Examples:** ▶ *packaged name-brand goods including food, cosmetics, and personal care* ▶ *entertainment (theme parks, mass-market toys, video games, marketing of movies)* ▶ *credit-card company loyalty groups* ▶ *global, diversified conglomerates (luxury spirits, clothing)*

"We're not in the business of producing video games. We're in the business of getting boys to take money from their pockets." This comment by a vice president of marketing captures the essence of this sector. Being profitable has as much to do with deciding how and to whom brands are sold, creating the "brand experience," and capitalizing on that experience as it does with the product. At the idea- or marketing-strategy (generation) phase, the work can be creative and intuitive. At the implementation stage, marketing plans and financials take over.

If the phrase "new and improved" describes the marketing strategy, it also often describes the approach to staff. Frequent restructurings mean that staff, as well as the products they are marketing, can have a short shelf life. As one finance professional for a credit-card company commented, "You leave work at the end of the day, and you do not know who your boss will be the next morning." Because of the intense competition internally and externally, there is little tolerance for failure. Sports metaphors with their vocabulary of winning and losing are used frequently. Many young overachievers in a hurry, clutching their MBAs, call this sector home. Lots of young blood is brought in each year.

These fast-paced and fluid environments can be exciting and rewarding for talented career builders, especially in global organizations. They are also a good fit for personal developers (as long as the profession is valued by the organization), novelty seekers, or creative authenticity seekers. They can be daunting for contemplative stability seekers and distasteful for value-hungry, authenticity seekers. Many bonus-driven Type A's work here. They thrive working at an everything-needed-yesterday pace. Touchy-feely people do not last long. These prestigious, hire-the-best environments provide diverse opportunities for top performers.

*"What is the brand experience?"*

## Scientific/Research and Development

**Examples:** ▶ *pharmaceutical* ▶ *petrochemical* ▶ *aerospace* ▶ *agribusiness,* ▶ *biotechnology* ▶ *aquaculture*

The common ingredient in these organizations is an emphasis on research and development, whether into aerospace, drugs, plastics, or practical applications of scientific discoveries. These organizations are prestigious, employing a significant number of highly skilled research scientists. Non-core staff (marketing, human resources) similarly tend to be clever and accomplished in their fields—they need to be in order to be effective and taken seriously in interactions with core staff. These organizations are financially cautious—it is very expensive to produce drugs that take years to come to market. Intuition does not play a role—everything is evaluated through measurable results and statistical outcomes.

Work in Scientific/R&D environments is team-based, and the atmosphere is warm and collegial. However, these teams can be experienced as arrogant and cool by noncore staff or outsiders. Environments are highly professional and prestigious. Knowledge and skills are at the base of the scientific end of the business, and there is intense competition for talented workers. To land that talent, many of these employers have sophisticated benefits and are sensitive to staff needs for career-development opportunities, transfers, fitness, and work–life balance.

Compensation in the global organizations reflects the importance of the individual knowledge worker. For example, a staff scientist might be paid the same as a vice president because he is "Mr. Polymer."

There are significant cultural differences between organizations in this sector. Consider, for example, a multinational of 50,000 employees with sizable finance, marketing, sales, and human-resources departments in each geographical location and a commitment to underwriting the development of a product that can take 15 years to break even. Now imagine a laboratory connected to a university, with 200 staff struggling

*"We need a full, in-depth analysis before we move ahead."*

### Environmental work
*Scientists take their work seriously. They are capable of putting in long hours with intense focus. They often work on projects in field environments.*

for funding, dealing with questions of ownership of patents and scientific freedom, constantly under pressure to publish. Or imagine a start-up biotechnology firm, founded by a team of scientists with little business and management expertise. The scientists in this company are continually looking for the new idea to pitch to investors and struggling to find venture capital. They feel the pressure of a discovery's short shelf life.

Personal developers can find wide scope for applying their skills at high levels; top-performing career-builders in global organizations can find significant challenge and advancement opportunities.

Evidence and measurable results are what count in this sector. Think twice about applying for a job here if you are a touchy-feely type. Most scientists are not sociability seekers, even though their working environments can feel very much like a family. Noncore staff who are sociability seekers may experience these working environments as cold. Autonomy seekers may be happier in an independent or quasi-independent lab than working for a multinational where their assignments are less closely tied to their academic interests.

Many organizations in this sector have large manufacturing and marketing and sales divisions, each with its own subculture. These divisions will have many of the characteristics described respectively under Marketing and sales (*see page 93*), and Engineering/Manufacturing (*see page 96*).

## Engineering/Manufacturing

**Examples:** ▶ *oil* ▶ *automotive* ▶ *electrical and utilities* ▶ *engine/turbine manufacturers* ▶ *steel* ▶ *construction* ▶ *nuclear-power plants* ▶ *mining* ▶ *the operations and manufacturing end of transportation (railroads, airlines)* ▶ *defense*

Airplanes cannot be manufactured according to specifications "more or less." Nor can they arrive and depart whenever the pilot feels like it. There is no room for error in this sector, with companies ranging from multinational automobile manufacturers to local energy utilities. They may be manufacturing anything from oil to missiles to cars to plastics to network-hardware components; typically they have large capital investments and a low ratio of people to machinery. If they are not manufacturing something, then they are managing highly leveraged infrastructures such as roads and telecommunications networks.

Because of the need for extreme predictability, tight timelines, and demanding budgets, work is scrutinized against clearly defined processes. Precision and attention to detail are key. These organizations have manuals to describe everything, and zero tolerance for failure. You are under the gun to meet budgets, quotas, timelines, quality standards, leading to constant problem-solving. Organizations focus tightly on the bottom line, always looking for efficiencies and opportunities to cut costs. "More, better, faster, with less" is the mantra.

Think twice about working in this sector if you are creative, thin-skinned, reflective, or intuitive, or if you are an authenticity seeker or sociability seeker. These are tough, male-dominated environments. Sometimes there are adversarial relations between management and hourly staff. Challenge-seeking personal developers and career builders can find significant advancement opportunities. Novelty-seeking project managers can feed their need for change. Many of these organizations are subject to economic shifts resulting in plant downsizings; they usually have a stable work force with many long-tenured, stability-seeking employees. Many of these environments are unionized.

*"On time, on budget."*

## Agents/Brokers/Deal-makers

**Examples:** ▶ *investment and corporate bankers* ▶ *venture capitalists*
▶ *leveraged buyout specialists* ▶ *commercial real estate* ▶ *consolidators*

It is all about the deal and the adrenaline rush when you get it. The bigger the deal, the bigger the rush. "What are my options worth?" Money is the way to keep score. With intense pressure to make the deal, there will always be winners and losers.

Being a player and being seen as a player is the measure of self-worth. When you are not playing, you feel dead. Hence the true stories of brokers checking the market within hours of undergoing bypass surgery. You are only as good as your last hit. Rather than feeling good about the mountain that has just been conquered, players look at the mountain that has not been conquered—yet. Time-urgent, driven Type A's call this area home. The work is fast paced and intellectually challenging, with short bursts of intense problem-solving. Intelligence and effective decision-making are revered. Everyone needs to be able to adapt and fend for themselves. Quick-thinking, resourceful, clever, confident people do well. They are able to move on after mistakes, and can integrate a lot of information and make a call quickly. They are cocky and tend not to follow the crowd. Weaklings do not last long. People in this environment can be demanding and intolerant of those who cannot keep pace (lifestylers and contemplative thinkers, take note).

There is little room for sentiment. Your allegiance is to yourself, not your employer. The product being marketed or traded is not important. You may like the people you work with, but in the final analysis what counts is their usefulness. People measure their success quantitatively: the size of the deal, the cost of the car, the number of electronic toys. There is a lot of social comparison. "I want to be sure I get the credit for that" is a common cry.

That said, there can also be tremendous camaraderie. Traders, for example, can be fiercely loyal to each other, while suspicious of outsiders and non-investment types.

*"What are my options worth?"*

*"Let's evaluate the situation and give you our recommendations."*

## Advisory/Professional services

**Examples:** ▶ *public-accounting and legal firms* ▶ *benefits consultants* ▶ *strategic planners* ▶ *large management- and human-resources consulting firms* ▶ *client-services organizations*

Many different types of professionals work in this sector, from public accountants to lawyers, actuaries, and management consultants. What they have in common is that they are selling expertise and knowledge.

The cultures of firms vary both within the particular professional sector (between different accounting firms, for example) and between professional sectors. As firms scramble to attract and retain the best and the brightest, they try to distinguish themselves from their competitors by selling their "unique employee brand." They trumpet that they provide the best training and development, the best work–life balance, or the best international opportunities.

Many of these firms depend on the availability of a large pool of young professionals whom they can leverage. These in-demand knowledge workers are looking for learning opportunities and work–life balance. As a result, many firms invest heavily in learning and development and are sensitive to staff needs.

That said, often there are value conflicts between older partners and the young professionals. The latter complain about schedules and unreasonable expectations for billable hours. The partners respond, "We're in the business of serving clients and meeting their needs when they need it—not when it suits your needs."

Although people are competing for the great assignments and for promotions, they are collegial and often develop social friendships. This can also be a source of tension: "We're all one professional team here, but only one of you is going to be promoted." People in this sector are not known for their effusiveness. Feedback tends to be negative. Positive feedback is qualified—"that was quite good" (translation: "that was great"). Words like "brilliant" and "amazing" are rarely used. People in this sector are under constant pressure to increase their billable hours, as well as to sell and cross sell. This can be a challenge, particularly for staff who are motivated to practice their craft and are uncomfortable in marketing roles. Fact and evidence, rather than intuition, underlie the work, which makes this kind of work a challenge for intuitive professionals. Authenticity seekers find it difficult to disengage their intuition and use fact and evidence for decisions. The repetitive nature of the work can also be challenging.

Tension arises from "who gets the recognition?" On the one hand, the firm is selling its reputation, not the reputation of individual contributors. On the other hand, its fortunes depend on the talent of the individual contributors. And many of these individual contributors have strong personal needs for recognition. When they become famous, by writing a book or becoming the leading expert in the field, for example, they often move on.

Many of the large firms, particularly those in public-accounting and human-resources consulting, have a number of professional disciplines lodged under the same umbrella, leading to good opportunities for lateral movement.

These are professional environments. Reputation is everything. Your leading-edge technical skills, ability to manage yourself, and talent for building relationships with clients will determine your success.

The greatest number of workers in this sector are personal developers and lifestylers, although career builders, autonomy seekers, and stability seekers are also well represented. Novelty-seeking professionals may disdain the repetitive nature of the work, although this may be modified by the opportunity to do increasingly complicated work with different clients and to move across practice areas.

The tools of these type of workers are their laptops, their brains, their pro formas and protocols.

*Although people are competing for the great assignments and for promotions, they are collegial and often develop social friendships.*

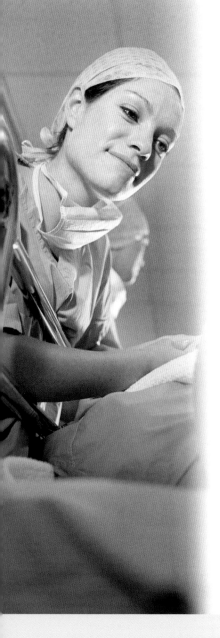

*"You try this job for a month with the kind of money and resources I have."*

## Government/Health/General welfare

**Examples:** ▶ *hospitals* ▶ *government services* ▶ *NGOs (environmental agencies, foundations, community organizations, charities, service organizations)*

Although organizations in this sector vary widely from small community-based nonprofits to large government bureaucracies, they have in common a mandate to satisfy the needs of multiple stakeholders—some combination of the public, the community, volunteers, clients, elected officials, and a board of directors, for example. They are accountable to an external body, have to manage competing demands from stakeholders for programs and policies, and are often cash-squeezed. They deal with complex issues, often under a siege mentality. Frequently they feel their work is unappreciated by the public—in fact, that they are working under negative public scrutiny.

Not surprisingly, a comment you often hear from people in this sector is, "This problem is much more complicated than you realize."

Historically, many have shunned working in this sector, saying, "Who wants to work with a bunch of self-satisfied bureaucrats who spend their day drinking coffee and pushing paper?" For the most part, this image has little to do with today's reality. Yes, there always were, and always will be, pockets of stifling bureaucracy and cautiousness. Some of the most interesting work I have ever done, and with some of the smartest people, however, has been in such contexts. This sector is undergoing revitalization, with the wave of baby-boomer retirements freeing up opportunities for young people.

These are collegial environments where individual differences are respected and cultural diversity is embraced. Although there are significant career-development opportunities for ambitious career builders, most people who work here do not do so for the money, which typically is lower than in the private sector. (Note that the pay gap is closing, especially in large government institutions and well-funded agencies.) You will find authenticity seekers who believe in the importance of their service, novelty seekers who appreciate the breadth of opportunities, personal developers who are attracted to the scope of professional challenges, and sociability seekers who like the often-friendly environments. Although some people work very long hours, there is greater opportunity to work a normal workload, which attracts lifestylers. Although these sectors have experienced frequent large-scale restructurings, and will continue to do so, public services are also home to many stability seekers.

For mid-career changers, work in this sector provides an opportunity for rejuvenation as well as to do work in sync with personal values. Older workers coming to the end of their career will look at nonprofits as a way of giving something back before they transition to retirement. For younger workers who put down "socially responsible" as an essential for employment, this kind of work can both satisfy personal needs and provide skill-building and challenge.

Perhaps surprisingly, many autonomy seekers also call this sector home. They avoid larger, more bureaucratic government departments, which can feel like death to them, in favor of field environments where they can "own" a program or work in plucky community agencies or other NGOs. There are significant differences between the cultures of government departments and between types of organizations in this sector. Cultures vary as well between frontline service providers, who are subject to burnout, and those in policy roles.

"I never get to finish anything. I never get a sense of completion." I hear this kind of comment frequently from people who work in the public sector where priorities constantly shift. This can be a major source of frustration, particularly for stability seekers and personal developers. Also frustrating to government and NGO staff is the need for constant consensus building. Nonetheless, the scope and importance of the work, along with the collegiality of the environments, are such that people in this sector are less restless and less interested than their private-sector counterparts in making a career change into a new line of work.

## Career counsel

Watch this sector. In the coming years you will see significant growth in career opportunities in NGOs and community-based organizations. Governments are cutting back social programs and are getting out of the business of direct-service delivery. Meanwhile, citizens are becoming more aware of the need for social infrastructure. Services such as meal deliveries, shelters, and recreational programs will be in greater demand by an aging population and by people who socially have fallen through the cracks.

## Educators/Helpers

**Examples:** ▶ *organizational and management-development firms* ▶ *edutainment (video- and web-based learning, e-learning)* ▶ *psychiatric, psychological, and social services* ▶ *human-resources departments* ▶ *personal trainers* ▶ *educational institutions* ▶ *coaches* ▶ *massage therapists* ▶ *nutritionists*

People in this sector sell their expertise and skills, and reputation is all-important. They need to develop long-term relationships with clients or to add value by establishing relationships with internal clients. Their focus is on helping people to be better, do something better, or know something better, not on business (although their interventions may contribute to the bottom line). People tend to be warm and collegial, although, interestingly, most are not sociability seekers.

People in this sector, mostly legacy-driven personal developers and lifestylers, set high professional standards and are not motivated primarily by money. "It's not just a job—it's about people's lives." Leaving work at the office is a challenge. Burnout is an occupational hazard, particularly for professionals and paraprofessionals working for large publicly funded institutions. They often feel under siege as they struggle with government cutbacks and sometimes-negative public perception. Equally challenging for many is the repetitive nature of the work, though people and levels of responsibility do change. The rewards are also significant: being able to make a difference in someone's life and watching someone change as a result of a personal intervention.

While employed individuals in this sector often feel under pressure to justify their existence, the self-employed—among whom there are many personal developers and autonomy seekers fed up with organizational politics and cutbacks, lifestylers looking for flexibility, authenticity seekers looking for freedom to express themselves—can also feel the pressure of spreading themselves too thin. Doing professional work while continually having to pitch new business and manage unreasonable client expectations takes its toll.

*"I want to make a difference in people's lives."*

## Service/Custodial

**Examples:** ▶ *credit agencies* ▶ *retirement residences* ▶ *nursing homes*
▶ *schools for children with disabilities* ▶ *security agencies* ▶ *baggage
handlers* ▶ *nurses aides* ▶ *fast-food chains* ▶ *telemarketing agencies*
▶ *some forms of tourism* ▶ *nontechnical support* ▶ *inbound call centers
(reservations, customer fulfillment)* ▶ *facilities management*
▶ *housekeeping and maintenance departments* ▶ *supermarkets*

Consisting largely of low-skilled, low-paying necessity jobs, the work is
routine and transactional and requires little independent thought or
initiative. Some workers are treated shabbily. That said, many people
who work in this sector enjoy their work and the fact that they do not
have to take it home at the end of the day. They may take pride in their
employer and have a sense of belonging.

Relationships can be collegial or rife with small and not so small
animosities. As many of these workers feel powerless, and management
in this sector is not known for its sophistication (there are notable
exceptions), there can be an adversarial relationship between
management and workers. Workers are usually closely supervised.
("This call is being monitored.") Profit in this sector comes from
maximizing production, minimizing costs. There is high stress, especially
for frontline service providers.

Many students work in this sector, at least for a short time. So do
lifestylers looking for flexible work schedules that enable them to pursue
their real interests; older and returning workers; and people hurt by the
permanent loss of better jobs or physical disability. Although there are
many long-tenured staff, these jobs are particularly vulnerable to changes
in the economy. Many workers in this sector are unionized. For the most
part, there is low investment in staff development.

The challenge for savvy managers in this sector is creating positive
environments where individual workers feel valued. Managers also need
to be sensitive to demographic and cultural diversity.

*"It's just a job, but
it pays the bills."*

*"I really like the people I work with."*

## Customer service/Administration

**Examples:** ▶ *stores* ▶ *retail banks* ▶ *hospitality and tourism (travel agencies, hotels, flight attendants, and restaurant personnel)* ▶ *call centers that provide technical support* ▶ *back-room administration involving problem-solving and technical knowledge (payroll departments, insurance claims, and bank loan approval)*

"I enjoy my job, but I like the fact that I can leave it at the end of the day." "I really like the people I work with." These are the kinds of comments I hear most frequently from people who are happily employed in this sector.

Not surprisingly, many people-pleasing sociability seekers and lifestylers looking for jobs that will not spill over into their personal life work in these environments.

Jobs vary in the amount of direct customer contact. What they have in common, in contrast to jobs in the service/custodial sector, is latitude for individual initiative and problem-solving and a need for technical skills. The latter may include anything from being able to sell a high-end dress to a demanding customer to understanding the impact of government legislation on payroll deductions.

Although this work is governed by standards and procedures, in progressive organizations being able to take individual initiative is critical to success. As the head of human resources for an international hotel chain said, "There are rules, but the rules are there to be broken." This may mean refunding a charge to an unhappy customer or upgrading a hotel guest, without getting permission from management. Also important for success are enthusiasm, good client relations, and professionalism.

A significant difference between front-of-the-house work and behind-the-scenes administration is the pace. Customer-service jobs, particularly in retail and hospitality environments, can be extremely fast-paced, with multiple demands thrown at staff simultaneously—five clients wanting your attention while your boss is breathing down your neck waiting for inventory numbers.

Equally challenging is managing the "down" times—going from a frenetic spell to a lull. Gossip, not necessarily kind, often occurs during these periods. People in the back of the house—checking contracts, designing schedules, balancing the books—appreciate the greater predictability of their work. Although some people, in particular stability seekers, like the routine nature of the work—no hassles, no surprises— others complain of boredom and feelings of anonymity. This can lead to low morale.

Although jobs in the front of the house are more directly sales-oriented ("I see, Mr. Jones, that you have considerable money sitting in your checking account. Would you be interested in one of our savings tools?"), most jobs in this sector have a sales component, as every contact with a customer can be considered a sales contact, and an unhappy customer is not a repeat customer.

Smart employers in this sector are attentive to staff needs for training, work–life balance, and career opportunities. That said, many do treat workers shabbily, especially in the lower-paid service sector, where turnover rates are high. Many part-timers (students, people who are "between jobs," displaced workers) work in these jobs, and they are particularly vulnerable.

This sector attracts people-pleasing sociability seekers and expressive authenticity seekers who believe in the product—for example, fashion workers and salespeople in music stores. Incomes vary widely from minimum-wage sweatshops to high-end commissioned sales.

People who do well in commissioned sales are self-managing, responsive to financial rewards, have strong egos, and are resilient. They are customer-focused and take pleasure in providing tailored interventions to meet client needs.

*In progressive organizations being able to take individual initiative is central to success.*

## Media and cultural

**Examples:** ▶ *mass media* ▶ *publishing* ▶ *music* ▶ *film* ▶ *new media* ▶ *art departments* ▶ *museums and galleries* ▶ *ad agencies* ▶ *fashion* ▶ *creative end of entertainment*

People in media and the arts usually get their kicks from creative activity and expression or practicing their craft, rather than from financial rewards. They like working with ideas, words, and pictures. Numbers bore them (although obviously this does not apply to people in sales, marketing, production, and other noncreative roles in these industries, which are focused on revenue generation). Many are disdainful of "the corporate world."

People in the media and cultural sector strongly identify with their work. They derive their status from being recognized for their creative contributions, from their influence on public opinion, or from being associated with prestigious institutions and publications. While some measures of their work's success are objective (book sales, newspaper circulation, television ratings), most are subjective and qualitative. They may be very ambitious for higher-profile assignments in bigger arenas, but generally have little interest in upper management: they would rather stay on the creative front lines. They are gossipy and always interested in "the buzz," and they love to be "in the know."

There is no defined career path; everyone makes her own. Reputation, contacts, and fit are more important than a résumé in landing a new job or assignment.

Most people on the creative side of the business—directors, columnists, authors, performers—are intuitive rather than analytical thinkers, lateral rather than linear. Most come from liberal-arts backgrounds. They tend to be curious, irreverent, skeptical of authority, easily bored, adaptable, and novelty seeking. They may also be insecure, with a constant need to prove their value through their work. They are competitive—for bylines, mentions in the press, reviews, awards. Most of them are highly verbal.

*"You're only as good as your last hit."*

Originality and fresh approaches are extremely important to get ahead. It is not all about creativity, however. There is also a heavy craft component to many jobs in this sector—for example, editing, fact checking, producing, researching, reporting, curating. On the craft side of the business, the opportunity to hone and apply skills at a high level is a major motivator. Workers in this sector move frequently between different vehicles—between different magazines or radio programs, for example—in the search for new challenges. Young people interested in the creative side of the business usually need to earn their stripes on the craft side.

Ultimately, success depends on creating media products that can find an audience in a marketplace that changes rapidly. People in these fields can have a short shelf life. Some have long-term, secure jobs, but many are highly mobile and move frequently between employers, or between different units of one employer. Work in this sector is competitive and often insecure: you are judged on what you can do and you are only as good as your last hit. Younger workers scramble to break into the business by taking whatever work they can get; older workers feel pressure as a result of their age: this is a youth-obsessed industry.

Team leaders (executive producers, senior editors) have the talent to recognize, recruit, and reward other talented people. There are many freelancers and contractors. Incomes range from very low to very high. A large number of personal developers, autonomy seekers, authenticity seekers, and novelty seekers work in this sector.

Cultural fields require people with a wide variety of strengths, preferences, and aptitudes. Some mainly work alone (some kinds of book editors); others work in small, close-knit teams (television producers). Some jobs demand a high degree of accuracy, precision, and daily deadline consciousness (newspaper copy editors), while others are driven by the "big idea" and projects with a longer timeline. Many people are happy to work "behind the scenes," contributing their particular technical expertise to the success of the project. Most people identify with their craft or profession, not their employer.

**Assessing** yourself

**Finding the right work match**

▶ Identifying the match
*pages 108–109*

▶ 12 features of a a great organization
*pages 111–112*

**PORTFOLIO**    **Identifying** the match

Think about each industry sector. Ask yourself, "Can I imagine myself working in this sector or in this role?"

*In what sector(s) have you identified the most appealing features, and the fewest negative features?*

.......................................................................................................

.......................................................................................................

.......................................................................................................

.......................................................................................................

.......................................................................................................

*What roles/functions might be a good match for you? Which industry sectors?*

.......................................................................................................

.......................................................................................................

.......................................................................................................

.......................................................................................................

.......................................................................................................

.......................................................................................................

*Which sectors, at first glance at least (remember these are guidelines only), should you be wary of?*

.......................................................................................................

.......................................................................................................

.......................................................................................................

.......................................................................................................

.......................................................................................................

.......................................................................................................

If you are currently employed, to what extent is your work a good match (regardless of its organizational sector). List the descriptors you have identified as appealing and unappealing. Evaluate your work against them.

*Characteristics that appeal to me*

*Characteristics that do not appeal to me*

.................................................... ....................................................
.................................................... ....................................................
.................................................... ....................................................
.................................................... ....................................................
.................................................... ....................................................
.................................................... ....................................................
.................................................... ....................................................
.................................................... ....................................................
.................................................... ....................................................

*Get feedback: Who can you speak to who would have insider knowledge of the sectors that appeal to you?*

....................................................................................
....................................................................................
....................................................................................
....................................................................................
....................................................................................
....................................................................................
....................................................................................
....................................................................................
....................................................................................
....................................................................................

### The right organization

*Great organizations meet the needs of the new worker. People in these environments enjoy working with each other. They are stimulated to grow personally and professionally.*

# Working for a great organization

Wanted: One terrific employer that is committed to personal and professional development and does not treat workers like interchangeable units.

What makes a great employer?

I am asked this question frequently, in particular by young people. As we have already seen, the new employment contract means that today everyone needs to take responsibility for their own employability, managing the boundaries of their professional and personal lives, and ensuring their economic survival. You also have your own set of specific needs related to your career situation, life stage, personal career motivators, and so on.

Opposite is a list of 12 potential benefits, policies, and features. I have yet to encounter an organization that has all 12. If you study the list of the best employers, however, you will find that many have a good number of these features.

### Size matters

Organizational size plays an important role in shaping what work "feels like," with people tending to feel more engaged in their work in smaller organizations. They feel more accountable for company outcomes, compared with people in large organizations who are less likely to feel that their contributions matter. Very small organizations also face challenges, however. The personality of the leader always has an impact on organizational culture, but that impact is experienced intimately in small organizations. A great boss will create a fabulous work environment; an egotistical, temperamental boss will wreak havoc. There are also more petty rivalries and tensions. A toxic co-worker will create a toxic work environment, and their presence is not muted by the fact that people are coming and going, doing multiple things.

**Assessing** yourself

**Finding the right work match**

▶ Identifying the match
   *pages 108-109*

▶ 12 features of a a great organization
   *pages 111-112*

**SELF-ASSESSMENT**   **12 features** of a great organization

Check off the characteristics that are most important to you. Underline the specific features within the descriptions that are most appealing.

| Characteristics | Features |
| --- | --- |
| ☐ **Learning opportunities** | Development is provided in good times and bad, not just when retention of staff becomes an issue. Everything from formal training and on-line learning to cross-departmental movement and opportunities to shadow someone in another job are offered. You are given assignments that stretch you out of your comfort zone. Work assignments and developmental activities are designed to play to your strengths and stretch you. The organization supports your learning by underwriting educational tuition and conference participation. Some organizations give each of its employees a "personal learning account"—a percentage of their salary to use on professional development, including courses, conferences, and books. Staff do not need to justify or explain their expenditures, and there are no expectations that the investment will pay off immediately on the job. |
| ☐ **A collegial environment sensitive to your needs** | Managers are sensitive to your personal issues and concerns. Your workload is manageable. You like the people you work with. People help when you are going through a difficult patch. Individual talents are recognized and celebrated. If the employer uses competency profiles (lists of desired behavior or skills for a particular job), they are treated as guidelines only. Your uniqueness is valued. |
| ☐ **Policies are actually implemented** | Some companies ensure that staff get a minimum number of hours of training and receive their annual performance review by penalizing their manager if they fail to get it. |
| ☐ **Career planning and coaching** | The organization does more than pay lip service to career self-management. It provides the tools and time to reflect on accomplishments, developmental needs, work preferences, and personal and professional goals. As a result, you can have meaningful career discussions with your manager. |
| ☐ **Mentoring** | People can benefit from the opportunity to be counseled in everything from career development to how to solve tricky political problems. Formal relationships involve matching potential candidates with mentors, while informal ones promote the concept of partnering by having people select from a pool of potential mentors. |

## SELF-ASSESSMENT | **12 features** of a great organization cont'd

☐ **Life-friendly**
Sensitive to the needs of all staff, regardless of their age and whether they are parents or not. Some organizations do a good job of supporting parents with young children but are not as sensitive to the needs of older or childless workers. Just because you do not have young kids does not mean you do not have a life. Life-friendly companies offer not only daycare subsidies, on-site daycare, or emergency baby-sitting, but also help with elder care, opportunities to bridge to retirement, and benefits for gay partners.

☐ **Personal services**
Some organizations provide an on-site concierge to assist, for a small fee, in personal services, whether it is having your dry-cleaning picked up or taking your car to the garage.

☐ **Flexible work arrangements**
Flexible hours, work from home, part-time work—they are all okay. People's careers are not derailed when they take advantage of these policies, as witnessed by the number of part-time senior staff.

☐ **Sabbaticals and extended vacations**
With so many today working to the point of exhaustion, some organizations encourage staff to take sabbaticals to recharge themselves, reflect on next steps if they have come to a career crossroads, or pursue a personal passion.

☐ **Wellness initiatives**
These could include personal trainers, Pilates and yoga instruction, aerobics classes, fitness centers, ergonomically designed workspaces, massage therapists. Vegetarians are welcome in the cafeteria.

☐ **Flexible benefits**
Complicated personal and family configurations mean that people have different benefit needs. Great organizations provide staff with a menu of benefits they can choose from, be it tuition assistance, dental coverage, extended parental leaves, or disability insurance, rather than assuming everyone is a member of a nuclear family with the same risk tolerance and needs for protection.

☐ **Opportunities to own a project**
Today, many people who are employed want to have the same kinds of experiences they might have if they were running their own businesses. That means owning their own work. They are prepared to take risks in return for a greater stake in the profits or losses.

Small-business owners often have fewer professional-management skills. They are under financial pressure to make their business a success. Their business is their "baby," so they may micromanage. However, they may also be "hands off" in their management style—they are too busy with other parts of the business to bother with each individual contributor.

Depending on your needs for autonomy, this hands-off approach can be a good or bad thing. Small businesses tend to be more entrepreneurial, great for people who prefer fluid, fast-changing environments, a challenge for stability seekers.

## Get a great boss

Most people do not quit companies, they quit their boss. A great boss will create a great working environment, while a bad boss will decimate your sense of competence and self-esteem. (For more on toxic bosses, *see* Overcome your career challenges, *pages 254–259*.) A great boss will coach and mentor you, put work–life policies into practice, and make training and development a fundamental part of your work. She will also thank you for a job well done, acknowledge your accomplishments, and be sensitive to your needs.

Whether or not a particular manager is a good match for you, however, depends on your career motivations. For example, if you are an autonomy seeker reporting into a manager who is even slightly controlling, you may experience her as a micromanaging dictator. If you are a stability seeker, however, you may experience that boss as being helpful and giving good direction.

## Career counsel

Review your career motivators. Think about what you need in a boss.

- What characteristics would that boss have?
- What kind of management style best matches your preferences?
- If you are currently employed, how does your boss's style match with your needs?

# What is your best option ?

How do you want to live and work? The options are many, including working part-time, telecommuting, working your portfolio, and working for yourself. Then again, maybe you would like to change your career altogether. Which option is right for you? What is the nature of the work relationship you want?

## This chapter shows you how to:

**Find** part-time work that gives you flexibility while allowing you to stay in the career loop.

**Identify** whether you have the right temperament, skills, and type of work for telecommuting.

**Work** your personal portfolio of skills—creating a living from diverse arenas to fulfill all your values.

**Determine** whether you have the skills and temperament to brave the challenges of self-employment.

**Evaluate** careers and audition employers to find work and workplaces that are a good match for you.

**Identify** and evaluate the relative payoffs of a career shift vs. a radical career change.

## Case study

Linda could not keep up with all the demands placed on her between her work as a senior manager and her home life as the mother of three young children. She was ambitious and knew that in her company part-timers were not promoted. She struggled. Should she maintain the frantic pace and face burnout, or put her career on hold? After collapsing with fatigue one night, she had a flash of insight. "I realized that the great career would still be there for me in three or four years, but I would never get back those years with my kids."

# Working part-time

For most people today, time is the most valued commodity. Working part-time helps you to fulfill all your roles in life both professionally and personally.

The amount of time we have today is precious: for family, for pursuing a personal passion, and for self. With their overcommitted lives and grueling workloads, many people are managing their time-squeeze by looking for shorter work hours. Polls show a significant number of people would take a pay cut if they could work fewer hours. It is not only lifestylers who would consider such a thing: a shorter workweek is high on many people's wish list.

The chief benefit of part-time work is flexibility—the opportunity to produce income and stay professionally engaged while still honoring other life commitments. However, when people think about part-time work options, at the top of their mind is loss of income. Often what they forget are the costs of *not* reducing their workweek—to their families, their health, and their sense of wholeness.

A comment I hear frequently from parents is, "I need to work full-time in order to give my kids a good lifestyle." Yet I wonder how their kids really benefit. Sure they live in a fancy house and go on expensive trips. However, their parents come home from work grumpy and distracted, too tired to spend meaningful time with them. Who are the real losers? What is more important to a child's healthy development—time with parents or an expensive vacation? Happy part-timers cannot imagine going back to a full workload. As one told me, "I feel squeezed even now. If the only way I could keep my job was by going back to full-time work, I would quit."

Not being in the loop can be a source of frustration, or a benefit, for part-timers. For some, it means feeling left out, missing out on important information, or not being seen to be seriously committed to the work. But as one happy part-timer commented, "When I go in I do my thing. I'm liberated from the day-to-day politics, which is great."

# **Strategies** for finding part-time work

Although there are lots of part-time work opportunities in the service sector, finding part-time professional work is more challenging. Here are some tips:

▶ Shop at home. It is usually easier to negotiate a change in work status with a current employer who understands your value than to find a new employer to whom you are an unproven entity. Sometimes this may mean moving to a lower-level position, or making a lateral move to a new department in which management needs your skills.

▶ Get into your boss's head and develop your pitch accordingly. Does he talk about being an employer of choice? Is he concerned that the ball may be dropped when you are not there? Anticipate the issues that may bother him and show how you will manage them.

▶ Demonstrate your understanding of key deliverables. Write a business case showing how they will be achieved.

▶ Show cost savings—how the company keeps a valuable employee while reducing overhead, including benefits, without compromising deliverables.

▶ Change your boss. Unfortunately some managers still confuse the amount of face time with work commitment.

▶ Be the right person for the job, but not too expensive. Employers sometimes cannot afford to hire full-time the person they really want. Some people successfully sell themselves into part-time work by showing how, by virtue of their skills and experience, they can do the job in a shorter work week, taking a reduced salary in line with reduced hours. Consider Sheri, a vice president of marketing. The company wanted to hire her as a full-time employee, but her salary expectations were 20 percent higher than they could afford. She also did not want full-time work. She convinced them that she could do the work in four days a week without compromising deliverables. In exchange, they paid her 100 percent of the salary they had budgeted for full-time work.

▶ Show flexibility. Demonstrate a willingness to modify your work schedule in the face of emergencies and changing work demands. One accountant, for example, rigidly enforces his 60 percent schedule for nine months of the year to spend time with his children. During tax season he works round the clock—a trade-off he happily makes.

▶ Look for family-friendly employers. You will be most likely to find them in the public sector and large financial institutions, and environments with younger work forces where talent is the core of the business, such as public-accounting firms.

## **Assessing** yourself

### **What is your best option?**

▶ Are you suited for part-time work?
*pages 118–119*

▶ Planning for part-time work
*pages 120–121*

▶ Are you suited for telecommuting?
*page 126*

▶ Planning for telecommuting
*page 127*

▶ Planning to work your portfolio
*page 129*

▶ Are you suited for self-employment?
*pages 134–135*

▶ Planning to work for yourself
*page 137*

▶ Planning a career shift
*pages 144–145*

▶ Planning for staying where you are
*page 149*

**SELF-ASSESSMENT    Are you suited to part-time work?**

Part-time work is not for everyone. Do you have the right circumstances and temperament?

| Suitability | Characteristics |
| --- | --- |
| ☐ **Can you afford to work part-time?** | Analyze your financial situation. Be realistic about what you really need to work part-time vs. what you merely like having, such as that second car. |
| ☐ **Are you prepared to trade advancement for lifestyle?** | Career-building lifestylers often face a difficult dilemma. They have to decide between satisfying career ambitions and lifestyle needs. Although some employers try to ensure that part-timers are not penalized in their career progress, these employers are probably still more the exception than the rule, despite whatever work–life policies they may have in place. There are some good reasons why part-timers are hindered. As one human-resources vice president of a bank, herself a part-timer, observed, "People get ahead because they are noticed by senior management. If you're only at work two days a week, there is less opportunity to be noticed." They also get ahead because they volunteer to take on extra work, especially if it is high profile. Ambitious part-timers understand these challenges. If they are savvy, they identify other vehicles for keeping themselves in the mind space of key decision-makers. |
| ☐ **Are you prepared to give up stability?** | Most employers are reluctant to guarantee a return to full-time work. Do not forget a reduction or loss of benefits can also be a challenge. Many part-time positions, particularly in retail and hospitality, do not provide any coverage, or else benefits are prorated to time worked. |
| ☐ **Are you prepared to give up a sense of belonging?** | If you are a sociability seeker or love being part of a group, working part-time may be lonely for you. If you do work part-time, build into your daily routine regular activity, such as going to the gym, or lunch with a friend. |
| ☐ **Does the work lend itself to being done on part-time basis?** | The work is stand-alone, with little knowledge transfer required on an ongoing basis. It does not overly burden colleagues to pick up the slack. If you are a manager, your staff is self-directed. The work does not require you to be in the loop. |

| | | |
|---|---|---|
| ☐ | **Are you a disciplined self-manager?** | Working part-time requires self-discipline. It means being able to discriminate between real emergencies that require your input—if you want this arrangement to be successful you need to show your employer that you are reasonable—and knee-jerk impositions on your unpaid time: "I can't be bothered to think about this, let's call Linda." Sometimes you will have to refuse unreasonable requests for help, which may require talking to your colleagues and boss about your expectations. |
| ☐ | **Do you have a clear idea of what you want to gain through part-time work arrangements?** | Can you act as your own "enforcer" in ensuring you meet your goals, whether it is time to look after a sick parent or going to yoga class? |
| ☐ | **Are your expectations realistic?** | Both you and your boss have a realistic understanding about what can be accomplished within your reduced workweek. |
| ☐ | **Can you deal with annoyed co-workers?** | Sometimes full-time colleagues resent part-timers because of extra work put on them. You are not around to do the work and someone has to do it. One veteran part-timer who cannot stand having people angry with her looks for work environments where other people are working part-time. |
| ☐ | **Are you taking a discount in pay for flexibility?** | Part-timers in knowledge work, for example, usually end up doing more work than they are paid for. Within reason, they do not mind. Sometimes the workload may be more than they bargained for, however. Instead of getting flexibility, they are giving work away for free. Be sure when you are putting in those extra hours that they are reasonable. As a general rule, a three-day workweek is more easily enforced than a four-day week. Work today is so fluid, it is difficult to get one's head around the difference between an 80 percent load and full-time. It is easier to put parameters around 60 percent, because it is so clearly different. |

*If you are only at work two days a week, there is less opportunity to be noticed.*

**SELF-ASSESSMENT**  **Planning** for part-time work

If you are considering part-time work, complete the following:

*Does your work lend itself to being done on a part-time basis?*

.......................................................................................................................

.......................................................................................................................

.......................................................................................................................

.......................................................................................................................

.......................................................................................................................

.......................................................................................................................

.......................................................................................................................

*Given your financial and personal needs, are you a good candidate? Why or why not?*

.......................................................................................................................

.......................................................................................................................

.......................................................................................................................

.......................................................................................................................

.......................................................................................................................

.......................................................................................................................

.......................................................................................................................

*What can you do to overcome areas of potential difficulties? (Brainstorm.)*

.......................................................................................................................

.......................................................................................................................

.......................................................................................................................

.......................................................................................................................

.......................................................................................................................

*What trade-offs will you need to make?*

Be specific, e.g., I will keep my car rather than getting a new one and give up my club membership.

........................................................................................
........................................................................................
........................................................................................
........................................................................................
........................................................................................
........................................................................................

*Can you live with these trade-offs?*

........................................................................................
........................................................................................

*What will you gain by making these trade-offs?*

........................................................................................
........................................................................................
........................................................................................
........................................................................................
........................................................................................

*How will you pitch a part-time work arrangement to decision-makers?*

........................................................................................
........................................................................................
........................................................................................
........................................................................................

*Being out of the loop can lead to surprising personal outcomes.*

# Telecommuting

Technology and greater work–life flexibility have made working from home a popular option. It comes with a very clear upside and downside.

Some people say, "I'm much more efficient working from home. I don't have to deal with endless meetings and office politics or spend two hours a day fighting traffic. I work on my own terms when I want to." Others say, "I don't like it. I miss the structure—I find it hard to discipline myself to work. And I miss the office energy."

While happy telecommuters love the flexibility they have to design their work day, be there for their kids, wear whatever they want, and avoid office time wasters, others find the lack of division between professional and personal space disturbing. As one person said, "When I work from home I feel like I'm still in graduate school, and when you are in grad school there's always more work to do on your thesis. You never have a sense of completion or that it is okay to hang out."

### Feeling disconnected
Many of the challenges facing home workers are the same as those for part-timers, for example, feeling disconnected from the group and

**Working alone**
*Successful telecommuters are self-disciplined and self-managing. They are capable of spending long periods of time working without social interaction.*

worrying about possible loss of career opportunities. "Out of sight, out of mind," as the saying goes, so how are you going to be noticed, if you are not there to be noticed?

Being out of the loop is a particular challenge for telecommuters. As one human-resources manager in a biotech company said, "Our information changes every day. The reason why some of our telecommuters become marginalized is because, quite simply, they can't keep up to date." Being out of the loop can lead to surprising personal outcomes. Many people I know who started telecommuting halfheartedly soon discovered they were freer to be themselves. In fact, they learned things about themselves—for example, that they did not like corporate environments or always having to be "in role." Going into the workplace now is a chore for them.

*One woman, a 14-year veteran of a telecommunications company, reluctantly decided to telecommute when her office relocated her department to another part of the country. Initially she experienced difficulties working outside the corporate environment that she understood so well. She missed getting up in the morning, putting on her suit, and going to meetings, which made her feel important and gave her a sense of belonging. But a year later when she was called to meeting at head office, she balked. "Do I have to wear a suit, panty hose? I've forgotten how to be a corporado."*

Most organizations, on paper at least, have policies that support telecommuting. They benefit by being able to attract staff who demand help in being able to balance their work and personal life. And they save on office costs. Telecommuting, however, can be particularly challenging if you are part of a virtual team—a group of geographically dispersed people working together. Virtual teams, which are so much a feature of the contemporary workscape, only work effectively if people can actually see each other periodically on some basis. So much of what we communicate is done visually through body language and facial expression. Email, and to some extent the same is true of phone conversation, does not encourage give and take, nor does it provide

## Career counsel

The problem of being called at home is common. There usually is a honeymoon period in which colleagues and bosses respect your work hours, and you avoid the temptation to call the office just to make sure there are no problems. But then things slip.

There is an emergency, and you are the only person who can deal with it. You respond helpfully. And then there is another call, and again you respond. And then before you know it, you have communicated that it is okay to call you at home anytime there is the slightest blip.

Or maybe you started it. You felt lonely. You felt out of the loop. You worried they did not need you. Whatever the reason, you started to call the office. First, it was just occasional, then it became regular.

*Telecommuters are happier and at least as efficient as their office-based counterparts.*

the same kinds of opportunities to pick up on nuances that contribute to being able to influence others.

In today's no-time-to-waste work environments, phone and email communications tend to be curt and to the point. Actually seeing someone in a meeting changes how you understand their personality. That is why many organizations use satellite teleconferencing and "real-time" meetings to maintain and promote the human connection and convey important information. So if you are thinking of telecommuting, you need both the right skills and the right supports.

## The right kind of work

Knowledge work that does not require extensive interpersonal interaction with clients and team members, such as writing, editing, financial analysis, and designing training programs, lends itself well to working from home. One woman, for example, a three-year communications specialist for an oil company, has only met her boss once; for that matter, she has never visited the offices of her employer, which are across the country.

Think twice, however, if your work requires "here and now" information or being able to influence others by reading nuances and cues. Other types of work can accommodate occasional telecommuting. Many senior managers, for example, stay at home one day a week to plan or play "catch up" without office interruptions.

The challenges do rule out some people as candidates for working at home. However, studies show that telecommuters are happier and at least as efficient, if not more so, as their office-based counterparts. If you are not ideal for telecommuting, but need to, consider:

- Going into the office two days a week.
- Working from a client's office.
- Scheduling regular phone conversations or lunches with colleagues.
- Preparing a to-do list at the end of the day for the next day and following it to the letter.

# Strategies for teleworking

▶ **Get a good boss**
Gail was shocked when her boss chewed her out after a day of home work. "I called you at noon. You didn't answer." Gail explained she had gone to pick up her son to take him for lunch. Her boss said, "I'm paying you to work, not to eat lunch." Avoid bosses who equate face time with productivity. Avoid bosses who think they are paying you for when you do the work, not the work you do. (A good principle, by the way, whether you are telecommuting or not.) Also, many extroverted sociability-seeking managers have difficulty believing that someone is really working if they cannot actually see them when they are talking to them. Your ideal boss is committed to promoting work–life balance and treats you like a self-managing professional.

▶ **Evaluate the fit with work requirements**
Does the work require you to be in the loop? Does it require face-to-face meetings and brainstorming sessions? Does important information get communicated "on the fly"? Does information you need for your work change on a dime?

▶ **Develop a business case**
Show how all work will be achieved with the benefit of a high-performing employee who is also a happy camper. Show you are a team member. Be reasonable.

▶ **Create office space**
Set aside an area of your home that can be devoted exclusively to your work. Get an ergonomic chair. Make the space your own whether with family snapshots or flowers.

▶ **Set boundaries**
Be vigilant in enforcing them. If you are a parent of young children, organize your childcare arrangements so you are not permanently on call. For example, if you have a care provider, let her be responsible for making decisions during the day. Decide what is a reasonable workday, and keep to it. That means no checking of email, or answering the phone after predetermined work hours. (For more, Determining your key, skills, knowledge, and interests, see pages 60–87)

▶ **Set up procedures for regular office/client communication**
whether prearranged weekly conference calls or regular emails to the boss. Be available in person for meetings and off-sites that require your input. Sometimes, even if your presence is not really necessary, being there is important because it communicates "I'm part of this team." Be sensitive to the needs of colleagues who may resent your lack of availability.

## Assessing yourself

### What is your best option?

**SELF-ASSESSMENT** **Are you** suited to teleworking?

Check off the items that are true of you. You are ideally suited to work at home if:

### Suitability

☐ You are a lifestyler who wants flexibility; an autonomy seeker or an authenticity seeker who wants to be free of corporate politics and "role playing"; a personal developer who wants to practice your craft without endless meetings or group think.

☐ You have considered the impact on your career advancement and are prepared to risk losing advancement in favor of flexibility and freedom, have found a supportive employer, and have developed mechanisms to stay in the loop: working on a high-profile assignment, attending weekly meetings, emailing messages to senior managers about your accomplishments.

☐ You are comfortable working by yourself—in fact you find small talk a drain on your energy.

☐ You are self-managing and self-rewarding—comfortable working with little or no direction or feedback and creating your own structure for the day rather than responding to one imposed on you (stability seekers take note). You can use words in email and phone conversations effectively, getting to the point quickly and clearly without preliminary social chat and at the same time without sounding curt; you can change communication style in the light of situational requirements.

☐ You can operate on a day-to-day basis without visual interpersonal cues; can interpret from voice tone on the phone how people are thinking or feeling; can modify your approach accordingly.

The more items you have checked, the better a candidate you are for telecommuting. If you do not possess many of the above characteristics but your situation is such that you need to work at home, identify the issues that will pose the greatest difficulty for you and what you need to do to minimize them.

## PORTFOLIO

## **Planning** for teleworking

If you are considering telecommuting, complete the following.

I am suited for telecommuting because:

*Issues that will pose challenges for me:*

...................................................................................................................................
...................................................................................................................................
...................................................................................................................................
...................................................................................................................................
...................................................................................................................................
...................................................................................................................................
...................................................................................................................................
...................................................................................................................................
...................................................................................................................................
...................................................................................................................................
...................................................................................................................................

*I will manage these challenges by:*

...................................................................................................................................
...................................................................................................................................
...................................................................................................................................
...................................................................................................................................

*I will pitch my boss by:*

...................................................................................................................................
...................................................................................................................................
...................................................................................................................................
...................................................................................................................................

## Case study

Maureen is a portfolio worker. She works on contract six months a year as a host on a woman's lifestyle show. In the summer she goes on a mission to Africa with her husband, a minister. Each year the mission is different: leprosy; orphans; water purification. She satisfies her need to give something back; she also values sharing the experience with her partner.

# Working your portfolio

A portfolio career is one of the most organic kind of careers you can have today. It allows you to play out multiple roles and satisfy your multiple needs.

"I like my work, but it is not enough to satisfy me. It stretches me in some ways, but it does not challenge all my complexities. I am a teacher, but I am also a writer, a thinker, a parent, and a member of the community. I need to satisfy all these roles."

This comment is typical of people who are part of a growing trend— portfolio work, that is, putting together a work package from multiple sources. Some do this out of financial necessity, others out of choice. Prominent in the former category are 20-somethings trying to get a foothold in the job market to acquire skills and gain résumé-building experience. For example, Peter, 24, has just graduated from college with a Bachelor of Arts degree. He is looking for a full-time job in journalism. In the meantime, he works as a courier four days a week, does occasional work as a lifeguard, and writes for free for a webzine.

You do not have to be young, however, to cobble together a living from a variety of sources. This category also includes lifelong freelancers, older workers forced into early retirement, and victims of downsizings who by virtue of their age or skill sets cannot find full-time work.

For others it is a life choice, born out of a desire for self-fulfillment in multiple arenas, not all of which are necessarily income-generating. This is particularly true of personal developers, novelty seekers, and authenticity seekers. Many mid-career personal developers who have reached a professional ceiling continue to ply that craft while they go back to school or explore new career territory.

An individual's portfolio might consist of volunteer work, artistic expression, income-producing activity in an area in which they are highly skilled, and lower-income-producing activity in an area that is professionally challenging.

## PORTFOLIO | **Planning** to work your portfolio

If you are planning to work your portfolio, complete the following:

*What work and life roles do you need to play for a satisfying life?*

...............................................................................................................

...............................................................................................................

...............................................................................................................

...............................................................................................................

...............................................................................................................

*Which roles are you successfully carrying out now?*

...............................................................................................................

...............................................................................................................

...............................................................................................................

...............................................................................................................

...............................................................................................................

*Which roles are you not successfully carrying out now?*

...............................................................................................................

...............................................................................................................

...............................................................................................................

...............................................................................................................

...............................................................................................................

*How can you better fulfill these roles?*

...............................................................................................................

...............................................................................................................

...............................................................................................................

...............................................................................................................

...............................................................................................................

*Even those forced into self-employment often discover that they thrive on it, to the point where they cannot even imagine going back to work for an organization.*

# Working for yourself

Being a free agent is one of today's most-sought-after work options. You are the boss. You decide what to do. You reap your own rewards. You are free of organizational politics.

*Jane had started her career as a very promising architect with a large international architectural firm. After winning a highly prestigious award to design a new cultural center in Japan, she was quickly promoted to associate. Now she has been with the same firm for 12 years and there is pressure to become a partner.*

*Instead of doing what she loves, however—"designing important, quirky buildings, being an artist"—Jane finds herself spending most of her time on revenue generation, client development, and management of the firm's young designers—all of which she describes as "a huge energy drain."*

*Jane has been thinking about going out on her own so she can do the design work that drew her to her profession. She has no debt other than a small amount remaining on her mortgage, and her husband has a good job with a great benefit plan. He is nervous about the loss of predictable income, but she is confident about her talent and the loyal network she has established. Although tired of a steady diet of client development, she is comfortable marketing herself. "I didn't go into this profession to make money for the partners," she says. "I'm not a profit center, I'm an architect."*

Some choose self-employment. Others fall into it through circumstance: by virtue of their age, their skills, or their geographical location they cannot find good full-time work. Even those forced into self-employment as a temporary measure, however, often discover that they thrive on it, to the point where they cannot ever imagine going back to work for an organization.

Some self-employed people are authenticity seekers disdainful of corporate values and the perceived need to wear a corporate mask.

Others are independent thinkers and autonomy seekers, sick of the politics and desperate to escape from the whims of mercurial bosses, or wanting to reap the rewards of their own efforts. For self-developers, self-employment means freedom to do the work they love. There are also many self-employed lifestylers who want flexibility to spend more time with family or on other personal pursuits.

According to forecasters, many of us will undertake some form of self-employment in the years ahead. Large organizations are increasingly concentrating on their core functions and outsourcing a range of services once provided in-house. Everything from corporate communications to sales to payroll and human-resources administration may now be handled for them under contract by freelancers or specialty firms. This means there are fewer positions available with large companies, but more opportunities for freelance and contract workers and for small, independent businesses.

**Working for yourself**
*Many people who are self-employed are lifestylers who enjoy having their own business because they can choose the number of hours they work.*

## **Strategies** for working for yourself

▶ People who go out on their own as a "soloist" often try to sell too many services. In their anxiety to get work, they do a bit of this and a bit of that, rather than focusing on areas where they have a unique expertise. You will be more successful if you focus on areas where you can be a star rather than one of a cast of many who do similar work. If you are doing several things, ensure that they are all linked in terms of their underlying themes.

Consider, for example, the difference between an organizational psychologist who does management training, opinion surveys, recruitment, psychological assessments, and coaching and one who says she has deep knowledge of how individual differences affect workplace success and therefore specializes in psychological assessments, recruitment, and coaching.

▶ If you are currently employed, how much time before you make the leap to self-employment? Try to give yourself at least six months (ideally one year) to develop your business plan, start to develop your network of potential clients, test out your business ideas, and do a first cut of your marketing materials. This way you will minimize the amount of time when you do not have income. If you are really savvy, you may be able to line up your first contract while you are still employed.

Do not burn your bridges. You may want your employer as a client or reference.

### People with structure

*Self-employed people create their own structure. They are capable of managing the anxiety of being responsible for generating their income and of working without a safety net.*

## Psychological challenges

There used to be a sharp division between self-employment and working for someone else. Today, with the erosion of the traditional employment contract, those differences are increasingly blurred. After all, everyone today has to take responsibility for their own employability and their financial continuity. There are still some important differences, however. When you work for someone else, you have a kind of safety net. While you do not have a guaranteed job, you at least have some protection under the law, along with a chance at a pension if you are of a certain age. There are psychological supports, too, in working with team members with whom you have a history and emotional bonds.

For those who have worked in large organizations for a long time, going out on their own can be a shock. They are often unprepared to operate with minimum resources, or for the fact that they are completely responsible for their livelihood today and tomorrow. As one woman who took the self-employment route after being downsized from two jobs commented, "I had spent my entire 20-year career working for large corporations. It took me six months to realize that I am 'it'—that I had no one to do the admin stuff for me, that there was a direct relationship between what I do and whether my family eats." Whether you are dreaming of being in charge of what you do and when you do it, or freed from office politics, remember, you have entered into a world where there is little protection and no guaranteed income.

The freedom can pose its own challenges. Yes, you have the flexibility to take time off from work to watch your child's soccer game, but you are also flexible to work until 2 A.M. to deliver your project on time. Achieving work–life balance can be particularly difficult when you are working, as so many self-employed people do today, from your home environment.

When your house becomes your office, you can never leave the office—and you can never come home. And because it is your business, it can be very hard to switch off. The danger is that your business will become all-consuming and you will end up working all the time.

## Myths about self-employment

It is a myth that you need to be an autonomy seeker to be successfully self-employed. Many successful small-business operators do not in fact have strong needs to be their own boss. They choose small business because it meets lifestyle needs or a desire to use professional skills. What is important is that you are self-managing.

It is also not true that you need to be an entrepreneurial, risk-taking visionary. This is an asset, not a basic requirement. There are many types of self-employment where being competent, organized, and offering a cost-effective service are the basic requirements.

### Points to consider

- If you are a sociability seeker, you may find self-employment lonely, and it may be difficult for you to discipline yourself. Compensate by building into your daily routine significant opportunities for social interaction; consider partnering either formally or informally with other professionals and sharing office space rather than working at home.

- If you are a stability seeker, think of your contract work or your business like a job. Establish relationships with clients and customers and cultivate a sense of belonging to a broader community. Carefully manage your risks.

- If you are a career builder, select a business opportunity that will give you enough scope and growth potential. Be careful, though. A common reason for business failure among career builders is their tendency to overdevelop their business or make it overly complex to meet their personal needs.

- Know when to stop. Running your own business requires tremendous self-discipline—there is always more work to do. (For more on setting boundaries, *see* Strategies for telecommuting, *page 125*.)

- For support, ideas, networking, and work opportunities, take advantage of the numerous networks of free agents that meet in real time and on on-line communities and forums. Self-employed individuals are usually generous in helping other self-employed individuals.

- Test out your ideas with potential clients and people who know you. Can you present a compelling pitch for your product or service?

### Assessing yourself

**What is your best option?**

▶ **Are you suited for part-time work?**
*pages 118–119*

▶ **Planning for part-time work**
*pages 120–121*

▶ **Are you suited for telecommuting?**
*page 126*

▶ **Planning for telecommuting**
*page 127*

▶ **Planning to work your portfolio**
*page 129*

▶ **Are you suited for self-employment?**
*pages 134–135*

▶ **Planning to work for yourself**
*page 137*

▶ **Planning a career shift**
*pages 144–145*

▶ **Planning for staying where you are**
*page 149*

**SELF-ASSESSMENT    Are you suited** to self-employment?

Each type of employment situation has its own constellation of success factors. That said, research shows that individuals who are successful in self-employment have many of the following characteristics:

| Suitability | Characteristics |
|---|---|
| ☐ Service or product people want | Talent to make them want it from you. You have tested your plans/ideas with potential clients. You have expertise, knowledge, and special skills that make you stand out. You have a business plan—you know it is viable. |
| ☐ Need for autonomy | Cindy, self-employed for most of her working life, never actually intended this as a career path. "It wasn't that I chose to be my own boss. It is just that at a fundamental level I never accepted the legitimacy of someone having the right to tell me what to do." Cindy's discomfort with hierarchy is typical of the psychological profile of the successfully self-employed. They are often uncomfortable with received wisdom. |
| ☐ Self-employed parents | Children of entrepreneurs learn early that income fluctuates. They also learn about marketing, cultivating client relationships, and going to the limit to get something out on time. |
| ☐ Comfortable taking risks | Have the ability to live with a lack of predictable income and without a psychological safety net. |
| ☐ Ability to hit the ground running | Self-managing and self-rewarding. Can maintain motivation and direction even through long periods with no tangible payoff. |
| ☐ Good marketing skills | Comfortable talking about your product, service; can articulate clearly and compellingly—getting to the point quickly about product's/service's benefits and features (there is a lot of competition); comfortable selling. |
| ☐ Enjoy thinking about business ideas and expanding a business | Entrepreneurs see possibilities where other people do not and get excited about them. Many are motivated to build and expand a business. |

| | | |
|---|---|---|
| ☐ | **"Trade" skills** | You have some early experience in entrepreneurship, whether trading Tonka cars in grade school, selling lemonade, or running your own band out of a garage, making you more likely to have the skills and interests to go out on your own. |
| ☐ | **The business reflects who you are** | Just as writers should "write what they know," you should do what you know. Many older people who have suffered a job loss panic and grab at straws, moving into franchises or other business areas they know little about. In choosing a business, much as in choosing a job, you are more likely to succeed in something that matches your own strengths, interests, and values. |
| ☐ | **Financial resources** | Have savings or a loan to realistically tide you over. Consider the impact of the loss of benefit plans. |
| ☐ | **Financial-management skills** | If you are hanging out a shingle as a PR consultant and working from your home without a bank loan, you need only basic personal financial-management skills. If you are taking out a bank loan, you need to be able to manage debt repayment. If you are starting a capital-intensive business and do not have financial-analysis skills (ability to understand a spreadsheet, interpret a balance sheet), consider taking a course in small business. Although a financial professional can help you, you need to understand your financials yourself in order to make sound business decisions. |
| ☐ | **Able to park your ego** | Some people experience marketing themselves as demeaning. You can withstand rejection and cope with people not returning calls or emails. You bounce back and persist. |
| ☐ | **Able to perform for the present, market for the future** | You do your current work at a high level while still keeping your eye on getting future work in the pipeline. You can manage competing priorities between carrying out work while pitching future work. |

The more checks you have, the easier it will be for you to successfully launch your own business. Identify areas of weakness. How important are these skills to running the kind of business you are interested in? What can you do to compensate for weaknesses? Consider, for example, taking a course; practicing new behaviors; finding a partner who can complement your strengths; redesigning your business to take advantage of your strengths and minimize exposure to areas where you are weak. There are many excellent resources online or in the community for setting up a business.

*I never accepted the legitimacy of someone having the right to tell me what to do.*

## Conduct an audition—try temping

In the past, contract workers and temps were mainly low-end clerical workers. Today, all levels of work in all sectors are carried out by temps, from Ph.D. chemists to management trainers to art directors, as companies manage their payrolls by buying skills when they need them. For example, a pharmaceutical company conducting a drug trial may hire a chemist on a temporary basis when their skills are needed, rather than keeping them on the full-time payroll.

Good contract work offers several opportunities. It is a great way to audition different types of employers, work, and workplaces and often leads to offers of permanent employment. You can do your job without being involved in the internal politics and still have some sense of belonging to a larger entity, especially if the contract is for several months. Easily bored novelty seekers appreciate the diversity of work, while strategic personal developers and career builders add to their skills portfolio with each new contract.

The work can also be safer than you think. During times of downsizing, temps are often kept on because they are not included in the company head count.

There is a well-known dark side to contract work. Select your employer with care. Look for organizations that use temps frequently, since they probably have better procedures in place to manage temp relations. The work can be low-paid and subject to abuse. Temp workers often feel they are treated like soulless, interchangeable units of productivity, who when abused do not receive a sympathetic ear (although today such treatment is not uniquely confined to temp workers).

Think twice about temping if you are particularly thin-skinned and need to be respected as a valued individual contributor.

## PORTFOLIO — **Planning** to work for yourself

If you are considering self-employment, complete the following:

*What are your areas of potential weakness?*

..................................................................................................................
..................................................................................................................
..................................................................................................................
..................................................................................................................
..................................................................................................................

*How can you compensate for these areas?*

..................................................................................................................
..................................................................................................................
..................................................................................................................
..................................................................................................................
..................................................................................................................

*What product or service would you sell?*

..................................................................................................................
..................................................................................................................
..................................................................................................................
..................................................................................................................
..................................................................................................................

*How are you specially qualified?*

..................................................................................................................
..................................................................................................................
..................................................................................................................
..................................................................................................................

**A new career**

*Changing careers takes courage, a belief in yourself, and hard work. It is a powerful source of career rejuvenation for mid-career managers and professionals.*

*Career change is becoming much more common today as jobs that never existed are being created even as others become obsolete.*

# Changing your career

Are you topped out in your field? Bored with your work? Looking for something more meaningful? Many find creative ways to reconfigure their careers into something more satisfying. Others jump ship entirely.

> *"I used to love this work, but I've been doing the same thing for 10 years and can do it with my eyes closed."*
>
> *"I'm sick of pushing useless product. I want to make a difference in people's lives.'*
>
> *"I don't know why or how I ever ended up doing this kind of work. I don't want to wake up one day consumed with regret about what I might have done or been."*

If you identify with any of these statements, you are in good company. As many as two-thirds of the work force, according to some surveys, say they would consider changing careers if they could. Not everyone who thinks about changing careers will actually do so. Still, career change is becoming much more common today as jobs that never existed before are being created even as others become obsolete.

Some change careers for economic reasons—for example, people laid off due to cutbacks; early retirees who discover they do not have enough income to live on; and artists tired of going from audition to audition who need to find a stable source of income.

Others change because they feel they cannot move up further in their current professions, are bored with doing the same thing over and over again, or are seeking work more in line with their values and interests.

Some, like Karen, the owner of a hip clothing boutique, make radical changes. Tired of living her life one year ahead, buying fabric, trying to second-guess what was going to be cool 12 months down the road, she closed her business, took studies in finance and massage and aromatherapy, and established an alternative health practice.

## Think career shift

*Take this career and dump it.* The idea of dramatic career change is compelling when you are experiencing a nagging malaise in your current work. You imagine yourself in a more exciting and fulfilling life. You want to get as far away as possible from your old work. The risk is that in the rush to start afresh, you may be rejecting the wrong things.

I frequently receive calls from lawyers, for example, who say they want to make a career change. Their story goes something like this: "I'm sick of practicing law. I want to do something else—recruiting, maybe, or perhaps personal coaching. All I know is, I can't stand what I'm doing anymore." When they go through a self-assessment, they discover that it is not the law *per se* that is bothering them, it is how they are practicing the law: the killer work hours, the pressure to increase revenues, the increasing specialization into narrow legal byways.

Although a few have made dramatic career changes, most have been able to leverage their knowledge of the law, and their problem-solving skills, into related areas. One started a conference company specializing in implications of government legislation on human-resources practices. Another became a career counselor specializing in unhappy lawyers.

### Using your talents

*Successful career changers build on their strengths and turn their interests and passions into new careers.*

**Fashion skills**

*If you are a talented dressmaker, consider transferring these skills to working for someone as a dressmaker or running your own small business.*

When you feel dissatisfied with your work, ask yourself whether it is what you actually do that is bothering you, or the environment or people. Or is it a conflict with your underlying values or a lack of balance between work and personal life? Correctly identify the source of your distress. Many people discover that their current work, with some adjustments, is actually a good match.

This may mean doing the same work in a different organizational sector. Mary, for example, a 38-year-old marketing manager for a large bank, was disturbed about the purpose of her work and its frenetic pace. She wanted to contribute to something important and still have a life. She became a marketing consultant to nonprofit organizations.

The nature of your career change does not have to be dramatic. Although we sometimes hear of remarkable transformations—the surgeon who becomes a pilot, the insurance broker who becomes an ice fisherman—such changes are actually quite rare. And they are often unnecessary to significantly rejuvenate professional lives. Rather than talking about career change, in most cases it makes more sense to talk about career shift.

Career shift means reconfiguring skills—applying existing skills and knowledge in new ways or with a shifted focus. Consider Peter, for example, a human-resources manager who was always complimented on his voice and his ability to draw people out. He made a successful transition to becoming a radio call-in-show host.

Many professions have shadow professions that use virtually the same skill set. If there are no obvious shadow professions, or none that appeal to you, identify core skills in your work that can be permutated into new situations. Transferable strengths may be developed at work or outside it. Jan, an artist, was always fascinated with old toys and used them in her sculptures. When she developed multiple sclerosis, she realized that longer-term she might not have the physical stamina to work on large-scale installations. She started an Internet business on the side selling old toys. It is now a thriving business.

Perhaps it is true that you cannot teach an old dog new tricks—but maybe what you require for a career shift is not a new trick at all but one already in your repertoire.

Of course, some people, upon reflection, do decide they need a major change. Many artists, for example, reach a point in their career when they are no longer satisfied with scraping through. They have gone as far as they can in their profession, or perhaps have had an accident or a health problem. Personal developers, who want to be challenged in a completely new domain, or mid-career professionals who want to turn an artistic hobby into a source of revenue generation, are similarly ripe for change.

## **Shadow** careers

Virtually every professional specialty has shadow careers. Here are some examples to kick-start your thinking. When you brainstorm you will be surprised at how many you can think of. Consult your professional association for their suggestions.

- **Teacher**
  Management trainer, curriculum designer, educational sales rep, market-research project manager, adult tutor, educational-assessment specialist
- **Journalist**
  Public relations, public affairs, speechwriter, copywriter, courseware designer, TV producer, editor
- **Nurse**
  Pharmaceutical sales rep, counselor, wellness specialist, recruiter of nurses, diagnostic lab technician, life-insurance agent
- **Lawyer**
  Legal writer, HR consultant on labor issues, intellectual-property specialist, policy developer in government
- **Public accountant**
  Compensation analyst, strategic planner, personal-finance planner, business analyst, government tax auditor, general management
- **Fashion buyer**
  Events coordinator, stylist, window designer, personal shopper, fashion editorial
- **Social worker**
  Policy development, clinician, administration, consultant to nonprofits, change management consultant, public-housing consultant.

## **Career** counsel

Consider a career shift rather than a dramatic change:

- Mine your skills and experiences—can they be reconfigured into more satisfying work?
- Look to make a lateral move inside your current organization.
- Consider incorporating personal hobbies and interests into your work.
- Consider similar work in a new environment.
- Be realistic—your age and financial situation make a difference.
- Look outside your work to reinvent your life.
- Get feedback: speak to people knowledgable about fields you are interested in. How do they see your skills, and the realistic potential for a shift?
- Learn about the skills and training you need to make a major career change.

# Career counsel

In your research, consider the following:

- Make things as convenient as possible for your interviewee. Remember how busy everyone is today. The promise of a free lunch will not usually cut it. You can get most of the information you need in 15 to 20 minutes. If you have been a charming interviewer, people will give you time—after all, most people enjoy talking about themselves.

- You also should make your interviewee feel important— there is a reason you have chosen him. If you ever received an email or letter from someone wanting to interview you about work, starting with "Dear Sir or Madam," you probably wanted to respond with, "And I want to do this because?"

- Do not ask questions just for the sake of asking questions. Ask questions that are of particular importance to you. For example, if you are a sociability seeker, gather information on the amount of social interaction at work.

# Doing your research

If you are thinking about making a major change, get the information you need to make an informed career decision. Consider:

- What kinds of credentials are needed? If you have to go back to school, consider whether there are qualifying courses, the competition for getting into the program, age biases in admission.
- Are there talent shortages predicted in this area?
- What will the demand be for the field in the future?
- What are typical starting salaries?
- Where and how do people in the field work, including self-employment opportunities, telecommuting, etc.?
- Most importantly, how will you feel if you do not pursue this option?

Speak to people knowledgeable about the field. Some questions:

- How did you get into your current work?
- What competencies, knowledge, skills, or experience are necessary for this work?
- What makes someone a "star" in this field?
- What type of formal training (if any) have you had?
- What do you like best/least?
- Do you think the need for this work is expanding or contracting?
- What organizational sectors employ people with these kinds of skills?
- What kinds of training or experience would be helpful to a person entering your field now?
- What other experiences or training were helpful to you?
- What advice would you give someone considering this work?
- What are the main problems or frustrations you encounter in your work?
- Are there related fields I should explore? Other people I should talk to?
- Given my skills and background, is it realistic for me to consider moving into this area?
- What is the culture of the profession?

## Is it too late?

I am often asked, even by people still in their 20s, "Is it too late for me to change careers?" The simple answer is "no." That said, if you are thinking of making a significant shift in mid-career, evaluate the opportunity cost of your move. Look at the cost of education and lost income, as well as the feasibility of putting your new skills to work in the face of younger competition. In choosing between hiring an older worker and a younger one, organizations often favor the younger one because they are cheaper and believed to be savvier technically. Your earlier experience may not be recognized as relevant.

Be realistic about your prospects of success. If you quit your job to do what you love, will the money follow, the way the self-help books tell us? Not necessarily. You also need the skills, personal attributes, and emotional wherewithal to make it happen.

In the future, we will see more mid-career changes and more people working beyond traditional retirement age, whether through financial necessity or to remain emotionally and psychologically engaged. We will no longer look at a career as having a finishing line such as retirement. Instead, people will constantly revamp their skills in new and inventive ways to meet changing financial and lifestyle needs.

### New directions

*Today's workplace is more welcoming of people who reconfigured their skills into entirely new careers.*

### Assessing yourself

**What is your best option?**

▶ **Are you suited for part-time work?**
*pages 118–119*

▶ **Planning for part-time work**
*pages 120–121*

▶ **Are you suited for telecommuting?**
*page 126*

▶ **Planning for telecommuting**
*page 127*

▶ **Planning to work your portfolio**
*page 129*

▶ **Are you suited for self-employment?**
*pages 134–135*

▶ **Planning to work for yourself**
*page 137*

▶ **Planning a career shift**
*pages 144–145*

▶ **Planning for staying where you are**
*page 149*

## PORTFOLIO        **Planning** a career shift

If you are contemplating a career shift or change, complete the following:

*Career options I would like to explore:*

.................................................................................................

.................................................................................................

.................................................................................................

*Skills I have acquired in my professional life that I would like to use:*

.................................................................................................

.................................................................................................

.................................................................................................

*Skills and interests developed in my personal life:*

.................................................................................................

.................................................................................................

.................................................................................................

*The organizational sector/environment I would like to work in:*

.................................................................................................

.................................................................................................

.................................................................................................

*Types of information I need:*

.................................................................................................

.................................................................................................

.................................................................................................

.................................................................................................

*People I can contact are:*

..............................................................................................

..............................................................................................

..............................................................................................

..............................................................................................

..............................................................................................

*Other sources of information:*

..............................................................................................

..............................................................................................

..............................................................................................

*The costs associated with making this shift are:*

..............................................................................................

..............................................................................................

..............................................................................................

*The benefits of making this shift are:*

..............................................................................................

..............................................................................................

..............................................................................................

*Given my age and financial situation, making a career shift is realistic/unrealistic because:*

..............................................................................................

..............................................................................................

..............................................................................................

*In the future people will constantly revamp their skills in new and inventive ways.*

*It may be unrealistic to expect any one domain of your life to satisfy all your needs.*

# Staying where you are

If your work is more or less a good match or allows you to meet other important needs, try "shopping at home" for career rejuvenation and personal development.

Many people discover that "shopping at home" is the best strategy for career management. After all, you are a known asset, and employers would much rather keep happy employees than incur the costs of replacing them. Obviously, if you do not like your employer, then leaving is the only option (see Know when to go, *pages 260–263*). But if you like your employer, look for ways to advance your career without moving on.

I have found that about 75 percent of employed people, on conducting a self-assessment, learn that they like their work more than they thought, or that they can modify their work and make it a better match. Some decide that staying where they are is the best career option because it enables them to meet other needs—for example, it is close to home, which gives them more time for family.

There is no fixed amount of time it is appropriate to stay with an employer, but you should consider:

- Your reputation: If you stay too long with one employer, you run the risk of being over-identified with your organization and organizational sector.
- Your employer: Does it spot and grow talent? Does it have broad opportunities for movement, learning, and development? Does it have a great external reputation?
- Your age: 20-somethings working for a great organization should leverage their opportunities before moving on; 30-somethings should consider moving on while other employers see them as mobile and as not entrenched in a particular organization; 40-somethings will have to find ways to overcome stereotypes if they have stayed in one organization or sector most of their career.

**Time out**
*Taking a sabbatical is popular today. Time out leads to significant personal discoveries and allows you to test yourself in new ways.*

# **Strategies** for career enhancement

Identify strategies in the list below that are meaningful to you.

## **Learn and develop yourself personally and professionally**

▶ Look for opportunities to develop new skills, and test yourself in new ways.

▶ Find an assignment outside your comfort zone—do something that feels risky, with an uncertain outcome.

▶ Do something surprising, something you have never done before.

▶ Understudy or work with someone who is doing work that interests you, or that you can learn from.

▶ Participate in a high-level conference.

▶ Get great training—become better at something you are already good at.

▶ Participate in an interdepartmental task force.

▶ Continue your education.

▶ Mentor younger staff.

▶ Learn a language.

▶ Volunteer outside the workplace to develop new skills, increase your network, and do something meaningful.

▶ Take on a completely new role.

▶ Make a contribution to something you care about.

▶ Rejuvenate yourself—take a sabbatical, go on a mid-career break, upgrade your education, test yourself.

## **Modify your work to make it a better match**

▶ Get rid of tasks that drive you crazy and replace them with ones that engage you.

▶ Make your work more challenging by increasing your involvement in some areas and delegating tasks to others.

▶ Change how you carry out your role.

## **Move across**

▶ Move across into another department or function to build new skills, increase your exposure to other areas, find new challenges, and refresh your perspective on your career.

## **Assessing** yourself

### **What is your best option?**

▶ Are you suited for part-time work?
*pages 118–119*

▶ Planning for part-time work
*pages 120–121*

▶ Are you suited for telecommuting?
*page 126*

▶ Planning for telecommuting
*page 127*

▶ Planning to work your portfolio
*page 129*

▶ Are you suited for self-employment?
*pages 134–135*

▶ Planning to work for yourself
*page 137*

▶ Planning a career shift
*pages 144–145*

▶ Planning for staying where you are
*page 149*

### Building on strengths

*Identify areas in which you want to develop yourself. Focus on existing strengths. Become better at something you are already good at, like presenting.*

# Strategies for career enhancement cont'd

▶ Reconfigure your skills in new ways, leverage existing skills (*see pages 139–141 for more tips*).

## Move up

▶ Position yourself for a promotion. Take on high-profile assignments, outperform expectations, make yourself an asset.

▶ Get exposure to senior management; be visible.

▶ Deliver the presentation yourself—wow them with your poise and passion.

▶ Develop an original idea.

## Identify strategies that are relevant to you

▶ Inform your thinking with ideas from unusual or unconventional sources. Marry ideas from different perspectives—for example, literature, the arts, politics, and either your business or your professional discipline.

▶ Participate in a high-profile task force.

▶ Develop a business case for an important piece of work currently not being done. Pitch yourself for the role.

▶ Speak up. People are sometimes passed over for promotions because no one knew they were ready and capable of a bigger role. Talk about your accomplishments. Show how you have added value.

▶ Increase your profile. Give a presentation at a conference; write an article for your trade magazine.

▶ Find a mentor. Model someone who has skills missing from your repertoire. Look for more than one mentor.

▶ Be a mentor. Share your wisdom and know-how with younger staff. Be generous in contributing to others' development.

▶ Relax. If you are feeling blocked in identifying what you want to do, relax. These decisions are complicated and take time. Spend the next month or so collecting job ads, media profiles of or references to people who are doing things that interest you. Then look for the underlying themes of what you have collected. What do these roles have in common? Even interesting ideas that emerge from dinner conversations count.

(For more on how to get ahead, *see* section 5, Boost your career intelligence, *pages 292–325*).

**PORTFOLIO**

## **Planning** for staying where you are

If you would like to stay with your current employer, consider:

*What strategies did you identify to increase your career satisfaction?*

.............................................................................................................

.............................................................................................................

.............................................................................................................

.............................................................................................................

*What personal and professional needs will they meet?*

.............................................................................................................

.............................................................................................................

.............................................................................................................

*Brainstorm: What do you need to do to implement your strategies?*

(e.g., have a heart-to-heart with boss next Tuesday about my career interests; speak to Jenny in Marketing about how I can leverage my human resource skills in her area; take conversational French.)

*Strategy 1*

.............................................................................................................

.............................................................................................................

*Strategy 2*

.............................................................................................................

.............................................................................................................

*Strategy 3*

.............................................................................................................

.............................................................................................................

# Turn your vision into reality

You have evaluated all your career and work options. You know the types of roles, industry sectors, and employment relationships that are right for you. Together these make up a vision of what you need to have in your life to feel engaged. Now you have to make it happen.

## This chapter shows you how to:

**Be purposeful**—focus on what you really need and avoid being overcome by inertia.

**Translate** your complex needs and desires into a vision of how you want to work and live.

**Develop** meaningful career goals that speak to your unique values, talents, and motivators.

**Get** to the finish line by breaking down your goals, identifying obstacles, and knowing the resources you need.

# Being purposeful

At this point in your search, keep active and motivated. Do not drift. Being focused is the key to making dreams happen.

Many of the people I counsel get lost at this stage. They determine what is important to them, identify meaningful options, and then drift. "I know what I care about and what I need to do, but somehow, every time I make a decision to do something, life gets in the way. I end up doing nothing," they say.

Today, with our overcommitted and complicated schedules, it is easy to be sidetracked in the process of just keeping our show on the road. Making a change is also frightening. It may significantly impact people we care about, affect our finances, and change how we live. It is critical that you develop a clearly articulated vision of yourself and what you want to achieve in order to lead a life that is purposeful and meets your most deeply held values.

If you are starting out in your career you may be particularly vulnerable. You may be anxious about student debts, and your parents may be

**Unique skills**
*If you are a young, talented musician and want to make music your career, apply commitment, discipline, and intense focus to achieving your dream.*

putting pressure on you to hurry up and get a job. "After all," they say, "you are an adult now and this is the real world. Get a foot in the door, and don't worry about whether you love the work." You may be overwhelmed by the choices available or the work involved in finding what you want, or be tempted to accept a job with a former summer or part-time employer, simply because it is offered, not because it is right for you. Exercise the self-discipline to stay on your path.

## Conduct an inventory

Some years ago I went through a difficult career patch: although I often loved my work, I was also often bored. I conducted an inventory of the previous seven years and analyzed the difference between the years I felt great and the years I felt "flat." I made three key discoveries:

- First, that I had been pursuing a portfolio career without knowing it: my life and work consisted of a combination of volunteering, speaking, organizational consulting, writing, home-related design.
- Second, that the "great" years were ones in which I had undertaken a project that tested me because its outcome was not clear.
- Third, that I was not making any conscious decisions about the configuration of different activities in my life. I loved speaking, for example, but I did not have a speaker's agent. Everything was done "by chance."

As a result, I became conscious of what I needed to feel engaged so that I could be more purposeful in the design of my life. Since then, every year I have deliberately taken on something outside my comfort zone or not on the menu of my daily activities. One year it was designing a garden; another, putting on a major conference on work–life balance to support a volunteer organization. Another year it was broadening my public-speaking activities.

Being purposeful means knowing what is important to you, and being focused on pursuing it.

*Being purposeful means knowing what is important to you, and being focused on pursuing it.*

**Assessing** yourself

**Turn your vision into reality**

▶ **Defining your ideal work**
 *pages 154–155*

▶ **Focusing your goals**
 *page 158*

▶ **What are your goals and trade-offs?**
 *page 159*

▶ **Action planning**
 *page 160*

▶ **Identifying skills for goal achievement**
 *page 161*

▶ **Overcoming obstacles to goal achievement**
 *page 162*

▶ **Identifying resources for goal achievement**
 *page 163*

## PORTFOLIO            **Defining** your ideal work

Reflect carefully on each of these vital questions before writing your answers. This is the distilled summary of all your learning.

*What roles do you need to play to have a full and satisfying life?*

..............................................................................................................

..............................................................................................................

*What do you want to accomplish? How will accomplishing this contribute to your sense of completeness?*

..............................................................................................................

..............................................................................................................

..............................................................................................................

*Where do you want to live?*

..............................................................................................................

..............................................................................................................

*What will your financial situation be?*

..............................................................................................................

..............................................................................................................

*What professional roles (specialist or generalist? manager or individual contributor?) will you be playing, and at what level?*

..............................................................................................................

..............................................................................................................

*Where (if anywhere) do you want to be working?*

..............................................................................................................

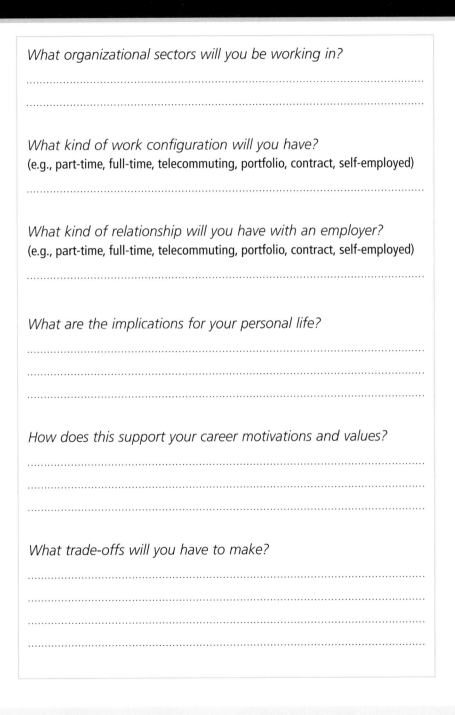

*What organizational sectors will you be working in?*

.................................................................................................

.................................................................................................

*What kind of work configuration will you have?*
(e.g., part-time, full-time, telecommuting, portfolio, contract, self-employed)

.................................................................................................

*What kind of relationship will you have with an employer?*
(e.g., part-time, full-time, telecommuting, portfolio, contract, self-employed)

.................................................................................................

*What are the implications for your personal life?*

.................................................................................................

.................................................................................................

.................................................................................................

*How does this support your career motivations and values?*

.................................................................................................

.................................................................................................

.................................................................................................

*What trade-offs will you have to make?*

.................................................................................................

.................................................................................................

.................................................................................................

.................................................................................................

# Setting and implementing goals

You have a vision of how you want to live and work. You want great work that will satisfy your most important values and talents. Make it happen.

Review your self-assessment summary (*see pages 84–85* and *pages 170–171*). Examine the work options you have identified as being a potential match. At this point, it may be absolutely clear to you what you need and want to do. Or you may have narrowed it down to two or more options. If the latter, research these options and get more information and feedback from others.

When you are thinking about your goals, they may be specific—for example, to accomplish something definite within a year: "I will be

**Personal goals**

*Set yourself some goals in your personal life as well as your work. If you have always wanted to be good at a sport, for example, organize some regular coaching sessions.*

working part-time for my present employer." "I will be enrolled in a Master of Education program."

Or your goals may be more general, and of a more investigative nature. In fact, you may be pursuing more than one option—for example:

- Speak to Jane and Peter about feasibility of moving into strategic planning role. Check out community-relations role—speak to VP, Public Affairs. Do before end of month.
- Look into marketing job for the symphony—good match for me? Check out ballet and opera as well—end of January.
- Look into certificate program for NGO/association management—competitive to get in? prerequisites? End of March.

## Considerations for setting goals

Four points to think about:

- **Goal or vision?**
  Most people need to set goals in order to turn their dream into reality. Some people, however, find the idea of a "goal" somehow diminishing when they think about their life's purpose. If the word "goal" does not work for you, replace it with the word "vision."

- **Big or small?**
  Remember, your goal does not need to be monumental. You can significantly enrich your life by identifying one small change—and acting on it. Small changes can have a huge impact on life satisfaction.

- **Work or personal?**
  Your goal does not need to be related to your work life. For example, it might involve volunteering or taking a night course or learning to garden. (See *pages 230–289* for more.)

- **Do you have a backup goal?**
  Do not put all your eggs in one basket. There is usually more than one way to achieve a career aspiration. Identify and pursue these other paths, in case your initial plan does not work out.

**PORTFOLIO**

# **Focusing** your goals

State, as precisely as you can, your goal or goals.

*Goal(s): To*

..................................................................................................

..................................................................................................

..................................................................................................

..................................................................................................

*By when?*
*I will know I have reached this goal if/when I (can/have, etc.)*

..................................................................................................

..................................................................................................

..................................................................................................

..................................................................................................

Check your goals against the following:

| Type of goals | Achievement |
|---|---|
| ☐ **Specific?** | For example, if they are learning goals, do they describe what you will learn? If they involve a move, do they describe your desired role? |
| ☐ **Measurable?** | Framed in terms that will permit you to evaluate whether you have achieved them. |
| ☐ **Time-framed?** | Do they include target dates? |
| ☐ **Realistic and achievable?** | Are they in tune with your skills, background, and abilities? |
| | Do your skills and qualifications compare favorably with others who are successful in this type of work? |
| | Are you likely to get what you want? |
| ☐ **Personally meaningful?** | Will you feel happy, satisfied, or proud when you achieve your goal? |
| | Will you have a sense of completeness? |

## Make trade-offs

Many of us have underlying career motivations that conflict with each other. You will have identified these conflicts (*see page 49*). For example, you may be a lifestyler who wants to spend more time with family—but at the same time may be ambitious to become a player in your profession, which may require a 10-hour day. You may not be able to satisfy these competing interests. People often get themselves into a knot when faced with these kinds of conflicts. At the core of their anxiety is a belief that if they meet one need, they are totally abandoning their other needs forever. This kind of second-guessing is debilitating.

Can you have it all? At any given time in our life we may need to make trade-offs. Generally, it is easier to get what you want by satisfying one need completely, rather than meeting each competing need in a limited way. You will probably be happiest if you completely meet one important need rather than living in a "gray" zone where all your needs are compromised.

## Career counsel

Commit to following through. Decide which of your needs are more important at this life stage. Be aware of what you are giving up, and more importantly, what you are getting instead. Accept your choice, and the trade-offs that may be involved in reaching your goal. Tell yourself, "At this point in my life, it makes more sense for me to do 'X' rather than 'Y' for the following reasons…" Write down the decision you have made and why. Put it somewhere you can see it. Read it when you waver.

---

### ● SELF ASSESSMENT    **What are** your goals and trade-offs?

Identify the trade-offs you need to achieve your goals. Be specific.

*What are the trade-offs I need to make?*

.......................................................................................................

.......................................................................................................

*Can I live with these trade-offs?*

.......................................................................................................

*I am making these trade-offs because:*
(This is one of the most important statements you will ever write.)

.......................................................................................................

.......................................................................................................

.......................................................................................................

## Make it happen

Many people become overwhelmed when they have set out large goals, such as a major career change or a business start-up. Break down your goal into manageable steps, such as networking with people in your desired field, taking a course, joining a professional association. Consider David, a graphic artist employed by a large ad agency, whose career goal was to do freelance work for small, creative companies where he could have creative control over his work. He gave himself nine months to make the transition to self-employment after determining the general steps he would need to take, including:

- Networking with industry professionals.
- Identifying creative companies with interesting ad campaigns.
- Developing a portfolio of his work to show to people.
- Finding office space to share with other designers.
- Saving a financial cushion for his first six months in business.
- Obtaining one small contract, with other possibilities in the pipeline.

**SELF-ASSESSMENT**  **Action** planning

List the steps you will take and timelines. Be specific.

1. ...........................................................................................................
   ...........................................................................................................

2. ...........................................................................................................
   ...........................................................................................................

3. ...........................................................................................................
   ...........................................................................................................

4. ...........................................................................................................
   ...........................................................................................................

5. ...........................................................................................................
   ...........................................................................................................

## PORTFOLIO

## **Identifying skills** for goal achievement

Do you currently have all the skills necessary to achieve your goals? Review your Skills workout (*pages 74–77*). Complete the summary below.

*Skills that are important to achieving my goal(s):*

...................................................................................................................................

...................................................................................................................................

...................................................................................................................................

...................................................................................................................................

...................................................................................................................................

...................................................................................................................................

...................................................................................................................................

...................................................................................................................................

*Skills I need to acquire or improve to achieve my goal(s):*

...................................................................................................................................

...................................................................................................................................

...................................................................................................................................

...................................................................................................................................

...................................................................................................................................

...................................................................................................................................

*Education and training I will need to get these skills:*

...................................................................................................................................

...................................................................................................................................

...................................................................................................................................

...................................................................................................................................

...................................................................................................................................

...................................................................................................................................

**SELF-ASSESSMENT     Overcoming** obstacles to goal achievement

Does anything stand in the way of reaching your goals? Identify potential obstacles. Plan how to manage them.

### Personal obstacles:

*What might you stop yourself from getting what you want?*
(e.g., an overly perfectionist attitude; procrastination; failure to communicate your goals to your manager)

...................................................................................................................

...................................................................................................................

...................................................................................................................

...................................................................................................................

### Other restraints:

*What restraints might external factors place on your progress?*
(e.g., the state of the economy, personal and family issues)

...................................................................................................................

...................................................................................................................

...................................................................................................................

...................................................................................................................

...................................................................................................................

### What can you do:

*How can you overcome or reduce the effect of these obstacles?*
*When will you do it?*

...................................................................................................................

...................................................................................................................

...................................................................................................................

...................................................................................................................

**PORTFOLIO**

# **Identifying** resources for goal achievement

What resources and learning opportunities are available to help you reach your goals?

| Resources and learning opportunities | How I will use this resource |
|---|---|
|  |  |
|  |  |

Identify the people who can help you attain your goals and the ways in which they can help.

| People who can help me achieve my goal | What I will ask of them |
|---|---|
|  |  |
|  |  |

# 3 Find great work

# Mapping your strategy

You now know what constitutes great work for you. You have identified the kind of organizational culture, industry sector, role, and type of employment relationship that represents your best fit. To find that great work, you must be able to exploit every work-search strategy available to you.

## This chapter shows you how to:

**Maximize** your search activities—expand your career options, mine every search vehicle, and use your time strategically.

**Overcome** the emotional impact of job loss—avoid common mistakes and make the right moves for a successful transition.

**Develop** a compelling leaving story and apply the master principle of work search to all your activities.

**Frame** your self-presentation in terms of the skills and attributes that employers are looking for today.

**Use** different search vehicles successfully, including following the dos and don'ts of effective networking.

**Boost** your response rate by developing and applying career intelligence in targeting your great work.

# Being a work-search activist

For some people, the prospect of looking for work is exciting. It is an opportunity to strut their stuff, meet new people, test themselves in new environments, and learn about other industries. For others, it is daunting.

**Explore and have fun**

*Find out about other work environments. Learn about important trends. Get connected to new people. Mine every opportunity to increase your marketability.*

If you take the activist stance you have learned from this book, you can minimize the stressful aspects of looking for work and turn it into an exciting journey.

Think of your work search as a challenge and a great learning experience. Think ahead to that moment when you accept a fabulous offer. Let that motivate you throughout your search.

## You are in great shape

You have developed a powerful and compelling way of articulating your special talents, skills, accomplishments, and aspirations as a result of the rigorous self-assessment you have conducted on key dimensions employers are looking for.

You have acquired insider knowledge of characteristics for success in different industry sectors. Now you can present what recruiters call a unique value proposition.

Finding great work is an art, not a science. The key factors? Self-knowledge; clarity of vision; understanding what employers are looking for; being able to "spin" your qualifications in words appropriate to what they need; and a compelling presentation.

This section, Find great work, builds on the in-depth self-assessment you have conducted in the first two sections of this book. Here I will show you how to take the results of your self-assessment and, step by step, use them as the basis of:

- Identifying and targeting work that matches your special strengths, values, and needs.
- Marketing yourself through networking, preparing a résumé and cover letter, and interviewing.
- Making the right career decision.

Read this section even if you are looking for a job with your current employer. Internal recruiters say that the most common mistake internal candidates make is operating on the assumption that they do not need to sell themselves because they are a known entity in their current role. They expect their career history to speak for itself. Remember, most people do not know the specifics of what you do and how you work.

When applying for work internally, just like an external candidate, you need to provide evidence that you possess the necessary competencies. Fortunately, you are already four-fifths of the way there.

*Think ahead to that moment when you accept a fabulous offer. Let that motivate you.*

*Remind yourself: people care about you and not your job title.*

## If you recently lost your work

"When I lost my job, I thought, 'This is a pain, but I'm strong, I can cope.' Then all of a sudden you feel completely disoriented, or like someone has punched you in the stomach. I didn't believe it would affect me so deeply. But it did."

I hear this comment frequently, especially from people who were in a job for a long time. Job loss is one of life's most stressful events. So much of our identity is wrapped up in our careers. If you have suddenly found yourself unemployed—whether you were fired or laid off—you probably are feeling a flood of emotions: anger, embarrassment, disbelief, and shame. These feelings are normal. Give yourself time to grieve and to digest the loss. (*See* Coping with failure, *pages 240–243*.)

You may also be anxious about finances and feel a sense of urgency. There is no shame in losing a job. It is simply a feature of the contemporary work landscape. Most people will lose their work at least once in their careers. Smart recruiters know that successfully weathering a job loss creates resilience and maturity.

You are not your job, and your job is not the centerpiece of your identity. Remind yourself: people care about you and not your job title.

### Bouncing back
*Although career reversal is painful at first, people do bounce back. In fact, most eventually describe their job loss as one of the best things that ever happened to them.*

# Dos and don'ts when you lose your job

Job loss can take a huge emotional toll on you. Take the necessary time to refocus your head-space and organize yourself for the future.

## Do:

- Take a week or two to come to terms with the emotional shock. Go easy on yourself.

- Consult an employment lawyer if you think you were wrongfully dismissed or want the severance package reviewed.

- Take a few days to think about any papers that you have to sign.

- Ask for counseling support (e.g., outplacement) if it is not offered.

- Negotiate terms regarding continuity of benefits. (If your spouse has the same benefits, trade the value of your benefits for money for the time covered.)

- Organize your finances. Allow margin for error. Develop a budget.

- Negotiate references from your employer.

- Develop a "leaving story" to explain to network contacts and potential employers why you left. Get permission from your former employer to agree to your leaving story so they will match it when a potential employer calls them for a reference check (a lawyer can help you negotiate this).

## Don't:

- Make rash financial or career decisions, such as selling your house or taking the first work offer that comes along.

- Think of your severance money as a lottery win to either save or go out and spend. It is designed as an economic bridge to new employment. Think of it as salary.

- Bad-mouth your employer to everyone you talk to.

- Tell everyone you know right away that you lost your job. You may sound understandably angry and bitter.

- Immediately get into job-search or résumé-writing mode before digesting the loss.

- Leave any personal belongings or electronic files behind.

- Start your work search before you have completed your self-assessment.

- Write a résumé before reading this chapter.

- Look for a job just like the one you had without thinking about it. It may not be right for you.

## Career counsel

If you were fired or laid off, the acid test of whether you are ready for networking outside your immediate circle is the ability to tell your leaving story without communicating any rancor.

# Career counsel

If you are currently employed, should you let your boss or co-workers know you are looking? Traditionally, the answer was a simple no. Today, the answer is not so clear-cut.

Every year I work with recently graduated public accountants in professional-services firms. They are concerned about looking for work outside the firm without letting their bosses know. Ironically, management stages my workshops precisely because it knows these professionals are at a decision-making point. Management prefers them to stay, but if they are going to leave, it would like them to leave on good terms—they may become clients, or may return. Use your judgment. Some bosses may marginalize you. Others know the score.

## Assessing yourself

### Mapping your strategy

▶ Thinking through your goals
*page 171*

▶ What are employers looking for?
*page 177*

▶ Identifying your network
*page 180*

## Search for great work

Your search will take time and effort, and at times may be dispiriting. The skills you develop and use, however, will be important throughout your career as you, like your fellow workers, frequently move in and out of new employment relationships or make a career out of doing contract work and working for yourself. Think of your search as a project. Think of yourself as the project manager. How long the search will take will depend on many factors, including your industry and level, the demand for your skills, the economy in your community, and your age and experience. If you are changing occupations or industries, expect the search to take longer.

## Think through your goals

When people have conducted the kind of in-depth self-assessment you have done, they usually identify two or three types of roles or opportunities that would be equally rewarding. Consider David, an autonomy-seeking marketing director who formerly worked as a director of marketing in a professional-services firm. He identifies three possible roles of interest: independent marketing consultant, manager of a small start-up, or manager of a public relations/marketing services firm.

Develop plans A, B, and C. The broader your goals, the more opportunities available. This also gives you a fallback position if you are in a difficult employment market, or if by virtue of skills or age your primary goal is more difficult to obtain. Review the goals you identified earlier (*see* Setting and implementing goals, *pages 156–163*).

## Evaluate the trade-offs

Know what trade-offs you are willing to make (*see* Find your perfect path, *pages 159–160*). Would you move to another location, compromise your personal life, or trade down financially if you found an otherwise attractive opportunity?

If you are just starting out in your career or are making a career change, would you be willing to work as a volunteer or intern, or in a poorly paid stepping-stone job, in order to gain experience?

## SELF-ASSESSMENT    **Thinking through** your goals

Identify two to three options. What needs will they meet? What will you have to give up as a result?

### Plan A

*Work in ...................... role in ......................................... sector(s).*
*This role would support the following needs and desires:*

...................................................................................................................

...................................................................................................................

*I may need to give up:*

...................................................................................................................

...................................................................................................................

### Plan B

*Work in ...................... role in ......................................... sector(s).*
*This role would support the following needs and desires:*

...................................................................................................................

...................................................................................................................

*I may need to give up:*

...................................................................................................................

...................................................................................................................

### Plan C

*Work in ...................... role in ......................................... sector(s).*
*This role would support the following needs and desires:*

...................................................................................................................

...................................................................................................................

*I may need to give up:*

...................................................................................................................

...................................................................................................................

*Try to identify at least one influential person who can introduce you to strategic contacts.*

## Develop a positive mind-set

You are looking for work for a reason, so take it seriously. If you are not working, your work search should be a full-time job. If you are currently employed, devote a certain number of hours a week to the search. It is not a hobby to get around to every now and then when the mood strikes you. Switch your brain over to work-search mode. Do not, however, think of yourself—or use the word with others—as being "unemployed." You are employed. Your job is to find work. Overcome the three common sources of derailment:

- Drifting. Many people start their work search with commitment—then life gets in the way, and they drift. This is particularly true of people who are currently employed and can easily be sidetracked by job demands. Maintain an activist stance. Stay focused.
- Procrastinating. "I'll call those people tomorrow." "I'll write my résumé next week when I'm feeling up to it." As you already know, it will not be any more fun or easier later. Do it now, if that was the original plan.
- Panicking. Although you may be feeling anxious, do not rush out to apply for every job you can find.

## Get organized

Create a devoted workspace. Keep all your files in one place. Record a professional-sounding greeting on your service (no children or pets in the background). Develop a filing system that works for you, whether file folders or recipe/index cards or on the computer. Organize bookmarks of useful websites of organizations, jobs boards, and professional associations. File:

- Notes on conversations with potential employers.
- Copies of cover letters you sent applying for work.
- Ads from the newspaper or Internet that interest you.
- Ads that you respond to.
- Business cards of network contacts.
- Information about organizations.
- Information on trends associated with targeted work.

## Develop a project timetable

Plot what you will do each week for the next four weeks. For example, in Week 1 you could set up a workspace and files, think about a leaving story, and start trolling advertisements for possible positions. In Week 2 you could start developing marketing materials (résumé, cover letter, etc.). Week 3 would likely be devoted to calling contacts in your network and setting up meetings with those contacts, and Week 4 to starting your active networking.

Do not worry if you end up doing steps out of order or spending more or less time on some items than others. Develop a routine such as checking ads at a certain time, answering the phone starting at 8:30 A.M., making a certain number of calls to contacts, and so on.

## Enlist support

Throughout the job search, you will need different kinds of support, including people who:

- Will serve as sounding boards to review your résumé and marketing pitch, and to whom you can debrief after interviews.
- Are sources of network leads.
- Can give you emotional support when you face rejection, employers do not return your calls, or leads seem to dry up.
- Can provide insider knowledge of the industry.
- Can give you advice on negotiating job offers.

Put together an informal advisory group of people with special skills in different areas. Indicate that you value their support and would like to be able to contact them occasionally for opinions and advice. Try to identify at least one influential person who can introduce you to strategic contacts.

## Create your leaving story

When you are looking for work, one of the first questions you will be asked by people in your network and potential employers is why you left or are leaving your employer. Your answer is important.

## Case study

David's wife was anxious about his loss of work. Every day she quizzed him about his job search. When he wanted to turn down a well-paying job because the work did not interest him, she even threatened to leave him. It was only with the help of a counselor that she realized she was imposing her own values and anxiety on her husband.

Your spouse or partner may be able to give you moral support, but they are not career counselors. Their anxiety about your employment may lead them to put undue pressure on you to find a job or to be unrealistic regarding the time it will take. They also often have different ideas about the nature of work, job level, or salary you should be targeting.

*Imagine yourself as the recruiter or employer. What skills, attributes, and accomplishments would you be looking for?*

If you have chosen to leave, take this as an opportunity to communicate something positive about yourself. For example, "Feeling good about my work is very important to me. I was no longer learning. I tried to remedy the situation by ... but it didn't work."

You should also establish just what it is you are looking for in work. For example, "I grew tremendously at ABC, but over the past year felt I had outgrown the professional challenges. I want the opportunity to apply my skills in marketing at a more strategic level."

If you were fired, there are many ways of being truthful without undermining yourself. Consider the following tips in describing what happened:

- Keep it simple. Stick to the key points, not all the "he said, and then I said, and ..." Do not bury your listeners in detail. If they want more information, they will probe for it.
- If you and your boss did not see eye to eye, that is okay. Do not show anger or slam your boss's personality, however. Ditto if you think your firing was unfair. Control your voice tone so that you do not sound bitter. If you were deeply upset, however, you do not need to come across like an android. You are a human being.
- Show how you are moving forward. You can say, for example, "It seemed to come out of nowhere, and as you can imagine, I was shocked. But I have digested it now and am looking forward to the next chapter." Sound like you mean it.
- Provide a positive spin, whether in showing what you learned from the experience or how you bounced back.
- Rehearse your explanation so that it sounds natural and credible. Get feedback from your advisers. Ask them, "Does this sound reasonable? Does it say something positive about me?"

For more on answering difficult questions, *see pages 211-215*.

## Apply the master principle of work search

Think like a recruiter. This principle applies to every aspect of your work search, whether mapping out a strategy, writing marketing materials, or going to interviews. Imagine yourself as the recruiter or employer. What skills, attributes, and accomplishments would you be looking for? Consider:

- The organization's goals.
- The industry sector.
- The challenges of the role.

As you develop your materials, continually review all your communications to ensure they speak directly to the employer's needs and provide hard evidence that you have "the goods." Use this protocol. If you were the recruiter for this position, what would you be looking for? Identify the desired attributes. Beside each attribute, cite examples of actions you took that demonstrate that attribute, and how your actions got results. If the past is the best predictor of the future, then it is your responsibility to show how your past behavior demonstrates that you have what they are looking for. (*See* box.)

**Spin your experience**

*Tailor your message about who you are and what you have done. The same story can be told in different ways to speak directly to the listener's needs.*

## Example: showing you have what is needed

| Desired attribute | Best example of action | Results |
| --- | --- | --- |
| Sensitive to needs of young workers | Introduced "buy vacation days" and completely redesigned office space | Opinion survey results showed 20 percent increase in employee satisfaction |
| Can adapt well to change | Streamlined recruiting process when plant added another shift | Hired 200 people so quickly that shift started two weeks earlier than planned |
| Risk-taker | Led move to acquire a competitor | Increased revenues by 12 percent in the first year |

## Career counsel

There are four sources of work:

- Personal and professional networks.
- Newspaper ads, organizations, recruiters.
- Internet: job bulletin boards, company websites, recruiters' websites.
- Professional-association newsletters and listings.

# Finding career opportunities

How do you find potential employers? Career activists do their research, they network, and they mine every other strategy from advertising to search consultants. Use these strategies effectively.

At the foundation of any search for great work is great research. Get the information on industries and organizations that interest you.

- Research companies and industries on the Internet and in the library. What did the media say? Do a search for news and magazine articles.
- Check out business directories to find employers in targeted industries. Read their annual reports.
- Contact the board of trade and industry associations. Read appointment notices in the newspapers and find out whether an employer has created a new position that could affect you. (For example, the appointment of someone as the head of a new marketing department signals that the organization is doing its own marketing and likely will be hiring marketing professionals.) Business articles will also tell you whether a company is taking a different direction with a new product line or is shifting its corporate culture.
- Talk to people in the industry or profession.
- Research whether government legislation will affect your industry or your targeted employers.
- Join an email discussion group in your profession and post queries about careers.

Find a great employer. You do not want just a job. You want a great workplace that understands your complex needs.

- Query potential employers about benefits, policies, and rewards that are important to you. Check programs and

## SELF-ASSESSMENT    **What are employers** looking for?

The contemporary workplace is lean, time-urgent, and bottom-line focused. Employers recognize that individuals have unique characteristics, but overall this workplace requires people who possess the attributes below to a greater or lesser extent.

As you proceed with your search – whether networking, writing your marketing materials, or talking about yourself in interviews – spin your experiences and accomplishments in the light of these attributes.

### Which attributes are true of you?

| Attribute | | Attribute | |
|---|---|---|---|
| Emotionally intelligent | ☐ | Opportunity seeker | ☐ |
| Resilient | ☐ | Challenge seeker | ☐ |
| Independent/self-reliant | ☐ | Results-oriented | ☐ |
| Self-managing | ☐ | Obsessive customer or client orientation | ☐ |
| Innovative/creative | ☐ | | |
| Continuous learner/ professionally curious | ☐ | Ruthless time manager | ☐ |
| | | Team leader/player | ☐ |
| Interpersonally sensitive/ people focused | ☐ | Problem solver | ☐ |
| Dedicated/focused | ☐ | Resourceful/enterprising | ☐ |
| Time sensitive/ deadline driven | ☐ | Accomplished/talented | ☐ |
| | | Savvy expert professional | ☐ |
| Market driven | ☐ | Think return on investment | ☐ |
| Leader | ☐ | High impact | ☐ |
| Compelling communicator | ☐ | Risk taker | ☐ |
| Visionary/strategist | ☐ | Top producing | ☐ |
| Professional | ☐ | Outstanding/ proven record | ☐ |
| Flexible/adaptable/ thrives on change | ☐ | Globally oriented | ☐ |
| Business acumen | ☐ | Leading edge | ☐ |

**Not in the cards**

*It is not only about handing out your business card. Think of yourself as an oral storyteller picking up information here and passing it out there.*

policies on organizations' websites. Look at independent surveys of the best employers conducted every year.

- Ask informed questions of potential employers and people in the know. Just because an organization has a policy does not mean it is actually applied.
- Quiz former and current staff.
- Be wary of studies that rank top-performing companies. A company can be very profitable but not a great place to work.

## Network! Network! Network!

Networking is one of today's most important career-management skills—not only as a source of job leads, but also as a way of gathering and sharing ideas for your work. In Find your perfect path, I showed you how to develop and use your network to look for career opportunities outside your current field or if you are making a career shift (*see* Changing your career, *pages 138–145*). In Boost your career intelligence, I will show you how to use networking as a lifelong career-management strategy (*see pages 307–309*). Here, let us see how to use your network for generating work leads.

Study after study has shown that up to 70 percent of people in new positions found them through networking. Networking is a simple concept. You communicate with a network of people you know either directly or indirectly. They, in turn, may let you know of possible opportunities, pass your name on to others, refer you to others, share information and trends in the field, provide you with inside information that can give you a competitive advantage over other job seekers, and let you know what it is like to work for a particular employer.

Networking is not about passing out business cards and then quickly disappearing, or starting every conversation with, "I'm looking for work." It is about developing professionally rewarding relationships where the goal is not to get an immediate payback but to reap long-term benefits.

Many people find networking uncomfortable or even distasteful, thinking it is an imposition on others. Most people, however, welcome the opportunity to talk about their work and to be helpful—especially if they have undergone a similar search. Networking will generate the greatest number of leads; spend at least 50 percent of your time networking.

## Identify and expand your network

When I ask people to write down the names of 25 people in their network, they often panic. "I don't really know that many," they say. Ten minutes later, having been asked to brainstorm using the categories below, they are surprised by how many people they do have access to. Start networking with people you already know to practice networking skills in a "safe" environment.

Ask people you know directly to recommend people they know. Aim to speak to people you think are beyond reach and would not be interested in helping you—they may surprise you, or at least refer you to people who could help. Think creatively and expand this circle, especially beyond your profession or industry. Identify an organization to which you would love an introduction. Ask contacts if they know someone, or know someone who knows someone, who could refer you.

*Study after study has shown that up to 70 percent of people in new positions found them through networking.*

## People in your network

| Category | Example |
|----------|---------|
| Family/friends | Family members, friends, neighbors |
| Social acquaintances; community/volunteering contacts | Members of clubs, associations, church groups, friends of friends, community groups |
| Professional associates | Current and former co-workers, former bosses, members of your professional associations, customers, suppliers |
| Educational contacts | Current and former classmates, teachers, professors, alumni associations |
| Service providers | Doctors, lawyers, hairdressers, plumbers, real-estate agents, estheticians, trainers |

**Assessing** yourself

**Mapping your strategy**

▶ Thinking through your goals
*page 171*

▶ What are employers looking for?
*page 177*

▶ Identifying your network
*page 180*

## SELF-ASSESSMENT   Identifying your network

List as many people as you know from each category below whom you could ask for career information and leads. Keep track of all your contact information, phone calls, and meeting appointments in your filing system.

*Family/friends:*

..................................................   ..................................................
..................................................   ..................................................
..................................................   ..................................................
..................................................   ..................................................

*Social acquaintances; community/volunteering contacts:*

..................................................   ..................................................
..................................................   ..................................................
..................................................   ..................................................

*Professional associates:*

..................................................   ..................................................
..................................................   ..................................................
..................................................   ..................................................

*Educational contacts:*

..................................................   ..................................................
..................................................   ..................................................
..................................................   ..................................................

*Service providers:*

..................................................   ..................................................
..................................................   ..................................................
..................................................   ..................................................
..................................................   ..................................................

## Send an email to people in your network

Networking through personalized emails is a powerful way to generate leads and provides an easy vehicle for people to be helpful. The email below was sent out by one work searcher to 100 people and generated 40 responses in two days.

---

**Subject:** Extra pair of eyes and ears

Hi David,

You have probably heard that GDF is not faring well. As a result, I, along with many others, have been laid off. I value my memorable working relationship with you and the friendship we developed at Koko's. If I may be so bold, I would be grateful if you could act as an extra pair of eyes and ears, alert to marketing management opportunities in media. I am attaching my résumé . . .

---

## Develop a marketing sound bite

Every time you meet someone, you have an opportunity to market yourself. What would impress that person so they will want to help you, whether by referring you to their colleagues or by meeting you to discuss opportunities in their organization? Based on your self-assessment, write a script that highlights your skills, experience, and career goals.

The script should be short (about 20 seconds), compelling, and to the point. Practice the sound bite on friends. Is it clear? Persuasive? If you are uncomfortable marketing yourself, *see page 310.*

## Sound-bite scripts

You will use your sound bite to get the conversation moving in your networking. Obviously, your sound bite will shift depending on your audience, what you want to communicate about yourself, and what support you want from them.

- Veteran worker: "I spent the last 10 years in progressively more senior positions in _____ and developed deep knowledge of _____. I am investigating opportunities in _____/looking for a

*see page 310.*

**Career** counsel

At every meeting, pick up an interesting tidbit—whether a trend, or insight into an industry, or the name of someone doing interesting work—that you can pass on to someone else. Most people involved in a work search forget how much insider information they are gathering.

*The questions
that you ask will
say a lot about
who you are.*

senior-management position in the _____ sector that
will use my _____ in an entrepreneurial environment."
- Recent graduate: "I recently graduated from the
  University of _____ with an honors degree in _____.
  I am looking for work opportunities in a creative
  environment/the _____ sector where my initiative and
  strong relationship-building skills will be recognized and
  where I can apply my professional skills in _____."

## Ask for a meeting

Make it easy for other people to be helpful. Although face-to-face
meetings are ideal, some prefer telephone or email. Indicate the purpose
of your call and how their expertise will help. Ask to set up a 15-minute
meeting on the phone or in their office. (Although some job experts
recommend asking for a 45-minute meeting, many people see this as an
excessive time demand.) Indicate who referred you. Say that you are not
looking for a specific opening. Although you may be looking for leads,
you are also gathering information that will increase your knowledge,
and hence marketability. Get in touch with the person who referred you
once you have made contact and thank them for the introduction.

## Use meeting time strategically

Outline your experience and the direction you are exploring—your sound
bite. Be clear about the purpose of the meeting. Use good listening skills.
Keep the meeting to the time limit suggested. At the end, ask the
contact if they can recommend colleagues who might be a good
resource. Follow up with a thank-you note. Sometimes people will offer
to show your résumé to others, but you are usually better off getting in
touch with their contacts directly. The questions you ask will say a lot
about who you are (*see pages 210–215*).

## Stay in touch

Keep your name in front of people. Update your network on your
progress. Inform them of developments in their industry or profession.
Email them articles you think would interest them.

# Mining other sources

Networking will be your most productive source of work leads, but career activists mine every search strategy, including career ads, employment agencies and recruiters, and job fairs.

### Respond to ads

Although the percentage of people who find work through paid employer advertisements is not as high as through networking, respond to all ads of possible interest. Even if you do not have the required experience or education as described, respond to ads for work that you think is a good fit for you. Show you possess the underlying skills they are really looking for. For example, if the ad asks for an MBA, describe your management skills and capacity for strategic thinking. The employer may be using the degree as a code for those attributes. Remember that employers often are not very sophisticated in understanding what attributes they really need.

### Pitch an employer

You have done the research and have identified an organization or person you would love to work for. You have exhausted your network for direct introductions. Although pitching organizations and people who do not know you is not a highly successful strategy, organizations are looking for talent, and you are talented.

Send a compelling pitch letter or email indicating that you have sought them out because of their special organizational culture or their unique expertise. Outline how you can provide skills or insight of value to them. Show you can solve a challenge facing their industry or profession. (*See pages 204–205* for more about the pitch letter.)

### "Net" a job

Most organizations use electronic media in some form as a recruitment strategy, whether it be on their own sites, advertising on job boards, or a combination. Check out job boards of professional associations as well.

## Career counsel

Cast your net broadly and strategically. If there is an opening in an organization you really want to work for, do not be put off by the stated qualifications. There may be another unadvertised opportunity.

For some professions, such as information technology, on-line ads are a top source of work.

## Use employment agencies and recruiters

Agencies and recruiters work for the employer, not for you. Do not assume you can simply sign up with a handful of agencies, sit back, and let them find you work.

Some agencies, particularly those sourcing more junior jobs, operate on a contingency basis. They are paid only if they fill an opening. Contingency agencies can be aggressive in their search tactics and may promise you the moon, but they are simply looking to fill the opening as quickly as possible.

Other search consultants usually conduct extensive research, casting their net widely to gather suitable candidates and conducting in-depth interviews before putting your name before the client. Beware of what I call recruiter break-up—the process of going from being very hot to being very "not." You are called for an interview with the recruiter, your name is put forward to the client, where you have several interviews, and

**Tough questions**

*Recruiters will grill you on your career history and will zero in on "weak spots." Before presenting you to their client, they need to ensure that you are a good match.*

then you hear nothing and calls are not returned. Employment agencies account for roughly 15 to 30 percent of all positions filled, with senior positions accounting for their highest percentages.

Never pay a fee to an agency that promises you work. Reputable ones earn their money from employers. Organizations that promise to find you work are little more than course factories. They will tell you that in order to find work, you need to upgrade your skills in X, Y, and Z.

### Job fairs

Employers in high-demand fields, such as information technology and healthcare, often hold advertised job fairs. Even if you are outside their target market, which usually is people with two to five years' experience, you still might benefit by attending. Meet with recruiters and managers at staffing booths, and develop relationships with hiring managers in various organizations. You may be interviewed on the spot. Bring several copies of your résumé to leave behind.

*Agencies and recruiters work for the employer, not for you.*

## **How to** work with recruitment agencies

Recruiters are not your personal talent agents. Find good recruiters and agencies that have proven, professional track records. Working with them requires skill.

▶ Ask networking contacts for recommendations of good firms.

▶ Monitor ads in newspapers and on the Internet. Which firms seem to specialize in your kind of work?

▶ Call recruiters. Ask questions about how they work and the kinds of positions they fill. Ask for a meeting.

▶ Ask for feedback on your marketing materials.

▶ Keep yourself in recruiters' minds. Be helpful when they are conducting a search in your field by giving them names of potential candidates.

▶ Follow up if you have been called in for an interview and have not heard back.

▶ When called by an employment agency, ask whether they have a specific assignment from an employer to fill a position or whether they are gathering résumés to send out to companies "on spec."

▶ Remember that the recruiter is not working for you—you are simply product with an attached price tag.

# Creating great marketing tools

Think of yourself as a unique "product" to sell to potential employers. Develop engaging, motivating marketing materials that speak directly and powerfully to what employers are looking for. Use all of these to provide evidence that you have the right skills and attributes.

## This chapter shows you how to:

**Write** a résumé that speaks directly to potential employers and clients, telling your story in a compelling and economical way.

**Showcase** your talent, whether you are starting out, returning from a career break, or entering the latter stages of your career.

**Tailor** your résumé by building on your insider knowledge of employers, industry sectors, and different work roles.

**Select** the right résumé format—functional or chronological—that tells your unique story with creativity and power.

**Capture** recruiters' attention with the right type of cover letters—your most important marketing document.

**Develop** and decide when to use other targeted marketing materials to support your search for work.

**It takes thought**

*Spend time on your résumé. You do not want an "identikit" résumé with so many meaningless superlatives and clichés that recruiters' eyes glaze over.*

# Writing a résumé that sells

Your résumé is a critical marketing tool—the narrative record of your skills, educational background, accomplishments, and work history. It must say, "I can be valuable to you."

Employers and recruiters spend as little as half a minute reading a résumé. You must capture their attention quickly, showing that you have the skills they need. Your résumé builds on four types of information:

- The results of your self-assessment (*see* Know yourself and Find your perfect path).
- Key information about industry sectors (*see* Find your perfect path, *pages 92–107*).
- Your understanding of what employers are looking for (*see page 175*).
- Your research on what a particular employer is looking for.

For examples and models of résumés, *see pages 166–199*.

## Steps to a powerful résumé

Write your résumé yourself. Once you have a good draft, you may want to go to a professional for polish, but only you can provide the content that really tells your story. You also need to "own" the words and ideas that you will expand on in interviews. Build on your knowledge of the industry sector to which you are applying (*see pages 96–111.*) Underline key words and concepts associated with that sector. Spin your experiences, skills, and attributes in that light. In this chapter you will learn how to:

- Write a personal profile.
- Describe your career history.
- Identify your accomplishments.
- Describe your education and other important information.
- Choose the right format.
- Refine, refine, refine—and refine some more.
- Tailor your résumé to fit the work you are applying for.

# CV dos and don'ts

Expect to write several drafts of your résumé before it showcases your talent and background in the most compelling and succinct way possible.

## Do:

- Focus on content, but make format attractive and easy to follow.

- Use lots of verbs, especially those that show off your accomplishments. Use active voice, not passive ("Managed a team of six" instead of "Was responsible for managing a team of six").

- Use a formal, professional tone.

- Be specific ("Am proficient in several programming languages, including C++ and Java" instead of "Have good computer skills").

- Explain long gaps in paid employment (e.g., full-time caregiver, work that was ended because of restructuring, return to school).

- Edit, re-edit, and have someone else proofread.

- Keep it short—no more than two or three pages. If you have published books or articles, list them in a separate appendix of a page or two at most.

- Avoid gimmicks such as résumés on T-shirts, mugs, or CDs. It only works in some creative fields—for example, advertising and design.

- Tailor your résumé to each position as much as possible. The basic architecture should stay the same, but you can emphasize or delete characteristics.

## Don't:

- Slap a résumé together quickly to start your job search sooner. Do it right.

- Obsess for hours over every word. Spend that time networking.

- Tell everything about your work history—leave some of that for the interview.

- Stretch the truth. Employers check the information on your résumé and some use verification services.

- Disclose your present or past salaries, or the salary you want. (Same applies for your cover letters.)

- Use acronyms or jargon—the person screening your résumé may not be familiar with your field.

- Overuse superlatives. Let your accomplishments speak for themselves.

- Write the month you started and ended.

*Only you can provide the content that really tells your story.*

*How much hyperbole should you use? It depends on the role and the sector.*

**Assessing** yourself

**Creating great marketing materials**

▶ Generating your profile worksheet
*page 191*

### Step One: Develop your personal profile

This short narrative paragraph or list of four or five bullet points summarizes who you are, what you have to offer, and the skills and attributes that would contribute to the organization you are applying to. Remember the master principle of work search (*see page 175*) and put yourself in the employer's shoes—what would they be looking for? In addition, use the attributes you identified as true of you from the list in the previous chapter (*see* What employers are looking for, *page 177*), as well as industry-specific traits, as appropriate.

The first point in your personal profile is a summary matching to the employer what you do professionally. Consider including role, level, special skills, and/or industry. Use the attributes you identified to describe roles and how you carry out those roles. For example:

● "Development-focused VP of Marketing with outstanding record for talent attraction and retention."
● "Strategic-thinking accounting professional with 10 years' progressive experience in the hospitality industry."
● "Client-focused Organizational Development consultant acknowledged for skills in creating high-performing teams."

Additional points will address key skills, attributes, experiences, and accomplishments directly relevant to the work. Include information that speaks to both technical and general competencies.

How much hyperbole should you use? It depends on the role and the sector. A therapist will use cooler words to describe herself than a sales rep. Draw freely from the attributes you identified in What employers are looking for, *page 177*.

Some people find it easier to write their personal profile after they have gone through the thinking process of generating their career history. (*See* Step Two, *page 192*.) Your profile can be written in bulleted points (*see page 195*) or in narrative style (*see page 192*). Bulleted profiles are easier to read and communicate the message more quickly than narrative ones.

**PORTFOLIO**     **Generating your** profile worksheet

List seven to nine of your key attributes. Include three core strengths or competencies. Use these tools:

- Your list of attributes (*see* What are employers looking for? *page 177*), e.g., "Resourceful, time-sensitive marketing professional"
- Your Summary of skills, knowledge, and interests (*see pages 78–79*)
- Your Accomplishments workout (*see pages 62–63*)

Use the examples opposite and the sample résumés (*see pages 196–199*) as a model.

......................................................................................................................

......................................................................................................................

......................................................................................................................

......................................................................................................................

......................................................................................................................

......................................................................................................................

......................................................................................................................

......................................................................................................................

......................................................................................................................

Review your list. Can you combine some of the concepts? Show them here:

......................................................................................................................

......................................................................................................................

......................................................................................................................

......................................................................................................................

......................................................................................................................

......................................................................................................................

......................................................................................................................

In writing your résumé, add or edit as appropriate from these lists. Tailor for different opportunities.

# Career counsel

Recent graduates:

- Show leadership skills and other talents by describing extracurricular and academic activities, as well as awards and scholarships. List internships and volunteer experience.

- Describe the kind of feedback you got from managers and peers in your jobs and student activities. For example, "Acted as a coach to co-workers" or "Was consistently praised by my manager for resourcefulness and initiative."

- Include information such as working part-time while completing full-time degree or setting up your own business.

- Keep it short. One page usually is sufficient.

- You can put "education" as the next heading after your profile.

---

**Example of Personal Profile, Narrative Style**

"A globally oriented senior bilingual consultant and trainer specializing in change management and individual effectiveness, with more than 20 years' experience in all industry sectors. Broad international experience includes working as a senior consultant for High Profile Learning Systems, leading numerous management development seminars in Paris, Hong Kong, and Thailand for global organizations. Praised by clients for clear and compelling delivery, meeting learner needs, and providing skills that are translated into on-the-job performance."

---

## Career objective or personal profile?

Job-search books used to recommend that a résumé begin with a career objective, such as "to use my financial-analysis skills in a challenging environment that rewards…" From the employer's point of view, there was a fundamental disconnect. Reading a career objective at the top of a résumé, they felt they were being asked to help the applicant. I prefer the personal profile. Some very technical professions, however, such as those in Information Technology and scientific research, do favor the career objective because the nature of their work is so specialized.

## Step Two: Describe your career history

This and the following step, Document your accomplishments, are the meat of your résumé. In your career history, list job titles. Describe overall responsibilities. Include information as appropriate to show scope of work and special challenges; for example, size of budget, number of reports, and special challenges—the company was going through a restructuring, was under bankruptcy protection, or had reported record losses.

If you had a senior job, include the title of the person to whom you reported, to demonstrate scope of work. List your experience in reverse chronological order, with brief descriptions of your responsibilities. Put the dates on the right-hand side of the page. Include any teaching or training experience. It demonstrates presentation and listening skills.

## Step Three: Document your accomplishments

List work-related accomplishments and relevant personal accomplishments. Describe results. Do not rehash job descriptions. Use power words. For example, "Designed and delivered customer-service training that led to a 50% increase in customer-satisfaction ratings. Consistently received top program evaluations." Review the accomplishments you identified in your accomplishments workout (*pages 62–63*).

## Step Four: Describe education and other important information

List degrees and courses taken toward degrees. If you are currently enrolled in a degree, show as follows: "B.A., University of Chicago, currently in progress. Completed two years." If you are an older worker concerned about possible age discrimination, do not include the date you obtained your degree. If you have more than 15 years of experience and accomplishments, you do not need to include early work experience—unless it is directly relevant. If, for example, you are applying for work with a pharmaceutical and your first job was with a company in that sector, include it. Otherwise, summarize: "Roles prior to 20xx included (list job titles and/or employers)."

List relevant managerial or professional training. This information is usually folded into material under the heading Education and Professional Development. If you have taken seminars in a similar area, summarize them:

> *"Have actively participated in professional development throughout my career. Have taken a broad range of courses in management areas such as team-building, coaching and counseling, and managing performance."*

Include information that speaks to your abilities, such as board memberships, volunteer experience, professional memberships, awards, speaking engagements, publications. Play your strongest card in the way you organize this information. For instance, if you are an award-winning journalist, use Awards as a separate heading. If you have played significant roles in the community, consider a heading Community Leadership.

## Career counsel

Career returners:

- Document personal accomplishments. One woman who described a two-year career sabbatical in which she sailed around the world received many calls from employers. They were impressed by the skills and attributes her journey showed: managing ambiguity, risk-taking, curiosity, love of adventure.

- Show what you did on your career break that enhanced your skills portfolio, including leadership roles in volunteer activities, courses taken, seminars attended.

- Show how you have upgraded your professional skills. Indicate the professional journals you have been reading or contributing to.

*Decide which format better tells your story in the light of the work you are targeting.*

## Step Five: Select the right format

Now you are ready to put it all together. There are two main types of résumés, chronological and functional (*see* samples on *pages 196–199*). Use the type that better highlights your qualifications.

## Types of résumé

| Résumé | Description | Use it when you |
|---|---|---|
| **Chronological** | Work history listed in reverse chronological order<br><br>Shows two to four key accomplishments or contributions for each role | Are applying for a position in the same industry<br><br>Are applying for a position with the same job title as you have had<br><br>Want to show how your jobs have progressed in responsibility<br><br>Have a consistent job history that reveals a stable record of accomplishments |
| **Functional** | Accomplishments organized by category or functional area with two to four accomplishments for each area<br><br>Brief description of work, employers, and titles in reverse chronological order | Want to emphasize your accomplishments and skills instead of job titles and career history<br><br>Are changing careers or have changed careers<br><br>Have spent much of your career with an employer that does not have a good external reputation<br><br>Have moved in and out of full-time or contract work or self-employment<br><br>Have gaps in your work history<br><br>Have changed jobs frequently<br><br>Have little paid experience<br><br>Are looking for consulting or contract work<br><br>Your job titles do not give a clear picture of what you did or can do |

Review your worksheets. Decide which format better tells your story in the light of the work you are targeting. Note that some recruiters are suspicious of the functional format, thinking the writer is trying to "hide something by burying their career history."

## How to write a functional résumé

A chronological résumé is easier to write. A functional résumé requires more thought and organization.

Review your accomplishments. How do they cluster? Organize by skill or functional category. For example, a director in healthcare targeting program-management work might cluster his accomplishments under these headings:

- Program Management
- Team Leadership
- Operations and Risk Management
- Organizational and Staff Development.

A financial professional looking to work as an investment adviser might cluster her accomplishments under these headings:

- Business Development
- Market Research and Analysis
- Client Development and Relationship-building
- Customer Service and Retention.

Write two to four accomplishments for each theme. If you have done the same work several times, summarize your accomplishments. An interior designer might write, "Have worked on numerous residential renovations from Victorian homes to edgy lofts. Am consistently praised by architects for getting the right feel."

**Tell the story**

*In the final analysis, your résumé is a storytelling document. Think about the story you want to tell. Select the form that best frames your talents.*

**Sample** chronological résumé

*This career builder's résumé shows a strong record of achievements in increasingly more senior positions.*

*Note how achievements are quantitatively substantiated; he pays greatest attention to his current position.*

*This manager shows hard business as well as leadership competencies.*

*Because Tony was seeking work in the automotive industry, he shows relevant interests. In his "generic" résumé this would be cut.*

**Tony P. Rodriguez**
**150 Main Street, Central City, Ontario M5E 1R4**
**Arodriguez12@sympatico.ca Tel:416-555-1212**

**Profile**

- Client-focused business-unit manager with proven track record in turnaround and change management.
- Visionary, results-oriented leader with significant accomplishments in corporate development, new technology development, and project management.
- Lead and motivate by creating high-performing teams and inspiring staff to develop new methods.
- Outstanding record for talent attraction, retention, and development.
- Over 15 years' hands-on, progressive experience in business improvement.

**Professional Experience**

**Diversified Corporation**                                                          1999–present
**Business Manager, Colorants & Textile/Leather Chemicals, Central City, ON**
Reporting to the Senior Vice-President, with a budget of $5 million, lead a national business team focused on corporate clients in the automotive coatings, architectural coatings, plastics, inks, specialty coatings, textiles, and leather industries. Manage department of 11 highly skilled industry professionals. Member of Diversified's Quality Management Leadership Team.

**Selected Achievements:**

- Amid year-over-year market price declines of 15%, increased net sales by 4%; increased sales per employee by 56%; reduced fixed costs by 18%; reduced selling expenses by 20%; reduced inventory as-a-percent-of-sales by 16%; increased operating cash flow by 118%.
- Aggressively restructured unit through product portfolio management, staff changes, activity-based costing models, market/customer-positioning changes, and overhead cost reductions.
- Executed a major divestiture and subsequently relaunched remaining textile chemicals brand, leading to a 37% increase in market share.
- Negotiated multi-year supply contracts with major clients. Identified new market niche in specialty textiles, leading to 15% year-over-year increase for one of the business unit's highest-margin products.
- Implemented a cross-business, key-account management program focused on clients with revenues in excess of $10 million, resulting in average increase in business of 7% and substantial profit improvement.
- Reinvigorated an underperforming, low-morale team by implementing performance objectives, incentive programs, and training and development. Employee satisfaction ratings improved by 15%, employee turnover decreased by 25%.

**Conglomerated Industries**
**Western Business Manager, Vancouver**                                        1995–1999
Assessed market opportunities in the Pacific Northwest region (US and Canada) and implemented structural changes by integrating the US and Canadian sales teams. Led a cross-

business sales, marketing, customer-service, and logistics team of 15 delivering products and services to the region with a total revenue budget of $3 million.

**Selected Achievements:**
- Restructured regional distribution and customer-service capabilities, resulting in improved service and saving of approximately $1 million in annual fixed costs.
- Developed a corporate customer-loyalty program to identify and retain top-tier corporate clients based on long-term value to Conglomerated, resulting in 15% increase in average order size and 10% decrease in churn.
- As a key member of the company's five-member restructuring task force, developed a plan that, when implemented, led to a 20% workforce reduction through leaving incentives, early retirement, and identification of poor performers.

**Consultant, Shift Change Consultants Inc., Toronto**           1994–95

Lead consultant on a major business-unit strategy case in the telecommunications industry. Analysis included customer survey, forecasting model, advertising and promotions, loyalty program, and international best-practices benchmarking. The implementation of recommendations led to a 15% increase in customer retention and a 17% increase in unit productivity. Recognized for client-management skills as well as exceptional analytic skills.

**Conglomerated Industries, Toronto**           1990–94

A series of progressively more senior positions

**Manager, Business Systems and Customer Satisfaction**

Directed four analysts in developing an automated business information system in 12 business units within six months. Managed purchasing and payroll budgets in excess of $2 million. Executed a corporate-wide customer-satisfaction survey and led implementation.

**Marketing Analyst, Specialty Chemicals**

Analyzed industrial markets and developed strategic business-unit objectives. Analysis and recommendations led to the merger of several business units.

**Project Specialist**

Assessed structure and marketing processes. Delivered recommendations to the company's executive committee.

**Financial Analyst, The New Bank, Toronto**           1986–89

Several positions in different divisions including corporate, small business, and retail.

### Education, Management Development and Interests
- MBA, University of Calgary, 1990.
- BA, Honors, History, Queen's University, 1986.
- Throughout my career have participated actively in management and professional development. Programs include Chemistry for Executives, Managing a Business Unit, Today's Executive.
- Certified in TQM; attained significant levels of quality and management accreditation.
- Go Kart Racer of the Year, 1998. Hobby—rebuilding automobiles.

**Sample** functional résumé

At a glance the reader sees Sandy's key skills in terms that speak directly to the employer's needs.

Sandy tailored this résumé for an editorial position with a lifestyle magazine targeting readers in their 20s (see *Profile* and *Interests*). She has various versions of her résumé, including one that emphasizes her writing skills—she is also investigating feature-writing opportunities.

Many personal developers and novelty seekers, particularly those who have moved in and out of full-time employment, contract work, and self-employment, find this format the best way to present their background.

The format—emphasizing her competency areas rather than where she used the competency—is ideal since she is sending the résumé to a "glossy," a type of magazine for which she has no hands-on editorial experience.

---

### Sandy Fowler
198 10th Avenue, New York, NY 10002  212-555-1212
sandy.fowler@email.com

**PROFILE**
- Multi-skilled editor and writer with commitment to editorial excellence.
- Fresh, creative, innovative—skilled in designing content that appeals to readers and advertisers.
- Deadline-sensitive and cost-conscious manager with proven experience in all aspects of periodical production.
- Compelling writer who can analyze and summarize trends and issues on any topic.
- Tuned in to the young-adult demographic.

**SKILLS & ACCOMPLISHMENTS**
Editing:
- Have edited a wide variety of materials, including consumer- and trade-magazine articles, directories, books, and websites. Have worked in all editorial positions including managing editor, section editor, and copy editor.
- Commissioned and led the redesign of *Human Resources Now*. Introduced new editorial features, including columns from freelance contributors and a new Careers section, increasing readership by 20% in the targeted demographic. At *Apparel Today*, increased market share by 10%, newsstand circulation by 20%, and advertising revenues by 15%.
- Praised by publishers for sensitivity to market challenges and reader demographic, and by readers for fresh editorial content.
- Identified and developed emerging talent. Have strong relationships with a stable of highly skilled freelance writers. Adept at matching story ideas with the right writer. Commissioned Dee Yung to write a story on the new workplace, which won the Young Writer Award.

Writing:
- Author of over 150 features and columns that have appeared in major magazines such as *New Woman*, *Clip*, and *Design*, national newspapers, and in broadcast media. Have also written book chapters, reports, background briefings, fact sheets, and news releases.
- Thought-provoking articles for *New Woman* generated record number of letters to the editor.
- Adept at capturing the essence of the subject, identifying sources and subjects, and producing compelling editorial. Sought after by editors for versatility and ability to translate technical content into engaging information and meet demanding deadlines.

Management:
- At *Human Resources Now* took over editorial reins of revenue-losing journal and relaunched with a new design. Revitalized staff of seven, reduced staff turnover. Boosted advertising revenue by 10% in first year.
- Have proven accomplishments in all aspects of editorial management. At *Human Resources Now* and *Apparel Today*, assigned articles to freelance writers and expert contributors; planned the editorial calendar; managed the freelance budget; approved the layout and design of each issue.
- Skilled in developing high-performing teams and building relationships.

- Managed production of award-winning cookbook, tracking all aspects of the project/production and managing an editorial budget of $300,000 with eight freelance contributors and editors.
- Sought-after mentor for emerging writers such as Erin Song, who subsequently became an award-winning columnist for *Ace Magazine*.

Electronic media:
- Initiated and oversaw the successful conversion of *Human Resources Now* to an Internet version. The site is one of the top five most-visited HR sites.

CAREER HISTORY

Managing Editor, *Human Resources Now*                                     2000–present
HRN Publications, New York, NY
Oversee the editorial budget and content for the journal. Manage a department of six. Hire and manage freelance writers and expert contributors. Oversee production.

Writer/editor (self-employed)                                             1994–2000
SJF Communications, New York, NY
Provided editing and writing services for clients including Diversified Industries, KYZ Radio, Conglomerated Financial, Central City Department of Public Health. Quadrupled revenues within the first three years of operation.

Editor, *Apparel Today* (quarterly journal)                               1996–1999
IBC Trade Publications, Newark, NJ
Assigned and edited all articles from freelance writers and expert contributors. Initiated a new column announcing appointments in the apparel industry that became the journal's second-most-read page.

City Desk Editor, *The Kingston Tribune*                                   1995–1996
Kingston, NY
Assigned all local stories to staff reporters. Decided which stories would be published in the newspaper. Instituted a computerized system for sharing files that shaved an hour off the previous deadlines.

AWARDS
- Michael W. Mason Award, American Trade Press, for Best Trade Article, in *Human Resources Now*, 2003.
- Prominent member of the team that produced the *Cookbook for Healthy Living*, which won three awards: two International Association of Food Communicators Golden Awards for writing and design, and one Editing Society Award for Editorial Excellence, 2002.

EDUCATION, PROFESSIONAL MEMBERSHIPS AND INTERESTS
BA, Honors, 1992 (Minor in English) Milton University. Member of the Editing Society and the Association of Journalists. Board Member, The Artists' Co-Op.

Interests:
Indie music, fashion, new business models.

**Be judicious**

*Get feedback from others, but be judicious in what you pay attention to. Everyone has a personal opinion on what a résumé should look like.*

## Step Six: Refine, refine, refine—and refine some more

Get feedback on your résumé from a few people whose opinions you respect. Ask them: "Do my talents and achievements shine through? Is it compelling? Does it show how I can add value?" Revise based on comments from interviewers and people you are networking with. Expect to write four or five drafts before your résumé is as clear and powerful as possible.

## Step Seven: Tailor your résumé

A résumé tailored to meet the special needs of an employer is a powerful marketing tool. However, if you are sending out many résumés, keeping track of which one you sent to whom can be challenging. Consider having a generic résumé that you can change for special opportunities. Modify your profile and make other minor adjustments to content. *See* the notes to the editor's profile on *page 198.*

## Getting "the look" on paper

You would be amazed by how often people send imperfectly merged letters. The letter is addressed to one person and company, but another company name appears throughout the letter. Using a word-processing template for your letter is dangerous. Double-check all names and addresses. After you have written your letters, double-check them against the Dos and Don'ts on *page 189.*

- Make it easy to read. Print it on plain white or ivory paper. No need to get fancy—in fact, employers may be turned off by a document that looks too slick.

- Use plenty of white space and keep margins at one inch all around. A typeface such as Times Roman or Arial, in 11 or 12 point size, is easy to read.

- If you work in a creative field such as advertising, marketing, or graphic design, and you are certain that the employer's corporate culture encourages it, present your résumé with more fun and flair.

- Many employers scan printed résumés to an electronic database. Make sure the letters in your résumé do not touch each other.

- When sending your letter and résumé by email, remember that computers vary. What looks good on your screen may end up looking ugly on someone else's. Therefore, use common fonts.

- Use a simple, easy-to-read layout. Do not add graphics that are tedious to download.

# Writing compelling letters

Letters, whether they are covers to résumés in response to ads or pitches to potential employers to hire you, provide the "big picture" of your special talents in words that speak directly to the employer's needs. Craft your correspondence with intelligence and care.

In your search you will be writing three kinds of correspondence—cover letters, pitch letters, and networking letters. The first two are described below.

## Cover letters

Grab the reader's attention. Write a letter that says, "Look at my résumé. I am uniquely qualified to meet your needs. You want to meet me."

The cover letter is first and foremost a marketing tool to sell yourself. It is often more important than your résumé. It shows higher-level thinking skills—that you can capture, in summary form, the essence of what the employer is really looking for. Spend the necessary time on this part of the process. This is your chance to make general statements about yourself that show how you can add value. Cover letters give the employer the big picture of your career highlights and allow you to tailor your application to a particular position or employer.

Keep your letter brief—three to five short paragraphs. Use power words to pack as much punch as you can in one page. Think back to your networking sound bite or pitch that you developed in the previous chapter (*see pages 181–182*). Rework that material.

What is the purpose of your letter? Many letter writers make the mistake of failing to ask for what they want. Do you want to set up a meeting to discuss how your skills are a perfect match for an employer's needs? Do you want to talk to them about industry trends? Do you want an interview? As you did with your résumé, follow the master principle of work search (*see page 175*) and think about what the employer would want from you. Show that you have it.

*Write a letter that says, "Look at my résumé. I am uniquely qualified to meet your needs. You want to meet me."*

## Parts of a cover letter

Personal coordinates: Name, address, and contact information.
The employer's information: Name and title of employer contact, organization, address.

**Opening line**: Grab your reader's attention and get to the point quickly.

- "Ten years as a management trainer in public-accounting and legal firms make me an ideal candidate for your management-consulting role, professional services."
- "As an accomplished gardener with proven marketing and leadership skills, I am uniquely qualified to be your Marketing Manager, Outdoor Products."

### Be tone-sensitive

*Consider what the employer is looking for. Add a personal touch. Present a compelling value proposition by adding something novel or unconventional that captures their attention.*

**Body:** Highlight important accomplishments, skills, personal traits, and relevant experience. Use words different from those in your résumé.

**Summarize:** If applying to a job ad, repeat key words that it lists as requirements. Show how you meet the criteria and your understanding of the issues or industry. If you are applying for work in a new sector, note the key words and concepts related to that industry (*see pages 96–111*) and cast your experience in that light. The cover letter opposite shows how a woman translated her experience working in an NGO into relevant concepts for the hospitality industry.

**Closing:** Close the deal and have the employer take action to invite you to an interview or let them know what your next step will be. For example, "I know my background in _____ (and/or) knowledge of _____ (and/or) enthusiasm for _____ would make me an important asset to the success of _____. I will take the initiative to call you next Wednesday to set up a time to meet with you and discuss how my skills and experience would be an asset."

## Sample cover letter

Sheila Kane
145 Sixth Avenue
Burlington, Ont.
L2C 1V7
905-551658

Diane Coutts
Paradise Hotels
P.O. Box 908
Toronto, Ont. M1T 6A5

Dear Ms. Coutts,

As a long-time admirer of Paradise Hotels, I was extremely excited when I saw the advertised opportunity for People Resources Manager (Ref. no. 12p). After hearing your Vice-President of Human Resources speak at a conference on work–life balance, I knew Paradise had become my number-one employer of choice.

I am an enthusiastic human resources manager sensitive to the needs of the new worker. I thrive in fast-paced, diverse environments and enjoy rising to the challenge of responding to multiple demands from many people. My customer-service dedication to meeting the needs of management, employees, and volunteers—our customers—has been recognized in three years of outstanding performance reviews. These attributes, combined with proven skills in all aspects of human resources, including employee relations, compensation, and benefits, would make me a great asset to Paradise.

My experience in the nonprofit world has been a wonderful training ground for working in hospitality. Imagine the skills and resourcefulness I developed in providing what has been described as "best in class" people strategies and programs while working to demanding deadlines with few or no resources.

I would welcome the opportunity to meet with you to demonstrate how my experiences and education would fit Paradise's mandate of being an employer of choice. I can be reached during the day at (416) 227-9221 ext. 438.

Sincerely,

*Sheila Kane*

Sheila Kane

*This letter-writer demonstrates her serious interest in and enthusiasm for the company. She has cast her experience in hospitality-specific language. She ends with a request.*

## Career counsel

Think benefits selling. Successful marketers target their message directly to the needs of the purchaser. They know the purchaser is thinking, "What's in it for me?" Before you write your letter, identify what the purchaser wants and needs. Now identify how your skills and experience can be packaged in that light.

## Covering letter dos and don'ts

Your cover letter is even more important than your résumé. After you have written your letters, check the content against the following.

### Do:

- Gather intelligence about the employer, the job, and the organization's culture. If you are responding to an ad, consider calling HR or the recruiter to get the job description.

- Show understanding of the industry based on your research.

- Show your enthusiasm for the position and employer. Flattery does work.

- Address the letter personally and double-check the spelling of the person's name. Make sure you have the correct address.

- Use a formal tone and address the recipient with Mr./Ms./Dr., etc., and their last name.

- Mention any job reference number if directed to do so in an advertisement.

- Omit pronouns and articles (I, you, he, it, they, etc.). It eliminates the need to begin sentences with "I," allowing you to brag without seeming boastful.

### Don't:

- Begin by saying, "Enclosed is my résumé in response to your job ad . . ."

- Address the letter to To Whom It May Concern. If you do not know the person's name or title, call the employer to find out to whom it should be addressed. If the name is not released, address it to Hiring Manager.

- Forget to include your contact information.

- Overlook addressing the stated needs of the position.

- State reasons for leaving a job until you are given an interview.

### The pitch letter

The pitch letter is designed to sell your services or ideas to a prospective employer or client with the goal of sparking an interest in your skills, abilities, and services. (*See page 183* for more on pitch letters.)

Follow the guidelines for a cover letter. The major difference between these two types of letters is that in a pitch letter you are selling yourself without having been solicited to do so. This means you have to be even more thoughtful and creative in developing a compelling value proposition and showing the relevance of your skills and experience to the employer's needs. Think benefit selling. Your research should shine through. Sheila Kane's letter (*see page 203*) would be a fine pitch letter. She would only need to modify the close to indicate that she would initiate contact.

Start the letter with an attention-grabbing statement or thought-provoking question. Consider, for example, how one successful job seeker started her pitch letter:

> *I was so impressed by the work you are doing that was written up in the* Times *that I conducted an extensive internet search on the industry. I discovered two future threats that most people are unaware of. Did you know that . . .?*

## Applying on-line

When applying for work on an employer or job website, you may be able to email your résumé as an attachment. Sometimes you may be required to use a standard electronic form on the site called a résumé builder, in which you type your career information on-line and the computer builds a résumé for you. They generally are easy to use.

Employers use résumé builders to search quickly for certain qualifications and terms and screen out applicants who do not mention them.

One way to increase your chances of getting your electronic résumé screened in is by using variations of job titles and experience. For example, if you are a computer programmer, also put "software developer" somewhere in the résumé builder.

**Pitch an employer**
*Although "cold" approaches usually do not work, many people succeed at getting potential employers' attention by offering skills or services framed in a way that says, "I understand you. I can meet your special needs."*

*Boost your chances of landing an interview by applying for jobs for which you are a good fit.*

# **Other** marketing materials

Depending on your occupation and industry, you may need other marketing materials. Although the formats vary, the key messages you want to send to prospective employers or clients should be the same as those in your résumé and cover letters.

## Bios

Many self-employed people and consultants use bios instead of or in addition to résumés because they sum up in one paragraph or one page what they can do. It is easy for potential employers and clients to understand a person's career when it is presented in a story format.

Your bio summarizes your career history, providing an overview of your background, services, clients, special areas of expertise, and educational credentials. As with your résumé, include relevant personal information, such as board memberships. Make your bio more powerful by tailoring it to your potential employer's needs.

For example, if you are pitching yourself as a consultant for a change-management project, write, "Carole has worked with numerous organizations in successfully managing change. Her clients include . . ."

## Articles

Include copies of articles you have authored or press write-ups with your correspondence. Having your name circulating in print as an authority is a wonderful marketing tool.

## Portfolio

Many people in creative fields such as advertising or writing take portfolios with them to job interviews. A portfolio does not have to be expensive, but it should be professional looking. Choose work samples that show the widest range of skills (for example, designing a full-color poster, a black-and-white newspaper advertisement, or a book cover). Do not include two samples that demonstrate the same skills.

## Website

Professionals in fields such as graphic design and Information Technology sometimes use their personal websites to post electronic and interactive work samples. Keep the work-sample pages separate from your personal home pages showing photos from your dog's birthday party.

Do not substitute your web page for a résumé. On your résumé, refer employers to your website to view additional work samples.

## Boost your response rate

Organizations are very specific about what they are looking for. Boost your chances of landing an interview by applying for jobs for which you are a good fit and by tailoring all your messages to their needs. Also:

- Follow up when you send a résumé. When you call, ask the manager if she has had a chance to review it. If she has, find out whether you are a possible candidate. Try to schedule an interview. If she has not, or seems unenthusiastic about your qualifications, ask when the organization plans to start interviewing candidates.
- If you cannot get through to a hiring manager or recruiter, leave a short, clear voice mail or send an email. Communicate your enthusiasm clearly, and outline why you think you are a great candidate for the work.
- Mine your own network. Try to find someone who has a personal contact inside the hiring organization. Contact them by email or voice mail. Summarize relevant career history and special qualifications. Indicate your eagerness to get the work. Ask if they would mind sending a note on your behalf saying that they know who you are and that they believe you would be a good candidate. Offer to talk to them. Recommendations from internal staff carry great weight. Many people are happy to do this for a "friend of a friend." Also, many companies pay a bonus to employees who recommend someone who ends up being hired—it is cheaper than paying an agency's fees.
- Continue to check in every two weeks or so with agencies and internal recruiters. Your persistence will communicate enthusiasm.
- Do not become a pest—calling more than every two weeks or so may be crossing the line.

### Market yourself

*Walk the delicate line between staying in touch and becoming a pest. Follow up by providing new and useful information, for example, that you delivered an important presentation.*

# Interviewing and negotiating

Show potential employers what you bring to the table. You do not know exactly what will be asked during the interview. You can, however, be prepared with answers that sell your unique skills and attributes. When the interview leads to an offer, negotiate the best deal for your dream work.

## This chapter shows you how to:

**Present** yourself effectively and respond to interview questions with answers that speak directly to the recruiter's needs.

**Answer** tough questions that zero in on weaknesses by being able to spin a negative into a positive.

**Apply** five proven strategies to make you shine, including auditioning the employer and being an expert.

**Decode** what you have seen and heard about the work and organizational culture to determine your fit.

**Make** the right career decision by meaningfully analyzing the match between your needs and talents and the offer.

**Negotiate** the best compensation package—know what the work is worth and understand all the elements.

**Speak their language**

*Learn the employer's lingo. There may be acronyms or buzzwords for different products, services, or company programs. Knowing these says, "I could be a member of your organization."*

# Preparing for the interview

Your research, networking, and self-marketing efforts have paid off. Now you have been asked to come in for an interview. Go in with confidence by preparing yourself to answer the tough questions.

The number-one mistake job hunters make in interviews is not knowing enough about the hiring organization and not identifying the behavioral implications for the role. Before you go to an interview, identify:

- The articulated requirements: the details, attributes, and qualities that fit the written or spoken requirements of the employer.
- The unarticulated needs: additional skills, attributes, and qualities that you believe will be required.

Think of real-life examples. Imagine you are being interviewed for a managerial role in an industry in which there is intense competition for talent. You probably would be correct in assuming that "attraction and retention" is a major challenge. You might reason as in the example below.

## Example: Showing you have the necessary attributes

| Challenge | Attributes that address this challenge | Examples of my behavior |
|---|---|---|
| Attraction and retention of talent | Understanding of the needs of the knowledge worker; ability to mentor; commitment to learning and development; sensitivity to work–life balance issues | Sought-after mentor in previous role: mentored five people; introduced learning accounts giving staff a portion of salary to use for personal development; created life-friendly work environment—two part-timers, two telecommuters |

# **Get ready** for the questions

Overcome potential objections by anticipating problematic areas. Practice your responses. For example, the ad indicates that industry-specific experience is desired. Show how you have the underlying skills they need, or that you will take an industry-relevant night course. There are many different kinds of interview questions. Some you can prepare for, and some you cannot.

## Behavioral questions

The assumption behind these questions is that past behavior is the best predictor of future behavior. Typically they will be prefaced with a phrase such as, "Tell me about a time when you…" or "Describe a situation when you…" For example, "Describe a time when you made a significant change in your previous work." These kinds of questions are the most common ones used by skilled interviewers.

DO provide real-life examples of when or how you demonstrated the behavior as shown above.

## Situational questions

These are hypothetical questions about how you would react in certain situations. For example, "How would you change the department if you were the manager?" Skilled interviewers do not use these questions frequently.

DO treat it as a behavioral question. Reference how you introduced change in a previous role.

## Stress questions

The purpose of these questions is to put you on the defensive. For example, "We need major changes around here. What makes you think you're tough enough?" Stress questions are unusual, asked only by very incompetent interviewers or for jobs in which being able to deal with tough situations or tough environments is important.

DO take your time. Respond coolly and in a matter-of-fact manner. Again, respond as if it were a behavioral question. Describe a tough change you stewarded.

## Conventional questions

These are traditional types of questions, such as, "How do you manage change?" or "Can you tell me something about yourself?" If possible, reference past behavior.

## Out-of-left-field questions

Some recruiters, tired of listening to over-rehearsed, canned answers, ask questions that seem to come from nowhere. "Your picture is on the front page of newspaper. What is the caption below it?" Obviously you cannot prepare for these kinds of questions.

## Career counsel

Be thoughtful. If you have trouble understanding the question, ask the interviewer to repeat it. Take your time. It is okay to say, "Let me think about that for a moment."

# Career counsel

Anticipate the questions an interviewer in the industry you are applying to might ask you.

For example:

- A public-sector employer might ask, "Tell me about a time when you had to switch priorities midstream."

- A brokerage firm might ask, "Tell me how you have handled yourself in a tough, competitive environment."

## How to answer common questions

These questions, although not inspired, are very common. Avoid raising a red flag to interviewers. Can you see the differences between the dos and don'ts?

**"Tell me something about yourself."**

Do not say: "I started my career in 1986" (going on with a blow-by-blow description of every job held). Or "Gee, I'm not really sure where to start." Or "I'm married with three kids."

Do say: "Three things about me that are most important in terms of this job are…" (briefly describing three job-related experiences or accomplishments that provide evidence of your fit).

**"How would you describe your strengths?"**

Do not say: "I'm not really sure" (this is no time to be modest). Or "I'm good with people" (horrible cliché).

Do say: "People describe me as…" (listing strengths pertinent to the job, keeping in mind the most important things employers are looking for; mentioning what others say about your strengths is even stronger. Give examples of accomplishments that speak to these strengths).

**"How would you describe your weaknesses?"**

Do not say: "My weaknesses include…" (proceeding to be devastatingly candid).

Do say: "I get nervous giving presentations, but I'm taking a night course" (describe honestly a minor and common problem that will not be damaging; show how you are addressing the issue).

**"What is most important to you in a job?"**

Do not say: "I need a lot of recognition and feedback," or anything else that would be a red flag to employers.

Do say: "I like to work in fast-paced environments that provide a lot of challenge" (use the results of your self-assessment to show that you are self-aware).

### Other common questions

Other interview questions you might be asked:

*"What is your management/work style?"*
*"How would you handle a failing employee?"*
*"How do you run meetings?"*
*"What do you think of committees?"*
*"How did you achieve your accomplishments? Why were they successful?"*

*"Why should we hire you? Why do you want to work here?"*
*(These are hostile questions, which are rarely asked*
 *except in stress interviews.)*
*"How do you know when you're successful at your job?"*
*"Tell me about positions you've held, and what your*
*responsibilities were. What did you like about those*
*responsibilities? What didn't you like about them?"*
*"How would you describe your last organization?"*
*"What other jobs or organizations are you considering?"*
*"If you could do it all over again, what changes would*
*you make in your career?"*
*"Would what your references say about you fit with what you*
*would say about yourself?"*
*"Describe the person who influenced you the most*
*in your career."*
*"What kind of people do you have difficulty with?"*
*"What are you likely to do that could annoy me? What sorts*
*of things could I do that would annoy you?"*
*"How can our company help you to achieve your goals?"*

**Say it out loud**
*Study your self-assessment results. Repeat out loud the words you used. If you are nervous or have been out of the market for a while, practice and record a mock interview with someone who understands the interview process.*

## Should you go to the interview?

Should you go to an interview for a job you are not interested in? The short answer is yes. It is an opportunity to practice interviewing skills and gather insider information. The work may also prove to be a better match than you think—you may be able to provide a perspective on business needs not identified by the employers or a redesign of the role more in keeping with your skills. There also may be another unadvertised opportunity or work down the road. If you know you are definitely not interested in the organization, you decide what is the best use of your time.

If you are dealing with a search consultant, initially do not indicate your lack of interest—after all, how can you really know until you have met the players? That said, be careful about pushing the envelope too far. Inform them of your ambivalence before they invest their time in setting up multiple interviews. After all, you want to develop a relationship with the recruiter and ensure that you are called back for future searches.

*If you quit your previous job, show how it speaks to your belief in your employability.*

# Common behavioural questions

Employers are looking for certain attributes in workers. Be prepared to answer many of these questions. Tell me about…

- **Innovativeness**

  …the changes you tried to implement in your area of responsibility. What have you done to get them under way?

  …some projects you generated on your own. What prompted you to begin them?

- **Teamwork**

  …a situation in which you helped a peer or co-worker.

  …a time when you needed someone's cooperation to complete a task/project and they were uncooperative. What did you do?

- **Ability to make tough decisions**

  …an unpopular decision you made. What was your thinking process?

- **Problem-solving ability**

  …the biggest problem you have had to face in the past six months. How did you handle it?

- **Leadership**

  …recent problems/issues in which you included staff in determining solutions. How did you do it? Were you successful?

  …a time when there was a change in the business priorities of your organization. How did you get your team reoriented?

  …a time when it was difficult to get people on board a project. What did you do?

- **Tenacity**

  …a time when your persistence in overcoming obstacles paid off.

- **Attention to detail**

  …the processes you follow to control errors in your work. When was the last time these methods helped you? How?

- **Emotional intelligence**

  …some specific situation that was frustrating. How did you manage it?

  …a situation in which you worked for or with someone you did not like or respect. How did you deal with it?

- **Flexibility**

  …how you have gotten around obstacles preventing you from finishing a project/task.

  …a situation in which your solution failed. How did you change your approach?

## Answering tough questions

Interviewers usually will zero in on your "weak spots." Be prepared to answer the tough questions. Use the following strategies.

- If you were terminated, answer honestly. Do not over-explain. In the objective tone of a third party, appeal to the recruiter's understanding of such common issues as the company's change of direction, conflicting views between you and management, housecleaning when a new manager arrives, a restructuring leading to terminations. You can start your sentence "As you know…"

- If you were part of a restructuring, explain the situation simply and show that it had nothing to do with your performance. For example, "There was a restructuring and my position was eliminated along with several others."

- If you quit your job or were fired as a result of "bad chemistry," describe the situation in an objective, analytical manner. Do not slam your previous boss's personality. Describe a problem area that would be a strength to this recruiter. For example, "I like to spend time analyzing a problem before taking action, but my boss liked to make decisions quickly."

- If you quit your previous job, show how it speaks to the value you place on being happy and challenged in your work and your belief in your employability.

- If you had a very long job tenure, you may be asked about why you are leaving now or why you stayed so long. Emphasize the varied experiences gained.

- If you have been a job hopper, try describing short jobs as contracts (you will have to negotiate this with previous employers). You can say, "I chose different jobs to add skills to my portfolio, and now I want to apply those skills." Other options include referring to a challenging economy, or having accepted a job without doing "due diligence" to see whether it was a good fit. Show how all these jobs have contributed to your skills portfolio.

## Career counsel

If you are asked to complete a psychological assessment, do not try to second-guess the test. Answer honestly, not based on what you think they are looking for. Some employers will give candidates feedback on their assessment—ask the recruiter if this is possible.

Psychological assessments are expensive. Employers usually use them once they have established a strong interest in the candidate. For employers, they are an additional source of data about the candidate. It is unusual for someone not to get a job because of their assessment results if they have shown that they possess the desired background and skills.

Some employers administer screening tests before the interview to see if the candidate possesses requisite attributes such as sales or problem-solving skills. You cannot prepare for most of these types of tests.

*Offer advice on an issue the interviewer has not thought of—for example, the reporting relationships, structure, or scope of the role.*

# Successful interview strategies

They have called. You really want this work. Use the following five interview strategies to make you shine. After it is over, you decide if it is still your great work.

### Establish a connection

Put yourself and the interviewer at ease. Build rapport. Start with an icebreaker, such as, "What a fabulous view," or, "I really like your artwork." Act natural.

Two candidates were shortlisted for an engineering position. On paper, Sophie was better qualified. In the interview, she was poised and polished and handled every question skillfully. She never paused to think, however, launching straight into reply mode. Her answers sounded scripted. It was like interviewing a robot. The other candidate, Jim, was less poised. He was nervous, but really wanted the job. He spoke with a lot of "ums" and "ahs," often saying, "Let me think about that for a moment." His answers sounded thoughtful and genuine. The interviewer could see this was someone he would like to work with. Guess who got the job?

### Be an expert

Offer advice on an issue the interviewer has not thought of. For example, do the reporting relationships, structure, or scope of the role make sense? Do you have experience to share that shows a different way of thinking about the work? Are there challenges or trends that have not been considered? Offer suggestions generously. Your ideas will show your special qualifications. Sound thoughtful, not "know-it-all" or judgmental.

### Be an equal

Speak to the interviewer as if you were a colleague or consultant, without sounding presumptuous. Ask about reporting relationships and where the position would fit in the hierarchy. Ask about challenges facing the organization. This creates an egalitarian exchange between you and the employer and sends the message, "I could be a member of your team." It also is a subtle way of showing your expertise.

## Audition the employer

Once you have established that you are an ideal candidate, ask questions about the work environment, organizational culture, and challenges of the role. A useful line of questioning is: "Will I be replacing someone in this position? What happened to the previous incumbent?" If the previous holder of the job was fired, try to find out why.

Also ask questions that address issues that are important to your needs. If you are a lifestyler, for example, ask about flexibility of work hours. If you are a personal developer, ask about money spent on training. You know what you want from an employer, so query items important to you. If they are clearly interested in you, ask for a meeting with future staff or team members.

## Know when it is over

Take your cue from the interviewer. They may say, "That is all the questions I have," or look at their watch, or start shuffling their papers. Close by summarizing your special assets. Restate your interest in the work. Ask the interviewer how long they think the decision-making process will be, what the next steps are, and when you will hear back. Ask if it is okay to call them in a few weeks if you have not heard from them. Thank them for their time. Shake hands as you leave.

# Career counsel

Not sure about what to wear? Imagine you were delivering an important presentation to management in this organization. You would want to feel comfortable but look great. What would you wear? Dress appropriately for the culture. Is it hip? Conservative? Freewheeling? What is the industry sector? Choose accordingly.

If in doubt, dress more conservatively. However, if the dress code requires clothes that make you feel ill, you probably do not want to work there anyway. If you are still not sure, you can also ask the recruiter about the dress code.

## Face the panel

*Public-sector organizations often use panel interviews. You need to impress each member. Make initial eye contact with the person asking the question, then with the rest, as you would in a presentation. (Refer to members by name if you can.)*

# Career counsel

If you have been working for one employer for a long time or are relatively new to the employment market, you may make certain assumptions about the interviewer's skill, job knowledge, and comfort level. Skilled interviewees know that the interviewer may be uncomfortable with the interview process. The interviewer may not have been trained to ask good questions, or they may have a limited understanding of the work role and challenges associated with the role. And no, most interviewers do not want to see you squirm. (If they do, you probably do not want to work there.)

## Dos and don'ts of interviews

Your body language, voice, dress, and general deportment communicate volumes about who you are. The interviewer will respond as much to how you say it as to what you say.

### Do:

- Arrive on time. Bring extra copies of your résumé in case the interviewers do not have them. Create a strong and respectful impression as soon as you arrive in reception. Yes, it is true: receptionists are often asked for their impressions of the candidate.

- Shake hands. Make eye contact. Smile.

- Sit straight, but be natural. Avoid irritating mannerisms, such as cracking your knuckles or drumming your fingers. Demonstrate energy and enthusiasm.

- Call the interviewer Mr., Ms., or Mrs. unless told otherwise. Use the interviewer's name from time to time.

- Be an attentive listener. Nod in agreement. (Resist the temptation to jump in and speak before the interviewer is finished.) Demonstrate active listening by occasionally rephrasing what has been said: "So you're looking for someone with experience in . . ."

- Be consistent in all of your messages about yourself, including dress. Determine ahead of time the message you want to leave behind. Coordinate the verbal content of your message with your personal presentation to ensure the messages are consistent with your desired impression.

- Read how the interview is going. Watch for signs of boredom or restlessness. Do not be afraid to ask, "Is this what you were interested in hearing?"

- Relax. Think of this as an interesting exchange. If you are nervous, do not worry about it—it will only increase your anxiety and interfere with your ability to understand the questions. Interviewers understand. It is human to be nervous.

### Don't:

- Be afraid to take initiative in the interview or to offer more information than you were asked for.

- Worry too much about trick questions. Most interviewers will be interested in hearing about you rather than playing games. Take their questions at face value.

- Raise the subject of compensation. Let the interviewer bring it up. If you are asked about salary expectations, give a general range such as mid-60s, as opposed to $64,000. Or "I'm looking for a competitive salary but it's not my major driver."

- Assume that the interviewer has studied your résumé in detail.

# After the interview

The interview is not really over when it is over. That is when you assess how it went—as a way of preparing for the next one, at the same company or somewhere new.

Record your own assessment of how the interview went as soon as possible *(see pages 220–221.)* Is there information to be gleaned to improve in future interviews? Make notes about your impressions of the organization. And do not forget to send a brief thank-you note. Summarize how you can make a great contribution.

## Managing your references

What former colleagues, staff, or bosses say about your skills and work style can play a critical role in determining whether you get the offer.

- Identify three or four people who can talk positively about your "style," skills, strengths, and accomplishments relevant to the work. As well as previous bosses, consider more senior managers to whom you did not report directly, current and/or former co-workers, external consultants, and, if you are just starting out, professors.
- Sound them out as references. Are they willing? Will they say good things? How will they answer the question about weaknesses? Outline the position and key points you would like them to communicate about your skills. Update referees you have not spoken to in a while on your career progress and goals.
- If the employer has a policy of not giving references because they do not want to be exposed to legal liability, is there a former employee of that organization who can give you a reference instead?
- If you need a reference from a former boss you did not get along with well, approach them and say: "I know we had our differences, but I would appreciate it if you would be willing to talk about what I achieved in…"

## Career counsel

Decode the corporate culture. How are people dressed? How do they interact with each other? What kinds of conversations do you overhear? Look at everything around you— the artwork, furniture, and office aesthetics. What is the organization or department communicating about itself? Does it say, "I'm big and arrogant?" "Creative and freewheeling?" "Struggling but having fun?" Consider, for example, the difference between a department housed in the basement where everyone looks depressed and one where clerical staff sit by windows and you hear a lot of laughter.

Note to lifestylers: Check out the number of cars in the parking lot at 8:00 A.M. and 6:00 P.M.

### Assessing yourself

**Interviewing and negotiating**

▶ Post-interview worksheet
*pages 220–221*

▶ Career decision worksheet
*pages 226–229*

**SELF-ASSESSMENT    Post-interview** worksheet

*Organization* ................................................................................
*Position* ................................................................................
*Date* ................................................................................

**General behavior**

*Was I satisfied with what I was wearing?*

................................................................................

*Was I calm and relaxed?*

................................................................................

*Did I communicate effectively?*

................................................................................

*Did I answer the questions well?*

................................................................................

*Did I ask good questions?*

................................................................................

*Did I get across my skills and experience?*

................................................................................

**Performance areas**

*Where did I perform best?*

................................................................................
................................................................................

*Where did I perform worst?*

........................................................................

*What questions gave me the most difficulty?*

........................................................................

*What did I accomplish in this interview?*

........................................................................

*What did I fail to accomplish in this interview?*

........................................................................

*How could I improve my performance next time?*

........................................................................

## Rating the organization

*Is the work a good fit? Do I know enough to decide?*

........................................................................

*Was I impressed by the general atmosphere?*

........................................................................

*Did the culture "feel right"?*

........................................................................

*Does the role match my current career goals?*

........................................................................

### Dealing with rejection

"We're sorry. We found someone who is a better match." Rejection hurts. It is also a fact of life. Maybe there was someone more skilled than you. Or perhaps you really were the ideal candidate but did not present evidence of that in your interview. Rethink the interview. Is that true? Consider calling the recruiter for feedback.

Then again, there are many other reasons for being declined that may have little or nothing to do with your skills and competencies. Someone younger or cheaper may have been selected, or the cousin of the president's best friend.

Often it is a question of fit—a vague word, granted, but a concept that drives most employment decisions: you talked too loudly or too softly, you smiled too much or too little, you were too friendly or not friendly enough. In other words, there is nothing wrong with you—someone else simply seemed to be a better fit. Think about it. You do not get "a good feel" about everybody. Why should everybody get a good feel about you?

### Do not get frustrated

*Multiple interviews—with co-workers, staff, HR, the boss's boss, an external consultant—and being called back for "repeat performances" are common at senior levels. Generate new stories for each. Do not read too much into not hearing back immediately.*

# Negotiating offers

You got the work. Should you take it? How can you get the best deal? The last thing you want to be saying to yourself three months into your new job is, "I sold myself out too cheaply," or worse, "I made a mistake."

Great news. At the end of your third interview the hiring manager said, "I think you will be a great fit," or the search consultant left you a voice mail—"It's looking great."

Accepting an offer is a huge move. Think it through. This is how you will spend the next chapter of your life. You have a responsibility to ensure that you will feel fairly compensated for the contribution you expect to make. Typically, employers respect a thoughtful discussion about terms when an offer is extended.

### Do you want the work?

You have the skills employers want. You know that great work is your right, not a luxury. Do not snap up the first thing that comes along just because it is there, or you cannot be bothered to keep on looking. I see too many people who take a job even though their gut tells them not to. This is particularly common when the job pays well.

Equally important, do not snap up the terms first offered. When evaluating the offer, make sure you have enough information about the job and working conditions to make a proper assessment. Reflect on what you observed about the organizational culture during the interview. Relate this information to what you know to be most critical to your happiness and effectiveness.

What if you accept your new employer's offer and when you give notice, your current employer presents you with a counteroffer? While it may be tempting to stay where you are and get a promotion, remember why you were looking elsewhere in the first place. Consider carefully whether you want to stay. These "carrots" will not change your work situation.

*You have a responsibility to ensure that you will feel fairly compensated for the contribution you expect to make.*

**Examine total package**

*When evaluating the offer over and above salary, consider such tangibles as benefits, car allowance, and bonus, and such intangibles as length of commute and investment in individual development.*

## Buying more time

Often everything bursts at once, and you receive more than one offer at the same time. Or offer A, though extremely attractive, is not your dream job—in your heart of hearts you really want offer B. Try these delaying tactics:

- Ask for an extension to have more time to consider the offer.
- Tell the employer you want the offer to be reviewed by a lawyer or someone else, such as your spouse or partner.
- Contact employer B if they have not offered you a job yet, and tell them you have another offer. Do not tell employer A that they are your second choice.
- Ask to meet with some individuals in the organization to further discuss the position.

## How much is the work worth?

Salaries fluctuate with industry, size of organization, scope of work, and importance of the work to the organization. Organizations have guidelines on where they want to be positioned in the market, such as top 10 percent, bottom quartile, and so on. Ask the employer how they position themselves in relation to the market. Salary will also be determined by your experience and the scarcity of your talent. Research salary ranges before you negotiate your salary. If you are not working with a search consultant, check out job ads for similar work, consult professional associations, review salary surveys published on the Internet.

Many people are uncomfortable talking about money. You are an adult. Talk about expectations in a matter-of-fact way. Do not assume that the employer relishes salary negotiations or is out to get you for the lowest price. For more senior positions, consider using a third party, such as a lawyer, agent, or recruiter, to act as an intermediary.

## Negotiating your compensation package

Your total compensation consists of many elements. Too often people fixate on base salary, or some other element, and fail to consider the real value associated with the complete package. Here are some things to consider when you negotiate your compensation.

- What is the minimum you will accept in terms of salary, benefits, vacation, etc.? This is the "I'm walking away from this offer" number.
- What trade-offs are you willing to make in favor of other gains? For example: Would you be willing to work for a lower salary if that bought you more vacation days? Can you trade off decreased benefits for increased salary, if your spouse's benefits cover you?
- What improvements to a less-than-ideal situation can you negotiate? If your salary is lower than you had hoped, can you negotiate a salary review after six months, or performance bonuses and perks such as stock options?
- What are you and the work worth? If an employer balks at your salary request, show why you think you are worth it. Point out average salaries in your industry or field, and mention your accomplishments and the value you bring to the employer.
- Can you negotiate down their expectations, convincing them, for example, that by virtue of your skills and experience, you can do the work in fewer days?
- What is the worst-case scenario? What would happen if you could not come to an agreement on the position? Do you have other possibilities, or do you really need this job? If you can walk away from the job, you are in an excellent bargaining position. If not, let the negotiations proceed. Know that you have made an informed decision.

Keep in mind that getting the right work for you is all about fit—both for the employer and for yourself. An essential part of a good fit is ensuring that you feel fairly compensated based on your skills, experience, and expected contribution. In too many cases, people compromise on some essential aspects of compensation and discover later that they do not feel good about the position they find themselves in. It is your responsibility to ensure that the total compensation being offered "fits" within your definition of fair.

## Career counsel

Put your acceptance in writing. You can sign the employer's letter of offer, or if there isn't one, outline your understanding of the offer in your letter. Include the start date and time, salary, location, and any bonuses or other items you negotiated.

## Assessing yourself

**Interviewing and negotiating**

▶ Post-interview worksheet
  *pages 220-221*

▶ Career decision worksheet
  *pages 226–229*

**PORTFOLIO** | **Career decision** worksheet

Before making this important decision, review everything you have said in Know yourself and Find your perfect path, about your needs and wants.

*My key career motivators (list):*

.......................................................................................................................

.......................................................................................................................

*My most important values (list):*

.......................................................................................................................

.......................................................................................................................

*My key competencies (list):*

.......................................................................................................................

.......................................................................................................................

**Does the opportunity represent a great match?**

| Not at all | | Somewhat | | A lot |
|---|---|---|---|---|
| 1 | 2 | 3 | 4 | 5 |

*Types of issues/problems I want to think about (list):*

.......................................................................................................................

.......................................................................................................................

*My ideal work role:*

.......................................................................................................................

.......................................................................................................................

*My desired features of the work environment:*

.......................................................................................................................

.......................................................................................................................

**Financial data**

*Base salary:*

....................................................................................................

*Commissions:*

....................................................................................................

*Bonuses:*

....................................................................................................

*Profit-sharing:*

....................................................................................................

*Stock options:*

....................................................................................................

*Signing bonus:*

....................................................................................................

*Other:*

....................................................................................................

**Benefits:**

*Medical insurance:*

....................................................................................................

*Life insurance:*

....................................................................................................

**PORTFOLIO**      **Career decision** worksheet cont'd

*Vacation:*

....................................................................................................................................

*Disability pay:*

....................................................................................................................................

*Pension plan:*

....................................................................................................................................

*Dental plan:*

....................................................................................................................................

*Car:*

....................................................................................................................................

*Relocation expenses:*

....................................................................................................................................

*Other:*

....................................................................................................................................

**Other important information**

*Does the work require long hours?*

....................................................................................................................................

*A lot of business travel?*

....................................................................................................................................

*Does the organization provide enough training and development?*

..............................................................................................................

*Is the organization growing?*

..............................................................................................................

*Am I comfortable with the management style?*

..............................................................................................................

*Do I understand fully what the work requires?*

..............................................................................................................

*Am I comfortable with the new manager?*

..............................................................................................................

*Am I comfortable with the work environment?*

..............................................................................................................

**General reflections**

*What are the advantages and disadvantages of taking this work?*

..............................................................................................................

*Trade-offs I will have to make: Can I live with these?*

..............................................................................................................

*What I will gain by making these trade-offs?*

..............................................................................................................

# 4 Overcome career challenges

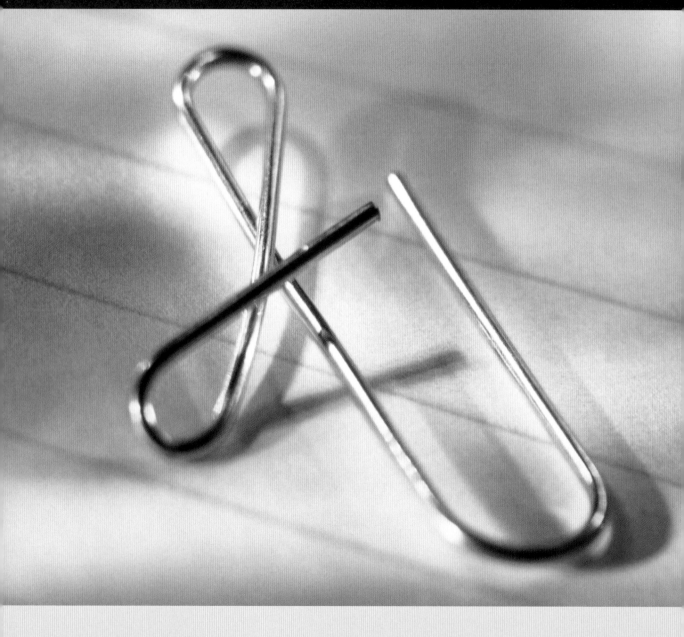

# Confronting career malaise

Most people will experience career malaise at some point in their lives. Learn to recognize the signs of career distress. Is it just boredom or are you experiencing something deeper? How should it be handled? Avoid the quick fix, examine the real issues, determine what you want, and get yourself back onto a positive career track.

## This chapter shows you how to:

**Determine** whether you are in the throes of a crisis by evaluating yourself against 12 symptoms.

**Understand** the complex psychological dynamics that underlie career and life distress.

**Identify** the kind of help you need— and changes you need to make—to resolve a career crisis.

**Make** creative, life-liberating changes that will give you a new lease on your career and your life.

*Sometimes, unknown to you, you have moved into a new life stage, and what you once thought important no longer has as much meaning.*

# Anatomy of a career crisis

You feel your work is meaningless. You despair at going in to work. You get depressed just thinking about it. The origins of a career crisis may not be what you think. Reflect on the issues. Be ready to move on.

*James, a 33-year-old management consultant with a prestigious international firm, had become increasingly agitated over the course of the year. He was tired of spending half his life on an airplane. His wife was complaining that she never saw him. He felt constant guilt about not spending time with his four-year-old son. He kept on telling himself and his wife that things were going to change. This would be the last project that would require so much travel.*

*One night, flying home from yet another business trip, he had an epiphany. He saw that there would always be another project that required cross-country travel. If he wanted to save his marriage, he could not go on living the way he was.*

*James came up with a wish list. He wanted work where he owned his own time, would travel very little, would experience less stress. Within a few months, James was offered another job—similar work for a local "boutique" consulting firm at slightly lower pay. The job seemed to be everything on his wish list, but he kept putting off making the decision. Frantically he sought advice from friends, partners in his firm, an outside counselor, but he could not bring himself to accept the offer. Paralyzed, he took unpaid leave to reevaluate his life.*

## Origins of career crises

A career crisis can be sparked by many factors. Perhaps you are passed over for a promotion you were certain was yours. Or, like James, you are faced with a decision you are unable to make. Perhaps the illness of a close friend pushes you to take a new look at your life. Although a career crisis can be triggered by an external event in your personal life, just as often, the crisis wells up from within. It may be due to a conflict between your motivators and underlying values. For example, a desire for challenge and career growth may be at odds with a desire to spend more time with family. There may be a conflict between your values and career motivators and the work you are doing, as when you are a personal developer who is insufferably bored with your work. Sometimes, unknown to you, you have moved into a new life stage, and what you once thought important no longer has as much meaning.

When you look at your situation more carefully, you will see that there were warning signs, and you probably drifted into the crisis imperceptibly. It may have started with a nagging feeling of dissatisfaction, but you ignored it, telling yourself that things would get better once you got a new boss or were given more resources to get the job done. Perhaps you wondered, "Is this all there is?" but you told yourself, "I can live with this, it's not so bad."

**Drifting into crisis**
*Although a career crisis can be triggered by a painful experience such as a job loss, just as often there is no obvious trigger, and we drift from mild distress— at regularly not getting home to our family on time, for example— into serious psychological crisis.*

Then one day, all of a sudden, you woke up and realized you hated your job or felt your work had no meaning. You were no longer experiencing mild career distress, but a full-blown career crisis.

Reflect on your emotions. Are you experiencing any of these symptoms of career malaise?

- The thought of going to work in the morning makes you queasy.
- You do not like the people you are working with.
- You do not like your boss.
- You are bored, distracted, de-energized, or agitated.
- You feel you are not accomplishing anything.
- You feel incompetent, inadequate, or that you have failed.
- You do not like talking about what you do.
- You feel better on the weekends.
- You think about choices you have made in the past.
- You feel that other people are happier than you.
- You have a nagging sense that something is missing.
- Your work feels meaningless.

> *There is no cure-all prescription for career and life crises. If it were that easy, there would be no art, no philosophy, no literature.*

## Determine what you want

What were the underlying causes of James's crisis? Why did he not snap up the offer? When James started to consider working for this new firm, all he could think about was the loss of status and the impact on his career goals. He had to confront something he really did not want to admit—that he loved the cachet of working for an international consulting firm, and the travel made him feel important. Worse, he had to recognize that he had been lying to himself and his wife about why he was working the way he was, that in fact it was his choice. This made him feel bad about himself. "If I am a good husband and father," he thought, "I should put my family first."

Underlying James's career crisis was a psychological crisis. He had to confront what was really true about himself. Faced with the competing job offer, James had been asking people, "What should I do?" instead of, "What do I really want? What gives me a sense of self-worth?" It took

**Sense of self**
*Often the roots of a career crisis are psychological—challenges to our core beliefs about who we are and how we want to represent ourselves to the world—and we may need help to explore them.*

James several months of counseling to come to terms with what he really needed, which in his instance was to keep his original job with renegotiated travel expectations.

## Examine your life

Most people's first response to career distress, however, is to look for a quick fix to their problem. They ask, "What should I do?" expecting an easy answer. When we realize we have a problem, we try to get rid of it immediately without thinking through what the real issues are. We think that if we only had the right career or job, we would be happy.

Sadly, there is no cure-all prescription for career and life crises. If it were that easy to rid ourselves of these feelings of discomfort, there would be no art, no philosophy, no literature—no bodies of work that wrestle with finding meaning and joy in life and work.

Solving a career crisis requires work. In particular, it involves taking a hard look at yourself. The unexamined life, Socrates observed, is not worth living. But given our never-ending busyness, it has probably never been harder to examine ourselves. Doing so can be scary. We dread the chaos of turning our lives upside down—stepping out of secure roles, challenging assumptions about who we are. At least what we have is secure and predictable. It is one thing to be forced into change—for example, by losing a job. It is quite another to set out to change our lives.

We may fear disapproval from people, whether family, friends, or colleagues. What would they think of us if we were to give up our current work in favor of something with less prestige or money? Would our families think we were being irresponsible if we tried something new? Would they think we were shirking our responsibilities? Old scripts, particularly ideas about financial needs, are very powerful.

As a result of these fears, we ignore and suppress feelings of discomfort until they implode. Only then are we are forced to confront the real issues in our careers and our lives: "What am I working for?" "What do I want to accomplish in my life?" Or more simply, "Why am I not happy?"

## Career counsel

It is unrealistic to think we can love our work all the time. There are irritants in every kind of work. They are simply part of the package, whether it is things taking longer than they should, working with people you do not care for, or dealing with irrational policies. You know which irritants you can live with and which are soul-destroying. Major irritants should be a cause for concern, but minor ones may have to be tolerated, a trade-off most people—including those who describe themselves as passionate about their work—have to make.

*If you experience an event as career-defining, embrace it and let it show you where you want to go.*

## Understand your career crisis

If you have reached a crisis in your career, look at what has changed. Has it been your own growth and development that render unsatisfying what you are doing now, or has the nature of your work changed? When was the last time you reflected on your values? What is most important to you at this stage in your life?

Look beyond your usual knee-jerk reactions to questions about what you value ("I want to make a lot of money," "I want a promotion") and reflect on what is really important to you now, today. When people do this, typically they discover that what they used to think important is no longer important, and that other needs and values have come to the fore. They also realize that other values were never that important for them—they just assumed they were.

Confront the possibility of making a change instead of avoiding it. Responding effectively to a crisis often requires making major changes

**New life patterns**
*The solution to a career crisis may lead to a significant reconfiguration of your life, affecting your most important personal relationships, sometimes with surprising outcomes.*

in your career and your life. Imagine living, working, interacting with the world in a new way. Ask yourself, "What are some of the rewards associated with this new way of being? How would it 'feel' to me and others in my life?"

## Get support

A career crisis can take a huge emotional toll, especially when you are accustomed to being competent in managing your life. You may think you can solve the problem by yourself, with minimal input from others. You may also see asking for help as a sign of weakness.

Sometimes complex psychological issues underlie a career crisis, and you may not be able to unravel them alone. You may need the help of a counselor or therapist. Unlike a friend or mentor, who may be too close to you or the situation, a professional can provide a neutral, third-party view of your situation to help you gain insight into the underlying issues, reframe the problem, and enable you to work through critical decisions.

## Career-defining moments

After a rave performance review, Kristin suddenly realized that she did not care about her boss's assessment and that she did not want a future in the company. Kristin had stumbled into a career-defining moment, a signal that she needed to take stock of where she was right then and where she wanted to go in the future.

Career-defining moments can be triggered by dramatic incidents—you lose your job or a close friend battles a life-threatening illness. Or they can emerge from a relatively ordinary situation, like a performance review, or getting a promotion and discovering that you do not actually want the job you have thoughtlessly been pursuing.

If you experience an event as career-defining, the chances are good that your work is out of line with your values and priorities and no longer gives you a sense of meaning and purpose, or you are moving into a new life phase. Do not shrug off one of these moments. Embrace it and let it show you where you want to go. It may be life changing.

## Career counsel

Ask yourself, "What is holding me back?" Often we are afraid of trying something new and failing. Change is always scary. Reconfiguring ourselves and our lives always involves some risks. Examine the trade-offs. Do not be afraid to test yourself in new ways, and do not underestimate your own capacity to rise to the occasion, or to find the internal resources that will allow you to withstand setbacks and reverses.

Have confidence you will resolve the crisis you are experiencing, even though it may take time and a period of self-doubt and questioning. The good news is that when people do weather a career crisis, they typically move forward into a new phase of their life with renewed focus and self-knowledge.

# Common types of career distress

Has work ceased to be a source of happiness in your life? Are you dealing with a career reversal? Are you suffering from the new career maladies? All of these will have a negative impact on your self-esteem but can be turned to your advantage if you know how. Identify the problem and learn how to solve it.

## This chapter shows you how to:

**Understand**, recover from, and ultimately benefit from different kinds of painful career reversals.

**Diagnose** and solve common career maladies, including boredom, burnout, crises of meaning, and feeling unfulfilled.

**Tame** the political manager, the taskmaster, the invisible manager, and other problem bosses.

**Know** whether the time may have come for you to move on—and the best way to do so.

## Case study

John was devastated when he was fired from his job after 10 years with the same company. Being fired also saved his life. "I had been a poster boy corporate warrior, but my marriage was in trouble, and I barely knew my kids." He went into a deep depression, but the experience was ultimately life-transforming. "It was the first time in my adult life that I wasn't a player. I could no longer believe in my own infallibility. The result was that I reconnected with my family and thought about what I really cared about." Like many who have experienced a failure, John said that he not only became more successful in his work, but also became a better partner and parent.

# Coping with failure

By the time most of us reach our mid-30s, we will have weathered some kind of career setback—whether being fired, failing to get an expected promotion, losing a business, or falling victim to office politics. Such a setback can be one of the most devastating experiences of our lives, but it also can be good for us. Learn strategies for bouncing back.

Even though it was almost two decades ago, I can still remember the sting I felt when I failed to land a job with a company for whom I was doing an internship. I was embarrassed and thought everyone in my broad network would know. I was sure the word on the street would be that I was incompetent.

My reaction was typical of how most people react to failure. Yet that experience proved to be very important to me. Up to then, I had never really thought hard about what I wanted to do as my next step, post-Ph.D.

Failure can be a valuable experience, one that strengthens us and sets the foundation for future career directions. When failure strikes, a world that once was clear becomes more confusing. We ask ourselves important questions: "What did I do wrong? What should I do differently?" We become more reflective and less certain about ourselves and our place in the world and more open to others' views. In fact, we are often more interesting and sympathetic as human beings when something has gone wrong than when we are convinced of our own infallibility.

## Analyze the failure

We all know people who seem to have a remarkable capacity to rebound from failure and disappointment and reinvent themselves. They are optimistic, with a strong belief in their ability to overcome difficulties. For them, failure is a problem to be solved, a temporary setback. This is not to suggest that they feel nothing. They usually do experience their failure at a deeply personal level. But they are able to rally their resources quickly because they have confidence that they will be successful in the future.

For others, however, failure is devastating, both to their sense of self and to their relationships. They ruminate obsessively: "It wasn't fair… What did I do wrong?… Why me?" Their self-esteem is seriously damaged, and it takes months or sometimes even years for them to recover, if indeed they recover at all. They become hypersensitive about their problems and feel everyone is aware of them. They interpret each new event as part of the fabric of a larger history of failure. They catastrophize, telling themselves, "I'll never be successful" or "I'll never be able to repair my reputation."

*Employers are less interested in whether a person has failed than in what they have learned as a result.*

## How to think about failure

It is popularly said that those who do not understand the past are doomed to repeat it. "Decode" the failure and learn from it.

- **Identify the cause.**
  How you respond to failure depends in part on how you explain it to yourself. Was it your fault, or was it a result of the situation? Do you say, "I'm incompetent" or "I've had some bad luck"? If you are able to blame your failure on the situation rather than yourself, you are likely to recover from it more rapidly. That said, most failures occur in a kind of gray zone, resulting from an interaction of external events and your own personal attributes and actions. This makes it difficult to identify a clear-cut cause.

- **Look at the failure in context.**
  When you have a career setback, you may find yourself focusing exclusively on what you think you did wrong and looking for underlying personal deficits. This will only create a downward spiral in your self-esteem. Step back and look at the failure in the context of your broader life-career history. Is this an unusual event you should not read too much into, or is it part of a recurring pattern— evidence of an Achilles heel? Thinking about past successes will also help you look at the failure objectively.

- **Analyze the situation to get insights for the future.**
  If the failure is primarily your fault, recognize that without going to pieces. Having failed at something does not make you a bad person. Analyze the situation to get important insights to modify future behavior. What could you have done differently? Are there any underlying themes common to other situations in which you have failed? What should you do about them? Keep in mind that employers are less interested in whether a person has failed than in what they have learned as a result. In fact, they often prefer to hire someone who has experienced a career setback.

# Career counsel

Often when people fail, they attribute it to external events. For example, they blame a series of business failures on a lack of start-up capital, or repeated job losses on bad bosses. When failure becomes repetitive, however, you should look at underlying themes. For example, the business person who has suffered several setbacks should ask, "Why do I always create businesses that require more capital than I can raise?" and at a higher level, "Why is my self-esteem so tied up with having a big, important business?" The person who has been fired many times should ask, "Why do I end up taking jobs for which I am ill-suited?" or "What am I doing to elicit this kind of rejection?" If they are unable or unwilling to address these questions, they likely will fail again.

# Strategies for dealing with failure

It takes time to recover from failure. There is no magic bullet. However, to bounce back, follow these tips.

▶ **Do not fixate on whether what happened to you was "fair."**
Fair or not, it happened. Now it is time to move on.

▶ **Do not ruminate obsessively and endlessly on what has occurred.**
If you find yourself doing so, you might benefit from counseling.

▶ **Allow yourself to be angry, particularly if you have suffered a business reversal or job loss.**
Mourning is natural, and so is some bitterness—as long as you can overcome these feelings with time and, in the meantime, manage how and to whom you express your anger.

▶ **Do not worry about your reputation or how other people see you.**
Do not catastrophize. "I'll never work in this town again" is a common sentiment people have after they are fired. Although your failure is front and center in your mind, it is much less obvious and important to everyone else. Even when others are aware of the failure, they usually have short memories. Although some people can be cruel, most will be sympathetic.

▶ **Do not overcompensate.**
There is nothing more grating than the false joviality of someone who, over-coached by misguided outplacement counselors, talks about what a great opportunity it was being fired. Although in the end it usually does turn out to have been a good opportunity, this is not the way most people react initially.

▶ **Know when to cut your losses.**
Linda found herself in a new job where institutional politics and a lack of leadership and resources meant she did not have a chance of success. She was miserable but refused to give up, telling herself, "I know I can turn this around." Both her mentor and her partner counseled her to quit, but she ignored them. On the job she was criticized as being aggressive and a poor team player, but the more the criticisms, the stronger her determination was to prove that she could succeed and restore her reputation. By the time she realized the situation was not salvageable, she had completely lost her self-confidence and believed the failure was her fault. Many job failures result from this kind of need to persist against all odds. When something just is not working for you, you have to know when to extricate yourself. When we are in a bad work situation, we often have the impulse to try to repair the damage to maintain our self-esteem and prove our competence to other people. Sometimes, though, the best option is to move on to the next chapter.

### "Why them and not me?"

Imagine that a professional colleague told you about a great career-related coup, such as getting a huge salary increase or a great new job. Would you think, "That's great, they really deserved that," or would you have fleeting feelings of envy or personal inadequacy? If the latter, you are not alone. Most of us are vulnerable to this kind of insidious social comparison. We look at others' accomplishments and think it is not fair that they are doing so well, because we are just as talented. We ask, "Why them and not me?"

Most of us measure our success in relation to others. Rather than looking at our own achievements with satisfaction, we look instead at how we have fallen short. Every profession has its own barometer for success, whether it is number of calls from headhunters, bylines, conference presentations, or mentions in the press. When we see others apparently outscoring us, we may well resent it.

If you are torturing yourself in this way, perform a quick reality check. Are you really underachieving? Even people who are successful by any standard, as well as those who have made conscious decisions to "trade down" in their career, can be prone to second-guess their competence. Consider also the possibility that these great accomplishments of your friends may reflect their self-promotional skills more than what they have actually done.

Sometimes good things do happen to less talented people. It may seem unjust, and often it is, but you have to accept it. Otherwise you will end up like many bitter people who have spent their lives bemoaning the successes of other people they describe as less capable than they are.

The fact that other people are doing better than you does not make you a failure. Set your own compass to evaluate your success. If you always evaluate yourself against others, there will always be someone doing something better than you or getting greater rewards for it. If you conclude that you really are underachieving relative to what you are capable of, analyze the reasons for others' success. What could you be doing differently? How can you get more of what you want?

*The fact that other people are doing better than you does not make you a failure.*

*One of the most powerful strategies to renew feelings of work engagement is taking on something that stretches you personally.*

# Overcoming boredom and burnout

Been there, done that, got the coffee mug. Boredom is a common problem today. So is burnout. Perhaps surprisingly, boredom and burnout are often two sides of the same coin.

*Gary is an excellent technical trainer. But he has become increasingly bored with his work. "I teach the same courses over and over again. I can do this job with my eyes closed," he says.*

*Gary is not sure how much longer he can keep going. "If I have to stand up in the classroom and say the same things one more time, I'm going to lose it."*

### Overworked and understimulated

Organizations used to hire people for their potential and move them around to broaden their development. In the contemporary workplace, employers are often reluctant to move people who are performing their work at a high level.

These employers should take note, however, that when these workers get stuck doing the same work for too long, they become stale and lose a sense of their own competence.

It is a paradox of our time that we can be both bored and overworked. You may wonder how you can be bored with so much going on around you, but it is quite possible to be both overworked and understimulated. You may be pushed to the max, but every day you are still talking to the same people, using the same skills, not learning anything new. In fact, at the extremes, boredom is a precursor to burnout.

Novelty seekers motivated by change, personal developers motivated to push themselves, and career builders motivated to keep moving higher are particularly vulnerable to boredom.

**Look outside**
*The solution to your boredom at work may be in your personal life. Set yourself a novel goal—such as running a marathon—that is outside your comfort zone.*

## Are you bored?

All work has its boring moments, but there is a difference between those inevitable moments and those that are mind-numbing.

- Does your day seem to crawl by, minute by minute?
- Has your work lost its luster?
- Do you feel like you are in perpetual reruns?
- Do you feel you are not being intellectually stimulated?
- Does the thought of doing the same thing one more time, or having the same conversations, make you ill?

## Strategies for overcoming boredom

There is nothing more soul- or mind-destroying than "dying of boredom." Get the stimulation you need by applying the following strategies.

▶ **Identify a challenge in your work life that will revitalize you.**
Do something slightly risky that will pull you out of your comfort zone. It is remarkable how something as minor as attending a two-day conference can rejuvenate feelings about work.

▶ **Mount a conference on a topic that interests you.**
Set up a discussion group.

▶ **Try "bartering."**
Get rid of boring parts of your work, or trade a boring task with a colleague.

▶ **Ask your boss for what you want.**
Gary's boss agreed to his spending two days a week working as an organizational consultant while conducting training the rest of the time. People frequently make assumptions about what their boss will or will not do, without testing them out.

▶ **Self-assign**
If you are self-employed, find an assignment that will take you out of your comfort zone, even if this means charging less than your usual fee.

▶ **Enrich your personal life.**
One of the most powerful strategies to renew feelings of work engagement is taking on a project that stretches you, whether volunteering or doing something out of character, such as snowboarding. (*See* Boost your career intelligence, *pages 300–323*.)

▶ **Find new work.**
Consider a career shift, doing the same type of work with different people in a new environment. (*See* Find your perfect path, *pages 86–163*.)

## Career counsel

Boredom is a warning signal. If you ignore it, your feelings of dissatisfaction will only increase. Pinpoint the source:

- Has your work changed to become less challenging?
- Have you been doing the same work for too long?
- Are you moving into a new life phase?

*Many people are too busy managing day to day to derive any pleasure from their lives.*

### Overcome burnout

*Sandra used to be a high performer. But these days she is listless and depressed. "I don't feel like I'm accomplishing anything. Before I can finish one thing I have to start another, or go out into the field to fight the latest fire. I'm not managing anymore, I'm just reacting."*

Besieged by relentless demands, producing what they fear is second-rate work, many people today are at the breaking point. They feel trapped in a never-ending routine of too much work and not enough recognition. They are too busy managing day to day, and reacting to events, to derive any pleasure from their lives. I have even heard people describe themselves as "one of the living dead."

Just as you can be bored and overworked at the same time, you can be overstretched to the point of burnout and yet still be understimulated—not learning anything new and feeling that you have nothing whatever to look forward to.

Burnout will often be expressed in your behavior—you flare up at the smallest cue or "lose it" with your kids. Alternatively, you may be so emotionally fatigued that nothing seems to matter, and you become withdrawn and apathetic.

### Are you burned out?

Understand what you are feeling. If you answer yes to two or more of these questions, you likely are well on the road to burnout.

- Do you dread going to work in the morning?
- Do you see yourself as having an endless "to-do" list?
- Do you feel apathetic and demotivated in your work?
- Do you feel that you have not completed any project to your personal satisfaction in the past year?
- Are you finding it difficult to respond to work demands?
- Do you have no energy left at the end of the day to do things important to you?
- Are you just holding on by your fingernails?

# **Strategies** to overcome burn-out

Fight back. Rejuvenate yourself. Do not allow yourself to be a victim of burnout. Use the following strategies.

▶ **Identify the causes of your distress.**
Is the sheer volume of your work too much for you? At some point you may have to "just say no," as in "No, I can't take that on," or "No, I can't meet that deadline." You may have to tell your boss or client, "If I take this on I'll have to give something up. What would you like me to drop?" (*See* Pushing back, *pages 286–287*, for more on standing up to excessive workloads.)

▶ **Follow good time-management techniques.**
Focus your attention on work that is most important and really adds value. For instance, have you had a lot of "administrivia" added to your workload? This has become an increasingly common problem and is a major cause of burnout—spending time thinking about and doing work that is uncreative and unchallenging. (*See* Strategies to restore balance, *pages 288–289.*)

▶ **Think about your pace.**
Are you moving too fast? Some people enjoy having a dozen tasks on the go at once. Others prefer to work on just one or two tasks at the same time. We each have our own individual rhythm. If the work is too fast-paced for you, can you restructure your job? If you cannot, then find work that provides a better match with your work style. Although people can sustain a grueling pace for a short period, over time they will begin to disintegrate.

▶ **Take a break.**
Studies show that vacations, even short ones, can be a powerful source of rejuvenation. Indeed, in one major study of cardiovascular health, researchers found that a vacation can be more effective than exercise when it comes to coping with stress.

▶ **Do something different.**
Many people discover that introducing something new into their weekly routine has a significant spillover effect in changing how they feel about something at work that is a source of burnout. Consider activities both at work and outside of work as sources of rejuvenation.

▶ **Accomplish something.**
Burnout is often caused by a lack of a sense of accomplishment. Find one activity that you can see through to the end. It does not have to be a significant endeavor. Many people find, for example, that something they can exercise personal control over—as simple as rearranging their drawers or cleaning their car—can provide a sense of satisfaction.

*The good news is, most people do not make 20-year "career mistakes."*

# Dealing with career vertigo

If you find it hard to explain to yourself how you came to be in your current line of work, you are probably suffering from what I have labeled "career vertigo"—one of the most common types of career distress I see today.

*Louis lies awake at night wondering, "Why did I become an accountant? Was it simply because they had a great recruitment campaign, or did I really want to do this? I feel like I never really chose what I've become, that it was just an accident somehow. And if it was just an accident, how do I know I wouldn't be happier doing something else?"*

## Are you wondering how you got from there to here?

Career vertigo is very common. If you answer yes to any of these questions, you are in the majority of managers and professionals.

- Do you feel that you just "fell into" your work?
- Do you feel that you never made an active choice to pursue your particular career path?
- Do you find it difficult to see the underlying logic that has led to you doing the work you are doing now?
- Do you often wonder if you would be happier doing something else?

When you suffer from career vertigo, you look back on your career and see no conscious choices, only an apparent sequence of accidents. You cannot find any underlying logic to what you have become. Asked how you ended up in your line of work, you say, "I just fell into it."

Suddenly, everything seems arbitrary. You see how the world might have ended up very differently, given only a relatively small change in circumstances. The very underpinnings of your life seem fragile.

Actually, our career choices, as we have seen in Know yourself (*see pages 14–85*), are rarely arbitrary or accidental. Typically, we have underlying themes that are repeated throughout our career. Most of us are doing work to which we are relatively well-matched, although that does not mean there is not something out there that would be an even better match for us at this stage in our careers. Often, people who go through the self-assessment process conclude that their work—with perhaps some adjustments—is fundamentally a good match. In other words, what feels like a career accident is actually the result of choices.

When we look at our career history, what we discover is that for the most part we have gradually moved toward what we are doing now through what psychologists call "successive approximations." That is, when we are good at something, we do it well and seek out similar work in the future, while if we are unsuited to something, we do not receive the necessary rewards to persist in that line of work.

The good news is, most people do not make 20-year "career mistakes." Occasionally, of course, people do continue doing work they do not like because they are frightened of change or cannot see any alternatives. More commonly, people find themselves in situations that are no longer a good match for them. But that does not mean they would have been happier doing something else all along, just that it is time to move on.

### Identifying core talents

*Your career may seem like an arbitrary series of accidents. However, if you dig down, you will probably discover that you have been building on core talents—such as being a good communicator—and that you did not just "fall" into your work.*

*A crisis of meaning may also reflect changes in your personal life.*

# Confronting a crisis of meaning

What good is my work going to do for me or for others? Where is all this frenzied activity leading? Feelings of meaninglessness are endemic in today's fragmented workscape. There are no quick fixes, but there are many strategies to make your work life personally meaningful.

*For years, Peter never really thought about the purpose of his work. All he cared about was doing work that gave him a general sense of accomplishment and allowed him to provide well for his family.*

*Now the sudden death of a parent had led him to think about what he is doing and why. "I can't see that anyone benefits from it other than the company's shareholders. I don't identify with the values of the organization. I don't like the people I work with. I make a good living, sure. But if I died tomorrow, what would I leave behind me? I can't help thinking, there must be something more."*

### Is your work meaningful?
Most people at times question whether their work is meaningful. There is a difference, however, between fleeting discomfort and persistent ennui.

- Do you sometimes feel your life is empty?
- Do you wonder if you could be doing something more meaningful with your life?
- Would you like to do work that contributes to your personal growth or that of the community or society?
- Do you feel that you should be serving something greater than profit?
- Do you feel out of sync with organizational values? Do you increasingly see them as driven by profits at the expense of human beings?

Today, people are listing "work that is meaningful" as a major criterion in their career choices. Many are looking for work that fits their personal values, work that allows them to contribute something important. Their ranks include young people who saw their parents downsized by what they describe as profit-hungry organizations; disaffected mid-career changers looking for work that better reflects their values; and older workers at the end of their careers looking to give something back. Many of these people describe their work environments as "soulless" or their employers as lacking integrity. They experience a spiritual hunger and are looking either to make a connection with the people they work with or to do work that contributes to society. They want to leave a worthwhile legacy.

Although many are authenticity seekers, a high number of people who fall into other motivational categories are also looking for greater meaning in their work. In some cases, they are prepared to make significant changes in their lives by trading down in their careers to accommodate their needs.

If you are wrestling with this issue, ask yourself whether your work really is meaningless. You may not be finding a cure for cancer, but you may still be enhancing people's lives.

A crisis of meaning may also reflect changes in your personal life—a mid-life crisis, an empty nest, health issues, the sudden death of someone close to you. That does not mean your concerns about your work are not real, only that you should think through what the issues really are rather than making any sudden moves.

There is no magic bullet to solve a crisis of meaning. Still, there are extraordinary opportunities for people who do want to contribute to the greater well-being of society. (*See* Finding the right work match, *pages 88–113*.) Many people have resolved these crises of meaning outside their work, making a huge difference in other people's lives by mentoring or volunteering. (*See* Boost your career intelligence, *pages 314–317*.)

**Why am I doing this?**

*Thinking about what you are really here for is a part of the human experience. Engage with your questions.*

*The new pursuit of personal fulfillment through work itself is in part a product of the times.*

# Feeling unfulfilled

**Many people do not look forward to going to work. They do not find their work personally fulfilling. How can you increase your sense of engagement?**

Do you feel you are doing something important or that you care about deeply? Do the content and challenges associated with your work enthrall you? Do you often find yourself surprised by how much time has flown by when you are working? Do you feel passionate about your work? If you have answered yes to one or more of these questions, you are in the fortunate position of being fully engaged by your work.

Unfortunately, feeling unfulfilled is one of the most common forms of contemporary career distress and one of the main reasons why people seek help from career counselors and coaches. People say, "I am not unhappy doing what I am doing, but there must be something more." For some, greater fulfillment means being happier and more satisfied. For others it means nothing less than being passionate about their work.

A generation ago, most people did not think about whether they were happy, much less passionate, at work. Instead, they looked on their work as a means to obtain the things that were supposed to make them happy—money, status, all the trappings of success.

The new pursuit of personal fulfillment through work itself is in part a product of the times, as self-help books and motivational gurus extol us to be passionate. It is also, however, a reaction to what many experience as a thankless contemporary work environment. People say, "If I have to work so hard for so little in return, shouldn't I enjoy and be passionate about what I do?"

**Go for flow**
*Where do you find flow? Look at experiences where you lose your sense of time and place. These may be caused by learning and intellectual stimulation.*

They want work that supports their personal values and allows them to express their authentic self rather than be part of a homogenized stew. They want personal fulfillment to be the major criterion in their work choices—in fact, they demand it.

# **Strategies** to promote passion

Do not allow yourself to die on the vine, or to continue doing work that is numbing to your soul. Consider the following to reignite your passion.

▶ **Know where passion comes from.**
People often say, "I want to find my passion" as though it was something they expected to stumble across in the woods or pick up at a department store. The fact is, passion is not a commodity, it is the by-product of doing something that really engages you. Look for what will truly hold your attention—psychologically and technically—and the passion should take of itself.

▶ **Take a clue from earlier work experiences.**
What originally attracted you to your line of work? Often, as we advance in our career, we move farther away from our original sources of engagement. Think about what has been lost. Many mid-career individuals experience their work as joyless and hollow even if they are very successful at it, because the very thing that brought them into their field of endeavor—whether making a difference in people's lives, or starting up and seeing through a high-risk project—is no longer a central feature of their work. You may also have "topped out" in your field. You have made significant achievements, but those achievements are no longer meaningful because they come so easily to you.

▶ **What was it that used to engage you?**
How can you find it again? Asking these questions can help you rediscover the original underpinnings of passion. Often, people who make successful career shifters are returning to work that more closely mirrors their earlier strengths and drives.

▶ **Seek new challenges.**
Today, employers reward us for mastery, not for our potential to do something new. Unfortunately, with mastery can come boredom. When what once was novel and exciting has become a dreaded routine, it is time to move on. Doing something new without promise of a safety net, testing yourself in a venture that involves a calculated risk, can be a route to finding a new passion. This is particularly true for personal developers and novelty seekers.

▶ **Go for flow.**
When was the last time you were so completely engaged and absorbed by your work that all of a sudden you looked up and said, "I can't believe it—five hours couldn't have passed!" This is what psychologists are calling "flow." When you achieve a state of flow, you feel a sensation of confidence, of being in control, of being engaged and focused. Flow is achieved when your work is performed in sync with your aptitudes and values. Can you remold your work so that it stretches you?

## Career counsel

People have read so much hype about passion that they feel they are missing something because they do not jump out of bed champing at the bit to get to work. They are afraid that if they are not completely engaged, then they must be dull and uninteresting at best, spiritually bankrupt at worst.

The reality is that not everyone needs to feel passionate in their work. Lifestylers, for example, want to have a general sense of professional accomplishment, but they derive their sense of personal fulfillment from activities outside their workplace, whether sports, hobbies, charity work, or family.

Many people fulfill vital functions in our society without loving their work, yet they are content in their lives. Perhaps it is only the current obsession with passion that leads some to worry that something is missing.

# Dealing with difficult bosses

Bosses come in all shapes and sizes, but the problem ones all have the same effect. They throw your work and your life into turmoil. There are ways to turn your situation around, though sometimes you just have to quit.

Today we are seeing more bad bosses than ever. As a result of institutionalized leanness, many overstretched managers are short-tempered and too busy or ill-trained to provide staff with the support they need. While some bad bosses are nasty by nature, others are simply a product of the times.

**Manage your boss**

*The key to managing difficult bosses is understanding their underlying motivation. Why are they behaving this way? How should you respond to their troubling behavior?*

As anyone who has had a bad boss—about 90 percent of those who have worked for more than 10 years—knows, a bad boss has extraordinary power to destroy your sense of competence.

What makes for a bad boss? Some bosses are just plain mean, but in other cases it is all in the eye of the beholder. One person's boss from hell may be another person's pinup. A sociability seeker will be miserable with an introverted manager. An introvert, on the other hand, will flourish under the same regime.

Then again, the problem may simply be bad chemistry. For whatever reason, you bring out the worst in each other. You like direction; she thinks you are "needy." You like to finish work at 6:00; she is just getting rolling. So before you assume your boss is a complete jerk, ask yourself, Does she get along with others? Does she pick on everyone, or just you?

The key to getting along with bosses is being able to manage them. This requires understanding the underpinnings of their behavior. Your boss may not be the cruel tormentor you think he is. In fact, his underlying motivation may be different from what you believe.

Here are some common types of bad bosses, their motivations, and strategies for dealing with them. (If you are a manager, you might want to ask yourself, "Am I described here?")

## The weak manager

She seems to go from strength to strength, even though everyone knows she has the spine of a jellyfish. She is vague, and her commitments have the sticking power of water. She studiously avoids taking risks. She will not lobby for the resources you need or stand up for you on critical issues. At the first sign of a conflict, she runs.

Although a constellation of behaviors describes the weak manager, the underlying causes vary. Often, she simply wants to be liked by everyone and cannot stand conflict. It is also possible she is too busy to understand when there is a problem, or too burned out to care. Frequently, such managers are reluctant to be managers at all. They would much rather be getting on with their own work as individual contributors, or may be ill-trained and lack management skills.

If you are dealing with a weak manager, identify the source of the problem. For example, if she needs to be liked by everyone, avoid communications that suggest contentious or highly charged emotional issues. Where you can, solve conflicts yourself.

If she is a commitment-phobe, cover yourself. Send an email after a meeting, saying, "Based on my understanding of what we just discussed, I will … and you will … Unless I hear from you, I will start on this …"

If your boss is simply spineless and cannot take on a leadership role, consider going to your boss's boss.

If your boss is too burned out to care or is a reluctant manager, work around her. Take initiative to set out the parameters of the work. Give yourself the feedback you need. Pin down your boss by email to a suggested meeting time. Talk to her only about critical issues. If she lacks management skills, tell her what you need from her to do your job.

*One person's boss from hell may be another person's pinup.*

# Career counsel

Political animals do not fool everyone. Smart senior management is tuned in to these aggressive self-promoters. They know that great bosses get their work done through others. Take comfort in knowing that most of these political animals will ultimately crash. Management wants to promote leaders who nurture and groom their staff. Bosses who take credit for everything are not real leaders because they are not talent growers.

## The stupid or concrete manager

He does not get it, either because he has the IQ of an eraser or because he is as concrete as they come. He does not understand context, nuance, or high-level ideas.

If his problem is intellectual deficiency, indulge him like a misguided child. Better yet, ignore him if you can. If the problem is one of cognitive style, however, shape your communications to his needs. If your boss is fact-oriented, do not waste your time painting compelling arguments based on ideas. Simply provide the information unembellished. Keep it simple and to the point.

## The political manager

She has an unerring ability to know what will make her look good. She will go to bat for you only on issues that serve her political agenda. She is sneaky. She plays favorites, and you likely are not one of them. She would not think twice about using you as a sacrificial lamb to further support her own career goals.

Support her high needs for recognition by making her look good on strategic projects. Focus your own efforts on "high value" work. Be prepared to share the limelight even if it kills you. Do not trust her to have your own interests at heart. Pitch her on work you want to do by emphasizing how good it will make her and her department look to senior management.

We like to believe the world is fair, that good things happen to good people, that political types eventually get their comeuppance. After all, why should we be punished for someone else's bad behavior? Some political bosses and co-workers do, in the end, crash and burn, while others just get by. The fact is, however, a few of them do extraordinarily well.

## The obsessive micro-manager

He trusts you the way he would trust a five-year-old behind the wheel of his car. No matter how much detail you give him, or how many times you redo a piece of work, it is still not right. You are completely demotivated. You have lost your sense of competence.

Why is he so untrusting? Is he anxious about failing to please his own boss, or is he simply a control freak? If the problem is one of his own insecurity, anticipate issues that will make him anxious by reassuring him that you have covered all the bases. Say, for example, "In completing this I spoke to … and, keeping the following issues in mind, I …" Write it down to further reassure him. He may be too anxious to fully process what you are saying.

## The invisible manager

You have no one to go to for direction. Your boss does not have a clue about the volume or pace of your work. You are killing yourself, but no one notices or gives you feedback.

The invisible manager shares many of the underlying motivations of the weak manager. She may be invisible because she is too busy or because she is a reluctant or unskilled manager. She also may be very introverted. If she is time-pressed, do your homework before you meet her. That way you can make the meeting as efficient as possible. Be strategic on issues where you want support.

Give yourself direction and feedback by setting milestones and regularly evaluating your effectiveness against them. Thank yourself for a job well done. Establish a mechanism for getting direction—perhaps weekly or monthly meetings at an agreed-on time. Hold your boss to her commitment to attend these meetings.

## The taskmaster

He does not have a life, so he does not expect you to. You are drowning in work, but he keeps piling more on. His timelines are ridiculous.

Sometimes an extremely task-focused manager is simply shy or preoccupied or is so focused on getting the work done that he is not aware of the impact of his behavior. Is he aware of your workload?

**Case** study

Carole, a 27-year-old autonomy seeker, liked her entry-level job because it was giving her great experience with a high-profile employer, but she could not stand her control-freak boss. She managed her own feelings of frustration by telling herself, "I'm choosing to do this for 12 months, which in the greater scheme of things is nothing, and then I'm out of here with great skills on my résumé." Before jumping ship, compare what you are gaining in the work experience with the frustrations of working with a bad boss. Remind yourself of the decisions you have made and why you have made them.

*Do not be
apologetic about
wanting time for
a personal life.*

If you have talked to him and he still does not get it, create your own standards for evaluating what is realistic and doable. Do not be apologetic about wanting time for a personal life. Work–life balance is a right, not a privilege. If your organization wants to be an "employer of choice," remind your boss of the incongruity between organizational policy and his behavior.

## The bullying manager

She is ruthless. She seems to take pleasure in watching you squirm. She has pets, and you are not one of them. She may be a bully, constantly threatening to fire you, invading your personal space, belittling you in front of co-workers, always yelling at you or making nasty remarks about you, showing so little respect that you cannot function properly. You may be her only target, or she may have created a generally poisonous work environment for all.

Sometimes apparently nasty bosses are simply so task-focused that they are oblivious to how their behavior makes staff feel. Underneath a very gruff exterior, as the saying goes, may be the heart of a pussycat. Workplace experts say that such bosses often do not understand the consequences of their own behavior. That is why you should confront them, no matter how uncomfortable it makes you feel.

Think about what outcome you want to achieve. Be very clear and specific about what is bothering you and what you expect your boss to do about it. For example, "Last week when you spoke to me, you said _____, and I felt it was inappropriate. I'd like you not to do that again in the future."

It is possible that when confronted, your boss will apologize. Then again, she may simply be nasty.

If her behavior is extremely offensive to you and shows no sign of changing, you may need to go to someone higher in authority and explain your concerns. Before you do, think about what you want to accomplish and what the ideal outcome would be. For example, do you want an apology? A transfer? Do you want your boss fired?

We like to believe we live in a world where people are honest and trustworthy and do not behave in irrational ways. Even in the face of provocation, we turn the other cheek or explain away bad behavior.

Sarah ignored colleagues' and friends' warnings that her bullying boss could not be trusted. "I didn't want to think that a person could just be plain nasty, so I gave her the benefit of the doubt. I thought maybe I was being overly sensitive, or that her behavior was the result of stress." By the time Sarah acknowledged the real problem, her self-esteem was very low.

### Make the choice

What if these strategies for dealing with your boss do not work? You have a choice. If you have good personal reasons for staying in your job—you love your work, you are learning a lot, you like the people you are working with—you can hold your nose and put your boss on remote, and refuse to allow her to define your worth as a human being.

Or you can quit. Life is too short to deal with this kind of abuse. You deserve better. Your self-esteem depends on it. Your life depends on it. Your relationships depend on it.

## Women: be assertive

Be assertive. Do not accept a bad situation or put up with unacceptable managerial behavior. You deserve better. Avoid the traps women often fall into.

- **Do not play "Ms. Fix-It."**
  When things go wrong, do not take on personal responsibility to "make things better." It is not up to you to clean up other people's messes. It is great to be helpful, but know when you have crossed the line from "helper" to "doormat."

- **Do not explain away bad behavior.**
  Do not look for excuses such as, "He doesn't really mean it. He's basically a good guy." Unacceptable is unacceptable.

- **Do not accept bones.**
  Do not tolerate unacceptable behavior simply because ever so occasionally it is laced with human decency. For example, do not interpret a boss's permission to take time off work in the face of a family crisis as going beyond the call of duty rather than something that is actually your right.

## Case study

Malcolm was so upset by his bullying boss that he was having trouble sleeping. He tried everything to improve the situation: he tried to mollify his boss, he confronted him, he spoke to his boss's boss. Nothing worked. Finally, after yet another sleepless night, he decided, "That's it. I'm out of here." The next day he told his boss that he was quitting and why. He did not pull any punches. He also sent an email to Human Resources documenting his boss's bullying tactics. He was not disappointed to learn, several months after he had moved on, that his boss had been fired.

*Today's new workers do not view quitting as a mark of defeat but as an assertion of their value.*

# Know when to go

**Perhaps the job that was previously engaging has changed. Perhaps you are burned out. Are you ready to quit? Leave the right way.**

Almost certainly, you will reach a point at some juncture in your career where you say, "Things aren't working, there's nothing I can do about it, and absolutely *anything* is better than this." Whatever the reasons, you cannot take it anymore.

I am not talking here about handing in your notice to accept another job offer, but about stepping out into the void, acknowledging that you have reached that soul-sucking, self-esteem-plundering point of no return.

Conventional wisdom used to be not to quit your job until you had a new one to go to. However, today's new workers, who see satisfying and meaningful work as a right, not a privilege, are much faster to take the plunge. They do not view quitting as a mark of defeat but as an assertion of their value. In job interviews they "sell" the fact they have quit as demonstrating their ability to recognize a bad work situation and their self-confidence to move on.

### Facing down doubts

Quitting goes against the bedrock belief in Western society that persistence is all and no one likes a quitter. This kind of learning starts early, with "the little engine that could" ("I think I can, I think I can"). We are taught to believe in the value of effort in overcoming obstacles and our own abilities. When children have difficulties in a particular subject, we tell them that working through the adversity will somehow make them a better person.

Quitting is never an easy decision. There will always be some uncertainty before the decision is made. You wonder if you will really find something better elsewhere. You may say, "Maybe I should give it another chance," or even bring out that old chestnut, "Better the devil you know..."

# SELF-ASSESSMENT **Know** when to leave

Leaving is never easy. It poses psychological and financial challenges. Use the following checklist to help you decide if it is time for you to go.

## You know you are ready to quit when:

☐ You have tried to make changes, either on your own or by speaking to your boss/clients, yet your efforts have come to nothing. Furthermore, you can see that it is clear that the situation cannot be improved.

☐ You are confident the toxicity of your work environment is not simply a blip—the result of a cost squeeze, for example, due to a temporary downturn. You are being realistic—not quitting in a fit of pique over some imagined slight, or because you think that you should be making twice as much money working half as hard. You understand that the grass is not necessarily greener elsewhere.

☐ You are sure that the price of staying (loss of self-esteem) is greater than the price of going (loss of income). You know that if you continue, you will suffer serious psychological pain—a price not only you but also your family members will pay.

☐ You can give quitting a positive spin—not as denial but as an affirmation of your own value. If a potential employer grills you about why you quit as if it is indicative of a major personality defect, you probably do not want to work there anyway.

☐ You have obtained an outsider's perspective on your situation, whether from a friend, mentor, or career counselor. Typically, the period during which we start to contemplate leaving is characterized by accelerating self-doubt and depression. We lose the capacity to see solutions to problems and we also lose perspective on our skills and marketability.

☐ Your finances are in order. If you do not have a cushion, you can reorganize your financial commitments so that you can withstand a period without income.

☐ You have evaluated the trade-off between short-term pain and long-term gain. If you are working with an incredible group of people or a new technology that will significantly enhance your long-term choices, it may be worth your while to stick it out a little bit longer. This is usually truer for younger workers and mid-career changers, who need to "put in their time" and establish their credibility, than for older workers, who may correctly conclude, "Life is too short to put up with any more of this."

☐ You have identified specifically what is not working for you, and you have determined exactly what you need more or less of, whether it relates to autonomy, social interaction, the skills you are using, or the amount of time you are working.

☐ You have a sense of your skills and people who could potentially buy those skills. You have conducted a self-assessment and can articulate your accomplishments and how they could contribute to a new enterprise.

**What do you say?**

*How much do you tell your boss about why you are leaving? Do you "tell all"? If you are quitting because of your boss's behavior, consider the ramifications for others before you "dump."*

Most professionals today are accustomed to making decisions based on data. However, you can never test the hypothesis that you would in fact be better off somewhere else. So there will always be some uncertainty. The moments before taking the plunge may be characterized by anxiety and doubt. This is natural, but avoid equivocating once you have made a decision. If you find yourself going back and forth, identify the pros and cons. Are the pros stronger? Write a statement about why you have decided to quit. Read it whenever you have second thoughts.

To face down your doubts and quit all the same requires a belief that you are worthy of something better and that your skills are sufficiently marketable in the current job market to find a better alternative.

Quitting requires courage. Be prepared to deal with being excluded from office banter. A common scenario when someone resigns is for co-workers to write that person out of the script. This "closing of the ranks" can be unsettling.

Manage your communications. If you are resigning because of a toxic boss, there is a good chance that co-workers would like to do the same thing as you. Be sensitive to the fact that they may not have the same financial, psychological, or skill resources that you have.

I have never heard anyone who has moved out of a bad work situation say, "I wish I hadn't quit." I have heard many say they regret they had not done it sooner. To quit is to acknowledge you are human. There is nothing wrong with you in not being able to change a bad work situation. There are no prizes given out for having stuck to a job you hated.

# How to leave

Turn quitting into a positive experience. Use the following seven strategies to minimize possible negative fallout, and leave feeling good about your act of courage.

- **Be gracious.**
  Quitting is not necessarily forever. In today's highly mobile work environment, many people return to an earlier employer. It is also likely that you will encounter former colleagues in the future—preferably as friends rather than enemies. Then there is the question of your references. Do not burn any bridges behind you.

- **Give reasonable notice.**
  There is no firm guideline as to how much notice you should give. It can take several months to replace professional and managerial workers. Negotiate a reasonable compromise between your urge to get out of there fast and your boss's need for transition. This may mean staying on at least a month to hand over files.

- **Try to avoid the negative.**
  If you are leaving because of a conflict with your boss, there is no need to get into detailed explanations. Try to keep the meeting brief and avoid getting drawn into a war of words. Indicate that you are prepared to stay on to tie up loose ends, and try to say something good about your experience there. What do you hope to achieve with a knockdown fight with your boss? The proper time for honest communication was while you were still employed.

- **Consider your responsibilities.**
  If you are leaving because of problems that have affected your co-workers or staff, decide if you have a responsibility to inform senior management of the difficulties. After all, your leaving and speaking out may be doing everyone a favor. On the other hand, consider whether "talking out" will bring the desired results for co-workers. What if the problem is a punitive boss? Unfortunately, this kind of boss often deals with feelings of inadequacy by lashing out at remaining staff. Consult co-workers about how they want you to handle it.

- **Do not put it in writing.**
  There is usually no need for a formal letter of resignation. If one is required, keep it short and neutral in tone.

- **Do not leave compromising information on your computer.**
  This would include copies of your résumé or potentially embarrassing bookmarks.

- **Know when to sign off.**
  Make yourself available for questions after you leave. Do not let the transition drag on too long, however. A few calls should be sufficient. Any more than that and you should start charging for your time.

*There are no prizes given out for having stuck to a job you hated.*

# Age-related dilemmas

We have many chapters in our careers. Each one presents special challenges, whether you are starting out, changing gears, or phasing down. And each one requires careful planning. Use these strategies to get the most out of your current career stage.

## This chapter shows you how to:

**Cope** with the uncertainty many people experience early in their careers about what to do "when you grow up."

**Learn** the answers to the five most critical career concerns 20-somethings grapple with.

**Avoid** common mistakes older workers make, using targeted strategies to ensure your continued marketability.

**Plan** for the next phase in your later career years, including solving the retirement conundrum.

*Many ask, "How do I know I'll like it if I haven't done it?"*

# Early-career uncertainty

**Young people are anxious about making the right career decisions. They wonder, "How do I know which work is best for me? How should I establish myself?"**

*Jill was everyone's golden girl—high school valedictorian, winner of academic scholarships, college athletics star. But after completing a master's degree in economics, her effortless progress began to falter. She enrolled in a doctoral program in political science but dropped out after six months. She entered law school, but that did not feel right, either.*

*Now she is contemplating an MBA. "But what if I'm wrong again?" she asks. "I look at friends who went straight into professional schools, and they're doing great. But I still don't know what I want to do."*

*Like many perpetual students, Jill is guilt-ridden about accepting any further financial help from her parents and worried about disappointing them yet again. She feels under pressure from them and from others to grow up, get a career, and get it right this time. Terrified of making any commitment, Jill marks time as an office temp, confused and depressed. Jill is suffering from 20-something career angst.*

"Should I go for my master's or start earning big money right now?" "Should I stay with a big public-accounting firm or get a job in industry?" "What kind of work would really suit me?" These are the kinds of comments I am hearing from 20-somethings these days. They are not the only age group prone to career confusion and indecision, but they are particularly vulnerable. The cost of a university education has spiraled at a time when many parents are cash-strapped. The pressure is on early to make the "right" decision.

This anxiety is exacerbated by a heightened awareness of careers. College students are bombarded with career advice. Newsstand magazines feature cover stories on where the hot jobs are. The clear implication is that you should know what you want to do when you grow up.

**Pressure point**
*You may feel huge parental pressure to make a career decision once you have left college and before you have been able to explore all avenues of interest.*

With the exception of an elite group with in-demand skills, such as engineers and computer technologists, 20-somethings face a challenging job market. In the past, organizations hired for potential. Today they are more likely to seek new hires who can hit the ground running and deliver value now.

For young people with limited or no work experience, making career decisions can present a real conundrum. As so many ask, "How do I know I'll like it if I haven't done it?"

## Manage early-career angst

Do not panic if you do not know what you want to do. Be in the moment and maximize your current experience, whatever it is.

- Recognize that there is nothing wrong with not knowing what you want to do. Do not overestimate the consequences of making a "mistake."

- Instead of chasing after that elusive "right" decision, understand that there are many possible career paths. When you are 45 years old, you are unlikely to look back and say, "If only when I was 25 years old I had done A, B, or C instead." The decision may appear momentous right now, especially if you have debts from student loans or parental pressures to contend with. But in the long term, it will have little or no impact on your prospects for success.

- Do not try to plan out your entire career—the fast-changing nature of work makes this impossible. When entering a workplace where a conventional job may last only a few years, and work is increasingly done by contract or external suppliers, you should focus on building a portfolio of skills and experiences that will ensure longer- term employability. There is no beginning line and no finish line on careers—and no right or wrong time to pursue a particular career option.

## Career counsel

There is no one formula for finding the right career. It is mostly a question of trial and error. Interestingly, the most successful and happy adults I know are ones who weathered some self-doubt while they tried to find the right field.

Career angst is itself a painful kind of experience, full of indecision and soul-searching. Some people try to avoid this process by closing down their options. Rather than seeking work that will best match their interests and skills, they surrender to the marketplace and pursue some "hot" career path whether or not they are suited to it. But if instead you engage your anxiety and struggle with it, you will come out on the other side with a much clearer sense of your values and priorities, well on the way to meaningful work.

*Remember that you are not in prison. If your job is not meeting your needs, look for better work.*

important. I know of few successful people who have not at one time or another had a really hideous work experience. It is simply part of growing up, and part of how we learn what we like and do not like. If you are not sure you want to pursue a particular line of work, conduct an "audition" (*see page 136.*)

- If you find yourself in work that is not a good match for you, use the experience to identify what it is that you do not like. There also must be some aspects of the job that you do like. What are they?

### Answers to common 20-something career issues
I work with hundreds of young professionals every year. Here are the answers to issues raised most frequently.

- **Should I take a job just for the money?**
  Major financial obligations may force you to do so. While the work may not be challenging or personally meaningful, all experience counts, and you can probably learn something. At the same time, consider the cost of taking a job that does not relate to your personal interests or the skills you want to acquire at this stage of your career. You may miss better opportunities you could have found through a more rigorous job search.

- **Should I quit this dead-end job?**
  The truth is, there are no real "dead-end" jobs—unless you plan on staying in one for life. Even unstimulating, low-paid jobs in the service sector can provide opportunities for accomplishments over and above the day-to-day work. It is up to you to be super-vigilant in identifying potential opportunities. Think strategically about how you can use your skills at a higher level. Look for opportunities to add value—for example, by finding a problem and solving it—and take advantage of every potential learning experience. Another strategy is "shadowing," finding someone

who is doing work that interests you and following them around as their "shadow" to learn about their skills and how they carry out their work. Remember that you are not in prison. If your job is not meeting your needs, look for better work.

- ● **What about when long-term plans conflict?**
  You are offered a prize assignment on the understanding that you will be staying around for the long term, when you know you will not be—you have been planning on going to Europe or taking time off to finish your Ph.D. Should you take the offer?

  As John Lennon observed, life is what happens when you are making other plans. The world rarely unfolds the way we expect. What if you should be forced to change your plans by unforeseen circumstances anyway? Rather than thinking about what would happen if you left in the near future, think about the learning experiences you would be losing.
  Organizations are made up of people who understand that life is unpredictable. So if you decide to leave, you cannot be

### Making the most of it
*Even if the job you are in is not your ultimate career choice, it can still provide opportunities. Find someone whose work interests you and become their shadow so that you can pick up new skills.*

# Case study

*"I'm planning on having children. Should I take this great job at the risk of alienating the employer?"*

Women thinking about having children often worry that people will assume they have only taken a job to collect maternity benefits. Bear in mind that it may take you a long time to get pregnant, you will likely be able to work throughout your pregnancy, and you could not possibly know now whether, or how soon, you will decide to return to work after the baby is born.

faulted. Note, however, that your job probably will not be held for you. But if you are doing an outstanding job, you definitely will be in a privileged position when you want to return. If nothing else, you have established good contacts for the future, not to mention marketable skills.

● **How do I escape professional stereotyping?**
No sooner do some young professionals receive their professional designation than they decide, "This is not what I want. I really want to do something else." They worry that their degree, whether in law, engineering, or some other profession, will pin them down in the eyes of employers, and they will not be able to move into new areas.

The easiest way to change disciplines when you are starting out is to establish your skills and demonstrate your value in your own professional area. Let us say you are an accountant who wants to move out of finance into marketing. Demonstrate your generalist skills to your employer before trying to compete with marketing professionals who hold specialized degrees in that area. You can then leverage the skills and experiences you have acquired to move into other areas.

● **Is there anywhere I can work where I do not have to be involved in office politics?**
Any place where you have people with different personalities, motivations, and points of view who are trying to influence each other, you will have office politics. And despite the term's negative connotation, office politics can actually provide a healthy and creative form of communication. Office politics can be an important source of information about what is really going on. It can help keep you "tied in" to the decisions that are being made. Information picked up at meetings does not always tell the complete story. The nuances of people's motivations, feelings about what has been proposed—all this adds color to information and helps you know what is important and what is not.

What is often thought to be negative about office politics is people complaining about co-workers who do not pull their weight, or unfair bosses.

Actually, this kind of exchange can be a useful way to compare notes and test whether your own perceptions are widely shared. If you feel inadequate because your boss is constantly criticizing your work, for example, it helps to hear from others that he is an extreme perfectionist who can never be satisfied.

If you find the politics really unpleasant—powermongering or petty whining about personalities—remember, you have control over your entry into the fray.

## Career counsel

Take a lesson from lawyers, who have a time-honored tradition of applying their legal skills to other areas. Consider three lawyers I know. One, after a stint with a law firm, parlayed her background into a career in journalism specializing in legal issues. Another used problem-solving and analytical skills to become a systems consultant. A third combined her curiosity about people, her appreciation of individual differences, and her broad professional network to move into executive recruitment.

### Benefit from politics

*Office politics is often thought of as a must to avoid. In fact, it can be a source of information about what really is going on. Share information. Test whether your views are shared by others.*

# How older workers can ensure their employability

Older workers can experience significant challenges. How can you protect your employability in the future? What strategies work?

"I've been looking for a job for nine months. I'm prepared to make less money than I used to. I've got great experience. But I'm not even getting to the interview stage. I'm sure it's because of my age."

**You are in demand**

*The talent shortage is good news for older workers. Smart organizations will look for creative ways to leverage the wisdom, experience, and mentoring skills older workers bring to the table.*

Despite the so-called skills shortage, some older workers feel that their age is holding them back. They are not being paranoid. We have become a youth-obsessed society, and some recruiters, unfortunately, do equate professional smarts, vigor, and the ability to think innovatively with youth.

Typically, hiring younger managers over more seasoned, older workers is done under the guise of needing to bring in fresh blood, appeal to young consumers, or think outside the box.

Older workers are thought by some recruiters to have bad work habits from having had it easy during decades of economic prosperity. They believe them to be less technically savvy and to lack stamina, and so on. They are also more expensive to hire. As one older manager observed, "From a recruiter's point of view, they can have two of them for the price of one of me and at the same time buy long-term potential."

That said, this trend is reversing. The good news is that organizations are now starting to court older workers, in part to compensate for the skills shortage caused by the baby boomers retiring, but also in recognition of their wisdom, experience, and proven management skills.

# What not to do if you lose your job

Losing work can be psychologically as well as financially devastating if you are in your late 40s and 50s. If you do lose your job and are looking for a new job or are setting up a business…

**Do not:**

- **Act out of panic.**
  Avoid the temptation to shift into panic mode—selling all your possessions, for example, or jumping at the first job that comes along, no matter how unsuitable. Remember that there is work for you somewhere. It may not pay as well, or it may involve other trade-offs, but it can be satisfying and still be reasonably lucrative. Think carefully about your resources, interests, and goals.

- **Look for a job exactly like the one you left.**
  If you lost your job because a whole industry was going downhill, it is probably time to move on anyway.

- **Tell old war stories.**
  Sure, you have a lot of history to reflect on in interviews or customer pitches, but no one really cares about that big turnaround you conducted 15 years ago.

- **Go into partnership with someone just like you.**
  It is understandable that people who have spent most of their working lives in a corporate setting often want to continue working with others. However, going into business with someone who duplicates, rather than complements, their own skills often means that instead of one person not producing enough income, now there are two.

- **Spend big money on electronic toys and office overhead.**
  Extravagant expenditures on brochures and the home office put you into greater debt without necessarily impressing clients. Most clients today want to buy your expertise, not the trappings.

- **Confuse endless networking lunches with effective marketing.**
  Having lunch with a senior vice-president is not necessarily twice as good as having lunch with an ordinary manager. The manager may be the one who is actually in a position to hire you, while the vice-president is focused on other business priorities. In any event, people are just too busy these days to have endless lunches. Chances are you will just spend a lot of money, put on weight, and end up without any prospects to show for it.

- **Have a victim mind-set.**
  It is natural to feel anger if you were let go in a restructuring, but potential employers do not want to hear about it. They are looking for someone ready for new challenges, not someone trapped in the past.

*Remember that there is work for you somewhere that can be satisfying and still be reasonably lucrative.*

*The truth is, we are constantly "retiring" throughout our lives and careers.*

# Strategies for older workers

Refuse to allow yourself to be a victim of age discrimination. Increase your employability by using the following ideas and techniques.

▶ **Make it easier for an employer to hire you.**
Consider contract work rather than waiting for full-time employment. It not only is a "foot in the door," but also gives the employer an opportunity to size up your potential. You are much more likely to get a yes to a first date than to a marriage proposal.

▶ **Think multiple income streams.**
You may not be able to produce enough income from just one source. Increasingly today people are putting together a living through a variety of work options. This may mean, for example, owning vending machines, taking on consulting assignments, and teaching a course at a local college. (For more, *see* Working your portfolio *page 128*.)

▶ **Identify the critical reasons why you want to work.**
Avoid the money-as-way-of-keeping-score trap. Ask yourself, "Am I continuing to work out of financial necessity, or primarily for psychological reasons?" If your primary motivation is a desire to remain fully engaged with the world, consider working for less, volunteering, or mentoring.

▶ **Rethink your relationship to money.**
How much do you really need? Carefully review your personal values and ask yourself what you really care about. Ruthlessly evaluate how your current lifestyle meets your real needs for a satisfied life. Do not get hung up on having the same salary or title as in your last job.

▶ **Join networking organizations catering to mid- and later-career workers.**
They are incredibly effective in helping people find work because their memberships are so diverse, representing managers and professionals from many fields.

▶ **Emphasize strengths associated with wisdom and experience.**
Find environments where your skills and know-how will count. Look at smaller companies that could benefit from your expertise. High-tech companies often shun older workers. However, I know of companies with an average employee age in the early 30s that have hired 60-year-olds on contract precisely because they "have been there."

▶ **Present yourself as a mentor.**
Organizations welcome the fact that many older workers derive pleasure from contributing to younger workers' development. This is very important today because many young workers do not receive sufficient developmental support.

## The retirement conundrum

Do you have a retirement plan? Do you look forward to your next phase? Do you plan to retire at all? Today, for many people, the answer to these questions is no.

Some simply cannot afford to retire at 65 or earlier because of large debts, ongoing expenses associated with supporting former spouses and kids who do not work, or inadequate savings. They will often try to stay in the workforce in some capacity, although they may have to settle for lower-paying and often part-time work to "bridge" their way to retirement.

Others want to continue to work primarily for psychological reasons. They want to stay engaged in the world, to continue to make a contribution, to be challenged and learn new things.

Still others fear and dread retirement because work has been the centerpiece of their lives, and they cannot imagine doing anything else. Their primary sense of identity is in doing and achieving. Retirement for them represents only loss—loss of status, structure, and identity. This is why so many people become depressed when forced into retirement.

### Redefine retirement

*Your next life phase may consist of a portfolio of income-producing activity, volunteer work, and the pursuit of personal passions. Few people really "retire" these days.*

*Start thinking about the next phase in your mid-40s so that you control work exit decisions.*

## Affirm retirement

When people fear retirement, they usually are focusing on the idea of retiring from something, rather than on moving on to the next phase in their lives. The truth is, we are constantly "retiring" throughout our lives and our careers each time we close one chapter and move on to another. Retirement itself is really no different. Rather than seeing it as a kind of death, we should look at it as an affirmation of life. Rather than focusing on what we no longer have and feeling deprived, we should focus on what we do have and celebrate our belief in the future.

## Plan your exit

I have seen legions of older workers devastated by corporate downsizing programs because they did not have plans, a fallback position, or a sense of self independent of their employer. Start thinking about the next phase in your mid-40s so that you control work exit decisions.

Consider putting together a portfolio of activities, consisting of paid work; unpaid work as a volunteer; personal and leisure interests. Your portfolio might consist of, for example, travel, directorships in for-profit or nonprofit organizations, mentoring, and teaching a college course. For more, *see* Working your portfolio, *page 128*.

This phase of life represents a major psychological change, with an impact on many aspects of your life—not least your relationship with your spouse or partner. You may be changing what is important to you, but it may not be realistic to expect your partner to be changing in exactly the same way. Your partner's identity may still be tied to work, for example, while yours has expanded—you want to play, to test yourself in new ways, to make a contribution. Then again, you both may be ready to begin phasing down, but discover than you have very different ideas on what that might involve—you want to raise sheep in the country, your partner wants to get a loft downtown.

Sometimes people hold back from discussing with their partner what they really want to do, fearing disapproval. A counselor can help a couple to talk about what they are feeling and what their needs are.

# **Preparing** for change

Planning for the next phase means thinking about the arena where you want to contribute, how you want to live, and where you want to live.

- **Initiate a dialogue with your spouse/partner.**
  "My husband and I have never really spent any unstructured time together in the past 20 years, except on vacation," one woman told me. "We have never developed a way of being together without external time constraints. We're going to have this blank canvas. How are we going to fill it?" The rhythm of this phase is fundamentally different—different kinds of responsibilities, different expectations, and often less structure to the day. This often requires renegotiating your relationship and inventing new ways of being together.

- **Rethink what is rewarding.**
  Allow yourself to think about activities that have no reward other than the pleasure they give you. Do not be tied down by your old ideas about being productive. Develop a new way of evaluating activities.

- **Explore your freedom.**
  At this point in their life, people usually feel good about themselves. They know who they are and no longer feel a need to try to please others, whether it is being responsible for kids, helping elderly parents, or "doing the right thing at work." There is no further need to worry about making a mistake or being disapproved of. This provides a great opportunity to test yourself in new ways, whether it is developing artistic talents or testing your physical limits.

- **Look at unfinished business.**
  Review where you have been, where you are now, where you would like to go, what is still missing in your life. Are there some pieces of yourself you have left behind that you would like to retrieve? Lives and careers do tend to come full circle. As we finish our careers, we tend to move into areas that reaffirm and reintegrate early impulses.

- **Rehearse now.**
  People who make the most successful transition to retirement are those who first try out new roles in advance to see how well they fit, and whether they are meaningful and energizing – volunteering, doing small consulting assignments, teaching part-time, taking up new artistic pursuits, and so on. In the process they begin to let go of notions of external rewards for their activities and find satisfaction from being engaged in the world and being themselves.

- **Think about the consequences of not moving on.**
  How will you feel if you continue working the way you always have? What opportunities will you be giving up?

## **Career** counsel

Start thinking about your transition well in advance. Identify areas where you may be able to use your skills and knowledge in part-time and contract work.

Do research. Talk to people who have successfully phased down. Find out how they did it. Inquire about organizations that employ semi-retired people, and the nature of their employment relationships.

Raise your profile in areas that interest you—for example, by taking on assignments, speaking at conferences, and writing articles. Keep your skills up to date and maintain your network of contacts to increase your options.

# Achieving work–life balance

Are you allowing important relationships to suffer because of excessive work commitments? Do you wish you had more time for family and friends? Do you feel your work is causing you to make significant personal sacrifices? There are many strategies that will enable you to design a life more in sync with your needs.

## This chapter shows you how to:

**Recognize** today's cult of busyness for what it really is—a destroyer of work–life balance.

**Play** all the roles that are important to you, instead of sacrificing your life for your work.

**Calm** your frantic, soul-destroying schedule by using the seven steps of "strategic laziness."

**Push** back, asserting your career rights and refusing to be a victim of over-demanding employers.

*Face the conflicts. They are what make us human, and what make us grow.*

### Satisfying your needs
*Today's new workers do not see work–life balance as a privilege but as a right. They insist on time for family and friends, their community, and personal pursuits.*

# Feeling the work–life squeeze

If you are feeling the work–life squeeze, you are not alone. Creative people learn to focus on what is most important to them and refuse to live in a gray zone where all of their important needs are compromised.

Throughout this book, I have used the term "work–life balance." This metaphor can be misleading, however, as it conjures up a gigantic mechanical scale on which you put all the pieces of your life and weigh them up, adding bits here and taking away bits there until they come out in perfect balance.

Our lives, however, are dynamic, not static. Children are born, loved ones get sick, we land a new job, or lose one… At different points in our lives, different priorities compete for our attention, and we focus on whatever is most important to us at that moment. You may be doing a piece of work that completely enthralls you or preparing for the birth of your first child.

### Competing desires
No matter how hard you strive to achieve balance, there inevitably will be tensions between competing desires. Whatever your main focus is, it will by definition take away time from other important things.

If you try to have it all, you will end up living in a gray zone—a bland compromise with none of your needs being met. Instead of compromising, face up to the conflicts. They are not necessarily bad—they are what make us human, and what make us grow.

Rather than searching for some mythical perfect balance, then, the real questions should be: Do you feel good about how you are spending your waking life? Are you able to play out all the roles that are important to you? If you are making sacrifices now, are you making them as part of a plan that will help you realize your vision of how you want to live and work?

It is difficult for most people at any given point in their life to have every need satisfied—great job, meaningful time for family, involvement in the community, time for physical, spiritual, and artistic pursuits. So at any given time our work and life will not be in perfect quantitative balance. Our lives are made up of many chapters. Focus on your priorities for this life chapter, whether it be work achievements or time for family. Qualitatively, as we move through the different chapters of our lives, our needs are met. Giving up something now does not mean you are giving it up forever.

## Challenge the cult of busyness

The most significant threat to work–life balance today is what I call the cult of busyness. Organizations demand improved productivity and competitiveness to please demanding shareholders and other stake-holders. And employees, uncertain about their job security, are forced to scramble to comply.

But somewhere along the way, we have become addicted to this relentless, hyper-metabolic pace of work. Even when we seem to be complaining about the pressure we are under, we are actually making a kind of boast: "I'm so busy, I must be important." We wear our busyness like a badge of honor.

Whether people embrace or resent busyness, however, they rarely stop to question it. If you ask people why they are working so hard, you find that most of them have not given it any thought. It is simply the way things are. Busyness has become a fact of nature, like the weather, or gravity.

Unlike the weather, you can do something about your busyness. Applying the principles of what I call "strategic laziness" and "pushing back" will enable you to enhance your work–life balance.

## Career counsel

Focus on what you are affirming in your choices, rather than what are you are giving up. In thinking about work–life balance, people describe making trade-offs—for example, "I'm going to work fewer hours and trade off my career to spend more time with my kids." The language of trade-offs, though, emphasizes the negative rather than the positive—what you are losing rather than what you are liberating. Instead of talking about making trade-offs, think "trade-ons."

# Becoming strategically lazy

Taking time for yourself is not a luxury but a necessity. It is not about being idle or taking credit for work you have not done. Make careful and conscious choices about how you use your time, rather than allowing yourself to be swept along in a mad, rushing torrent of busyness.

## Is your life in balance?

Most managers and professionals experience a conflict between their professional and personal desires. Take the quiz to see where you fall.

- Do you feel your life is out of control?
- Are commitments to family, friends, and other things you care about suffering due to work commitments?
- Do you feel guilty when you take time for yourself?
- Do you automatically respond to every work demand without thinking about its impact on other areas of your life?
- Is your employer getting the best of you, and everyone else the dregs?
- Do you feel you are doing everything in a half-baked way, and nothing to your satisfaction?
- Do the people you care about complain that you are never available for them, or make jokes that you "do not have a life"?

## Be thoughtful

When my friend Jane, a vice-president of human resources, developed multiple sclerosis, she said, "It made me realize how much we think what is necessary is actually discretionary. Understanding the impact of stress on my symptoms meant I had to think purposefully about every commitment—why I should be doing it, and what the consequences would be of not doing it." Many people today say they are working so hard because they have no choice. I ask them, "What would happen if you said you could not attend that Saturday-morning meeting or if you

**Fulfill life commitments**

*Belonging to the cult of busyness interferes with our ability to play out any of our important life roles, to the detriment of everyone.*

left the office today by five o'clock?" Typically, they have not thought about it. When they do, they realize that there really are no significant consequences. The company stays in business, the team meets its objectives, the work gets done.

## Know what is really important to you

Filter any demand through a template of what is important. Ask, "Do I want to do this? How will it cost me and the people I care about? How will I benefit? What are the consequences of not doing this?"

## Do not worry about being "selfish"

When I ask people in workshops why they do not take time for them- selves, many say that would be "selfish." Would you rather be selfish or burned out? Who are you helping by working to the brink of physical and mental collapse? Taking time for yourself is not selfish; it is a matter of personal survival.

Use the following additional strategies to protect your time. They will protect not only your time but also your sanity.

- **Distinguish between what is possible and what is desirable.**
  Some years ago I declined a lucrative speaking engagement a year down the road without even looking at my calendar. The engagement would have required talking about a subject that did not particularly interest me in a location that required two airplane changes. The meeting planner said, "I'm impressed that you know your calendar by heart for such a long period of time. Are you really busy?" "No, I just don't want to do it," was my response. Just because something is financially rewarding or professionally prestigious does not mean you have to do it. Turning down one opportunity often liberates another—even if it is just an opportunity to feel good about yourself.

*Taking time for yourself is not selfish; it is a matter of personal survival.*

# Career counsel

Identify one thing you can do that is important to you and gives you a sense of personal satisfaction—for example, working out three times a week; playing the piano; having dinner with your kids. Then complete the following statements:

- I will practice strategic laziness by…
- To do this I will need to…

## Assessing yourself

**Achieving work–life balance**

▶ What will you change?
*page 285*

- **Think before you say yes.**
  Saying yes to one thing usually means saying no to another, or at the very least delaying it. Every time you say yes, you make a choice. Consider what you may be saying no to.

- **Be sensitive to the feelings of others.**
  Being strategically lazy does not mean pursuing personal fulfillment at everyone else's expense. For example, if a boss who has been good to you asks you to do something you do not want to do, evaluate the request in terms of the cost to her if you do not do it.

- **Live in real time.**
  John, a highly accomplished mid-career professional, told me he was taking a job he did not really want, because it would look good on his résumé. I thought, "How sad. Here is someone who has nothing left to prove who is still pursuing challenges for no other reason than that it looks good." Many people evaluate taking a job or an assignment in terms of its prestige, its résumé-building potential, or what it will eventually lead to. You have to ask yourself, "At what point do I start to live in real time? When can I feel good about what I am doing now rather than what it will lead to in the long run?" Obviously there are times when we have to do things for financial reasons or to prove ourselves in a particular field. Saying no to well-paid or prestigious work in favor of time for self is obviously a luxury, but it is one that, on careful consideration, you may find you are able to afford.

- **Fire fair-weather friends.**
  Most of us have at least one person in our lives whose relationship with us consists of never-ending demands for help with career, family, romantic, or decorating

crises. When the crisis is over, you never hear from them again—until the next emergency. At any given time, most relationships are uneven—one person is more in need of support than another. A real friendship is mutually satisfying over the long haul. You do not need these soul-destroying, time-sapping "friends."

- **Pay yourself first—in terms of time.**
  Build in opportunities for something that has no reward other than personal pleasure. Evaluate all other commitments in terms of how they will affect personal time. "Why is it," asks a friend, a gifted career and life counselor, "that we have made personal greed a virtue, but we think laziness is evil?" Why, indeed?

*Every time you say yes, you make a choice. Consider what you may be saying no to.*

### SELF-ASSESSMENT **What** will you change?

Just because something is possible, or you have always done it, does not mean it is desirable. Identify the things you are doing now that are not adding value to your life. What will you do instead?

*I will stop:*

..................................................................................................................

..................................................................................................................

..................................................................................................................

*If you were to continue doing it, who benefits?*

..................................................................................................................

*I will start:*

..................................................................................................................

..................................................................................................................

..................................................................................................................

*"It's not like you decide, 'Today I want to be an idiot and work myself to death.'"*

# Pushing back

Corporate work–life policies are one thing. Whether they are acted out is another. Refuse unreasonable demands. Assert your right to have a life outside work.

Many organizations today support work–life balance, at least in theory. Despite their great-sounding policies, however, few of them actually have what I like to call "life-friendly" environments. (I use this term rather than "family-friendly." Not everyone has a family, but everyone has a life.)

Often people are afraid to take advantage of options like flexible work arrangements for fear that their careers will suffer. To achieve work–life balance, you need to push back.

It is not easy. As one woman, a manager of marketing, commented ruefully after three straight weeks of nonstop work, "It's not like you wake up one morning and decide, 'Today I want to be an idiot and work myself to death,' but the sheer volume of work carries you along."

### Key strategies for pushing back

Take control of your working life. Think about how you can apply the following ideas.

- **Communicate.**
  Just because you once told your employer about your need for work–life balance does not mean it will be front-and-center in his mind. Be clear about what is acceptable and not acceptable. Too many people assume it is their boss's responsibility to "get it."

- **Be reasonable.**
  Paying attention to personal needs does not mean having a knee-jerk reaction to any infringement on your personal life. The important thing is knowing what trade-offs you are willing to make and why you are

**Do not be a victim**
*You have choices. You do not have to fall victim to unreasonable work demands, such as working excessively late hours. Push back. Just say no.*

making them. There are times when it is necessary to rise to the occasion—for example, to meet an important deadline. If your boss puts you on a steady diet of important deadlines, however, then you need to have a conversation about how work is planned and delegated.

● **Train your employer.**
Does your boss call you at home or on your cell phone at all hours, or expect you to work late as a matter of routine? You probably helped create your boss's expectations by making yourself so available. Now you have to retrain your boss in a new set of expectations.

● **Find a good manager.**
Some managers will go to bat for their people. Others, either too mired in their own workload or lacking sensitivity, will not. One of the most common things I hear from people who have created flexibility in their work life is that they sought out a supportive manager.

● **Be a role model.**
Whether they are managers or not, everyone has a role to play in changing organizational culture. If you are a manager, recognize the complicated and overcommitted lives of your staff. Protect their commitments outside work by designing work accordingly. Push back with your fellow bosses for more resources and reasonable timelines.

● **Do not overestimate your own importance.**
Avoid the hubris of assuming that the whole organization will collapse if you do not respond to every request made of you. Do not let yourself get swept up in the adrenaline rush associated with ever-escalating work demands, or the validation of self-worth through sheer busyness. Be vigilant.

## Career counsel

So you miss the meeting—does the company fall apart? So you miss the soccer game—does your kid look sad? Parents, change your behavior:

● Be strategic about business travel. How important is the value of a face-to-face interaction? Would a telephone call or video conference suffice? When you travel, is it feasible to take your children with you?

● Involve your children in domestic tasks. It is good for them, and good for you.

● Have a standing "date" with your children to do something special—a movie, a meal out, some other excursion.

*Ask yourself, "Am I doing this because I really need to or just because it is there? How important is this work?"*

## Strategies to restore balance

As you read through these quick tips, select two you can act on right now. When will you do it? How will you do it? Make a commitment to follow through.

▶ Set realistic targets. One reason for our chronic busyness is that we overschedule ourselves. Our expectations for ourselves are out of line with what we can reasonably expect to get done. There is always more to be done than you have time to do. Even when you organize yourself with complete efficiency, additional and unforeseen demands on your time will threaten to throw you off schedule. Think back to yesterday, for example. How much time did you spend on unplanned activities?

▶ Set priorities. It is absolutely impossible to do everything very well. Learn to set priorities, focus on what is most important, and allocate your time commitments accordingly.

▶ Differentiate between the urgent and the important. Your boss may say it is urgent, but it may not be the most important thing you need to do it terms of its real value. Be dispassionate. Do not get sucked into the vortex of other people's busyness. Step back, examine your own priorities, and stick to them.

▶ Evaluate every time commitment. Ask yourself, "Am I doing this because I really need to or just because it is there? How important is this work? By spending time here, what time am I sacrificing by not doing something else equally or perhaps more important?"

▶ Know your limitations. Being busy is not an end in itself. Work strategically. If you are working excessively long hours over an extended period of time, are you still productive? Are you making good decisions? Are you creative? What is the effect of giving up sleep on your long-term well-being and effectiveness in all the important roles of your life?

▶ Refresh yourself on weekends. Turn off the cell phone. Go where you cannot be reached. Make at least one day of the weekend—and preferably two—sacred. If the new work realities mean that you must sometimes work odd hours seven days a week, learn to pace yourself. Take Wednesday off, or two half-days, if that is when the workload lets up.

▶ Make time for personal priorities. See if you can free up more time for personal pursuits by delegating less important tasks to others or not doing them at all. For example, at home, could your partner or children cook more, or could you buy more prepared foods? Involve your children in domestic tasks. It is good for them, and good for you. Some parents do this using a reward approach. They draw up a list of tasks on a chart and record their

## **Strategies** to restore balance cont'd

children's performance. For example, clearing the table after dinner might equal extra allowance. Try combining desirable activities. For example, if you want to spend more time with your children and make a greater contribution to your community, consider volunteering to coach one of their sports teams.

▶ Reduce commute time. Consider working at home or at a nearby customer's office one day a week.

▶ Set aside one night a week for an activity that is important to you. This could be getting together with friends, going to dinner with your partner, or attending a course. Of course, once you have set aside that time, you will have to guard it jealously.

▶ Reevaluate your financial situation. Do you need to earn as much money as you are making now? Could you simplify your life in some way? By working toward greater financial independence now, you broaden your career and life options in the future. You will know that you are working long hours because you want to, not just to support your financial needs. A financial planner can help you set long-term financial goals and figure out what you need to do to achieve them.

▶ De-clutter. If you have not used it for a year, you probably do not need it. Stuff makes demands on our time. You have to sort it, dust it, push it aside, maintain it. It is much easier to find a shirt when you are not poking through a closet that contains 30 others you have not worn in years.

▶ Consider a reduced workweek. Many people discover, after rethinking their financial needs, that it makes sense to trade extra dollars for extra time— one of the most powerful strategies for renewing work–life balance. (*See* Working part-time, *page 116,* for more.)

▶ Avoid the guilt trip. You do not get brownie points for feeling guilty. Know what choices you are making and then stick by them.

▶ You cannot really have it all. It is very difficult for most people at any given point in life to have every need satisfied—great job, meaningful time for family, involvement in the community, time for physical, spiritual, and artistic pursuits. Decide what you really need right now. Just because you are giving something up now does not mean you are giving it up forever.

## **Career** counsel

If you want to keep your life in balance, you need to be assertive about your life, and that means being prepared to say no.

● No to excessive overtime, missed vacation days, and bosses who expect you to show up for Saturday breakfast meetings.

● No to 70-hour workweeks, working on the weekend, behaving as if your work is more important than the well-being of your family or other people important in your life.

● No to assuming quality time is more important than quantity time. Your friends or kids or partner cannot make the distinction. They just know they want to spend time with you.

● No to feeling like you are uncommitted or lazy because you are only prepared to give your job 45 high-octane hours.

● No to trying to please everyone. It is not possible, so kill the guilt. Feel good about what you can do.

# 5 Boost your career intelligence

# Becoming a career activist

Craft a work life that is meaningful and supportive of your important values. Be your authentic self. Expect your work to stretch you and still allow time for a personal life. Test your activist quotient to see if you are managing your career with intelligence.

## This chapter shows you how to:

**Become** a career activist, shaping your work to fit who you are – not the other way around.

**Set** aside debilitating career passivity and take creative, active control of your career.

**Think** like an independent agent instead of defining yourself by your work or others' expectations.

**Test** your career–activist quotient and identify what you need to do differently to increase your career smarts.

## Career counsel

Most people assume extroverts are more likely than introverts to be successful in today's work world. After all, so much work now is done in teams, and people have to network and market themselves to let others know what they are capable of.

However, today you are more likely to engage in marketing yourself in non-extroverted ways—for example, by sending a quick email talking about a recently completed project, or reminding someone of your existence by sending a link to an article of interest.

The new work world is elastic. Some work favors extroverts, other work favors introverts. Your challenge is to find or design work that plays to your traits and strengths.

# Your work, your self

You have a right to expect your work to be an intimate expression of your needs, values, and talents. Be prepared to make the tough decisions. Refuse to deny important aspects of yourself.

*Linda, 31, has made a value proposition to a company. "On paper, it doesn't look like I have the experience, but I know I have the skills you need. I'll work on an intern's salary for four weeks, and then you decide if you want to hire me."*

*David, an entry-level professional, has not gotten around to getting a business card. "I look for people doing interesting work in the company, and then I sell my skills to them."*

*Susan, a 35-year-old single mother, has decided to trade in the security of her government job to pursue her dream of becoming an entertainer. "I've saved some money and put together a business plan. We'll live on very little. It may be risky, but I don't want to wake up one day ten years from now wondering what would have happened if . . . "*

## Be who you are

All of these people are demonstrating what I call career activism, one of the fundamental principles underlying this book. Being a career activist in turn is based on this book's other foundational principle: *Be who you are*. Have a vision of yourself as worthy of meaningful work and a fulfilling personal life. Understand that your work is an intimate expression of your needs, values, and talents. Refuse to hang up your personality at the door of your employer. Be prepared to take the tough decisions so that you do not deny important aspects of yourself in your work.

Indeed, if I had to condense into one the most common issues I hear from people regarding work, it would be this: How can I express my authentic self in my work? How can I find or do what is right for me, that is true to my individual uniqueness?

## The only certainty is you

Being a career activist means thinking about the landscape of work and opportunities in a radically different way. It means being prepared to live in an uncertain work world where the only certainty is you: your skills, your flexibility, your capacity to adapt to change. This requires optimism and a belief in yourself. Career activism means:

- Thinking in creative and novel ways about the workscape. This requires a refusal to accept received wisdom about how you should manage your career and what you should want to achieve in your career.
- Looking at all life domains—personal, educational, work— as providing opportunities for expression and satisfaction. One domain is not necessarily better than another.
- Becoming an independent agent—defining yourself in terms and concepts that are separate from your job title, your organization, or what other people think you should be.
- Writing your own script rather than waiting for someone to write it for you.
- Seeing yourself as being in an egalitarian relationship with your employer or client. You have in-demand skills and choices. You are choosing to rent your skills to your employer not only in exchange for revenue but also to meet other personal needs. If those needs are not met, you will vote with your feet and find another employer/client.
- Seeing yourself as worthy of being protected and ensuring that no work environment abuses your right to feel good about yourself.
- Acting as your own talent agent. Being vigilant on your own behalf—identifying and preparing for opportunities rather than expecting anyone else to guide you along or promote your interests.
- Being entrepreneurial—looking for opportunities and taking risks.
- Doing work that is true to your individual nature, supports your most important values, and your life commitments.

**Be your own agent**
*Career activists act as their own talent agents. They seek out roles in which they can shine. They advocate to make sure that their needs are met.*

*Becoming a career activist is the key to your future success.*

## Beware of career passivity

One of the best ways to understand career activism is to look at the contrasting—and much more widespread—phenomenon of career passivity, the failure to look out for your interests and control your destiny.

Most of us take an activist stance in our health, personal finances, and children's education. We do not believe other people or institutions can look after our best interests. In these domains, we act at the first sign of a problem. But work—which plays such a critical role in determining how we feel about ourselves and in our effectiveness as family members and members of society—has become the last arena for such personal activism. It is as if we do not see ourselves as worthy of protection.

Are you passive in your approach to career management? Do you recognize yourself here?

- You feel unhappy in your work but are unwilling or unable to do anything about it.
- You complain about being overworked and under-appreciated, of not spending enough time with your partner or children, of not having a life at all, but you make no attempt to change anything.
- You justify staying in a bad situation by saying such things as, "Better the devil you know than the one you don't," "I'm just waiting for the package," or "Maybe when X retires next year, things will change."
- You feel completely helpless and resigned to your fate. You say, "There's no point in trying to make a move. It's the same everywhere."

**Set high expectations**
*Avoid passivity. Expect your work to play to your strengths and motivational preferences. Be ready to move on when it does not.*

Some people do make career moves but base them solely on making more money, not on what kind of life they want to lead or whether their work will meet their personal values. They say, in effect, "If I'm going to have to go to the wall for my work, I might as well get a whack of money." This is really just another form of career passivity. It is, unfortunately, a very common form.

It is a paradox that many people who see themselves as independent, take-charge types demonstrate helplessness in how they spend their working lives. They act as if their work is an implacable force of nature, like the weather: something they are powerless to change. Perhaps we are too tired, too busy, too distracted, and under too much pressure to look after ourselves. Typically, however, we are ill-prepared to think like career activists and to recognize that we do have control over our working lives if only we choose to exercise it.

## The key to career success

As one woman observed, "I wouldn't allow myself to be abused in a relationship, so why would I put up with being abused in a job?" When you are doing work you are not well suited for, or that does not make you feel good about yourself, it starts to feel like abuse.

Career activism means becoming an intelligent actor in your own life. Become vigilant on your own behalf by routinely scanning your environment to ensure that your work continues to meet your needs. Ask yourself:

- Am I engaged? Am I feeling stretched in a positive way?
- Am I contributing to my employability?
- Do I feel I am doing work that is important?
- Are my personal needs outside of work being met?

Becoming an activist is the key to your future career success. The only security you can depend on is knowing that your own skills are strong, current, and marketable, and that you have the inner resources to manage through the ups and downs of life. To be a successful career activist, you need to understand the external economic and social landscape, educating yourself about changing work realities and knowing what you need to do to ensure your marketability. But you also need to be attuned to your own internal, personal world. What do you care about? What gives your life meaning? Only then can you think about yourself and your career differently. You can rise above the frenetic pace of working life to make choices in terms of your own agenda.

# Career counsel

To be a successful career activist you must behave more like a guerrilla fighter than like a regular soldier. Career activists are:

- Informed, vigilant, and flexible
- Passionate and engaged
- Unconventional thinkers with no preconceived concepts
- Opportunistic—always on the lookout for windows of opportunity
- Mobile, fast, and fluid.

**Assessing yourself**

**Becoming a career activist**

▶ Are you a career activist?
*pages 296–297*

**SELF-ASSESSMENT**    **Are you** a career activist?

Take this quiz to determine your activist quotient. Which of these statements are true of you?

| | Yes | No |
|---|---|---|
| I routinely ask myself if I am happy, involved, and learning. | ☐ | ☐ |
| I know how to leverage my skills to get better assignments. | ☐ | ☐ |
| I am aware of the sacrifices I have made, and made them based on a thoughtful analysis of pros and cons. | ☐ | ☐ |
| People think of me as someone who is passionate and engaged in my work. | ☐ | ☐ |
| I am aware of my strengths and the environment in which I am most effective. | ☐ | ☐ |
| I have learned something new in the past six months. | ☐ | ☐ |
| I define myself by my skills, not by my job title. | ☐ | ☐ |
| I am aware of what I am going to be learning over the next six months. | ☐ | ☐ |
| When I am unhappy with my work, I do something about it. | ☐ | ☐ |
| I am prepared to be seen as pushy if that is the only way I can have my work needs recognized. | ☐ | ☐ |
| I would not take on a project I am not interested in simply because my boss expects me to. | ☐ | ☐ |
| If a business acquaintance cancels a meeting three times, I will not rearrange it. | ☐ | ☐ |
| I am prepared to lose clients if the only way I can keep them is by doing work that compromises my professional standards. | ☐ | ☐ |
| Just because someone is a client or my boss does not mean he can treat me in a way that compromises my dignity. | ☐ | ☐ |
| I am prepared to vote with my feet if my needs for balancing my work and my personal life are not met. | ☐ | ☐ |

I am prepared to turn down a lucrative assignment if the work would be painful for me to carry out (unless I need it to pay the bills). ☐ ☐

I have searched out a select group of people as mentors and friends to provide me with professional and emotional support. ☐ ☐

I feel stretched in my work. ☐ ☐

I am prepared to do work I do not like if it increases my longer-term options. ☐ ☐

If my boss scheduled a last-minute after-work meeting that conflicted with a personal commitment, I would try to get her to change the meeting. If the boss did not, I would not go. ☐ ☐

I will not put up with being pushed around. ☐ ☐

If I am not learning or I am unhappy in my work, I will actively seek out alternative opportunities. ☐ ☐

*Become vigilant on your own behalf by routinely scanning your environment to ensure that your work continues to meet your needs.*

## Scoring

Give yourself one point for every yes answer. The higher your score, the more of a career activist you are.

### 19 or more
You are the epitome of a career activist. If you scored 100 per cent, however, you may want to lighten up. Other people may perceive you as being overly aggressive in managing your career. Balance your needs against the rights of others. There is more to life than your career.

### 10 to 18
You have developed some effective coping strategies but could significantly increase control of your work life by identifying challenging situations and developing a more activist approach to them.

### Less than 10
Do not be surprised if people treat you like a doormat. Use this quiz to identify the situations that are most problematic for you and formulate some realistic strategies to raise your activist quotient and increase your work and life satisfaction.

# Strategies for career success

You are it. Your skills and knowledge are in demand. You have the ability to think about yourself and your work in new and creative ways. Starting now, and in the years to come, use the 12 strategies for career success to take advantage of today's new employment realities.

## This chapter shows you how to:

**Apply** the 12 new strategies for career and life success and profit from the new work order.

**Redefine** what you do, understanding yourself not by your title but by what you do.

**Derive** your security from your skills so you are not vulnerable to the ups and downs of the economy.

**Prepare** yourself so that you are always ready for the next career move or career stage.

**Manage** your own life and career, moving smoothly between work, education, and personal pursuits.

**Develop** an action plan for constantly improving your career intelligence.

# Thriving in Tempworld

Welcome to Tempworld—a constantly shifting world with no guaranteed employment and no external protection. You are your own protector. Your skills and activist focus are the tools that will ensure that you thrive.

I like to describe the contemporary workscape as Tempworld, a world where you can make no assumptions of guaranteed work, where you will be moving in and out of different life arenas (education, revenue generation, time for family, sabbaticals, volunteering, contributions to the community), a world where you work with the activist mind-set of being in charge of your career. In this new workscape:

- Your work will shift rapidly—not only where you do it, but also how you do it, and with whom and for whom.
- You will have many competing pressures on you for your time and energy.
- You may have a so-called full-time job, but equally likely you may be working on a series of short-term contracts, on projects, or for yourself.
- You may be sitting at a desk in your own office or cubicle having regular meetings with colleagues and clients, or working at your home or country retreat interacting electronically with people you rarely meet face to face.
- You may be working with people who talk the same professional language you do, or on interdisciplinary project teams with people who have little or no understanding of your professional discipline.
- You may be working flat out, 24/7, or you may be taking a career break to contemplate your next career chapter.

No matter how you are working, following the Strategies for career success will ensure you succeed in today's workplace. Do you have what it takes to thrive? Evaluate yourself on these 12 key dimensions as you go along.

**Alone but connected**

*Even if you are working by yourself, you are only a click away from colleagues. Create your own community by staying connected.*

## Strategy 1: Think building blocks

▶ *Can you clearly and persuasively describe three to five key skills that contribute most to your employability?* ▶ *Can you articulate two talents or areas in which you excel?* ▶ *Can you describe your key strengths as others see them?* ▶ *Do you know your three underlying career themes?*

Like a child's building blocks, your skills, talents, and key strengths are components that you can assemble in new configurations as you move through your career.

We have all heard that in the future we will hold five to seven careers. Many people find this alarming. They think it means they are without substance, with no enduring value, programmed to self-destruct every few years. They fear they will be required to reinvent themselves constantly—today a banker, tomorrow a makeup artist. Actually, most people will not be embarking on new careers (architect becomes farmer) so much as reconfiguring existing skills and experience (architect/hobby farmer starts business designing and building greenhouses).

Revisit your self-assessment regularly to ensure that you are continuing to catalog talents acquired in new work and life experiences. (*See* Know yourself, *pages 26–55.*) Remind yourself of your unique talents, the special skills in your repertoire, and the skills you have added to your portfolio.

### Create a fallback position

Have you put all your eggs in one basket at work, or have you kept multiple options open? Could you readily change career directions if required? If you lost your main source of income tomorrow, could you successfully move onto another course?

It is critical today to have multiple options, multiple avenues, and multiple roles. This means that you can equally see yourself selling your skills as a contract worker, a freelance consultant, or a small-business owner. Develop a new mind-set. Redefine the way you work and your relationship to potential purchasers of your skills, to ensure your future employability.

**Reconfigure your skills**
*You will constantly reconfigure your skills in response to changing work demands. This will ensure your ongoing employability and engagement.*

**Stay on the edge**
*Continue your education to get the leading-edge skills you need. Intellectual stimulation is a powerful antidote to boredom and plateauing.*

## Strategy 2: Ensure your employability

▶ *If your current work assignment ended tomorrow, how quickly could you find a new one?* ▶ *Are your skills up to standards set by the external community and profession, or are you evaluating yourself against internal corporate standards?* ▶ *Are you confident that your skills and knowledge are sufficiently current that you could sell your services to another employer or client?* ▶ *Do you mine your work for opportunities to strengthen and enhance your marketability?*

I often meet people who have been good performers in their own organizations and who discover that they are not mobile. Because they have become so closely identified with a particular company or industry, their skills are not perceived as being readily transferable to other settings. Beware if you find yourself using words or jargon comprehensible only to the people in your organization. Measure yourself against community as well as internal standards. Your professional association and network can assist you.

The most important imperative in protecting yourself now and in the future is ensuring that you have choices. Do not be held back by a lack of skill portability ("I've been working for this department/company so long, I'll never be able to get another job") or fear of change.

We have always been responsible for developing skills needed to get ahead and for keeping our skills up to date. However, this used to be a shared responsibility between the individual and the organization: you would identify your needs, and the organization would provide the necessary tools, training, and developmental experiences. In our hit-the-ground-running culture, current expectations are that you will do whatever is necessary on your own time to ensure the currency of your skills.

### Continuing your education

"Should I get an MBA? Should I get more credentials?" In this era of lifelong learning, many people will consider this option. Many employed by client organizations, particularly those in knowledge-based industries,

# Keep on learning

With constantly changing work and shifting skill requirements, "lifelong learning" will be more than a catchphrase. It will be a necessity.

▶ Seek lifelong learning opportunities that play to your strengths. Become even better at what you do well.

▶ Stay current in your field. Develop skills and knowledge outside it.

▶ Associate with talented people. Understudy them. Seek them out as mentors.

▶ Benefit from your on-the-job experience.

▶ Seek opportunities for learning, both inside and outside your workplace.

▶ Take courses, read books and journals, develop and practice new skills.

▶ Look at periods of full-time education between periods of work not as diversions but as savvy career moves ensuring your future employability.

▶ Volunteer. Develop new skills by taking on roles outside your everyday work routines.

▶ Judge your progress not by your job title or level but by the depth of content of your work; its importance to the organization and to customers; and whether you are still learning and having fun.

## Career counsel

You are protecting your employability and ensuring that you are on the path to career satisfaction if you can answer yes to the following questions:

● Are you feeling stretched in a positive way?
● Can you describe what you have learned in the past six months?
● Can you describe what you will learn in the next six months?
● Are you aware of the most recent trends in your field and their implications for your longer-term success?
● Do you know what skills and knowledge you need to develop that are critical to your future success and employability?
● Are you strategic in your learning, focusing on something you are good at rather than on your weaknesses?

such as pharmaceuticals, government, marketing, and information technology, are strongly biased toward hiring people with a graduate degree or postgraduate diploma. Although the possession of a graduate degree is not synonymous with high-level conceptual or problem-solving skills, they treat it as a shorthand measure of these attributes. That said, other organizations are more interested in experience and attitudinal or psychological attributes. Consider:

● Are you being held back by lack of education?
● Do most people who do work similar to yours possess greater educational credentials?
● Are you employed in or interested in working for a knowledge-based industry?

- Are you interested in enhancing your knowledge of or abilities in a particular area?
- Are you genuinely interested in your academic area of study or are you just doing it for the credentials? If the latter, look at alternative routes to the same goal. For example, is there another credential that will have the same symbolic meaning?

Consider the quality of your experience. If you have a proven track record, you will have less need of the degree or diploma as a shorthand symbol of what you know and are capable of.

Do not pursue education simply because you imagine it is a "hot" qualification or an area where you think jobs will be in the future. The perceived value of and demand for MBAs, for example, is cyclical. Some years they are prized, while a few years later, employers say, "These people are great with spreadsheets, but they lack creativity and depth."

**Be selective**

*Pursue education in areas that engage you at a deep intellectual level. Be strategic if you are upgrading your credentials purely for employment purposes.*

Do not pursue something just because you think the market wants you to. Keep in mind not only the utility of the credentials, but also your age. Some older people love going back to school. Others find it difficult.

As one woman commented, "I'm rushing home to make sure my teenager does his homework, while my classmates are making plans to hook up at a club."

Look at the opportunity costs—what you are giving up by *not* going back to school vs. what you are giving up in lost revenue and neglect of other responsibilities by going back to school. Take advantage of the many educational opportunities today designed to meet the needs of adult learners through internet delivery of content and programs designed around work/study.

## Strategy 3: Think roles, not jobs

▶ *When you think about your future, do you think about jobs or areas of competence? (e.g., accountant vs. financial advisor; hotel manager vs. leadership role in hospitality or tourism)* ▶ *Can you describe three broad areas of competence in which you can apply your skills?*

I am not a great fan of preparing for the future by trying to guess where the hot occupations will be. I call this the "Top 10" or "What's Hot, What's Not" approach to career planning. Today's hottest jobs can be rendered obsolete by many factors, including global events and changes in government legislation, the economy, and technology.

Instead of preparing yourself for specific jobs, identify the areas where you want to contribute, whether they are technical areas such as software design or market analysis, or nontechnical areas such as team-building, leading knowledge workers, or relationship-building.

### Look to the future
Your career choices should be based on what engages you and where your talents lie. However, you can leverage an understanding of demographic, economic, and cultural trends to make informed career decisions for the future.

Look at the world around you and you will see many trends, including:

- Growing concerns about a resource-depleted environment.
- The aging of youth-obsessed baby-boomers.
- Continued crises in healthcare.
- Increasing anxiety over safety and environmental security.
- Parents wanting to give their children a leg up.
- Resource-squeezed governments.
- An increasing number of people looking for high-impact leisure activities to counteract chronic stress.
- Widespread concern about ensuring future employability.
- Frustration over the great time-squeeze.

**Choose your roles**
*Identify roles you want to play, and areas in which you want to contribute. Do not prepare for jobs that can be rendered obsolete tomorrow.*

# Career counsel

What roles do you want to play? Consider, for example the roles of: team builder; manager; individual contributor; change agent; technical expert; relationship builder; trouble shooter; someone who makes things happen; consolidator; problem solver; conceptualizer; big picture thinker; marketer; decision-maker; talent spotter/nurturer; mentor; turnaround artist; mediator.

the following fields to be buoyant: medicine; biotechnology; human sciences; pharmaceuticals; esthetic services; security services; education/training/coaching; "edutainment"; graphics; communications; software development; recreation/ecotourism; and environmental sciences.

Consider, for example, how these trends might play out in the field of medicine. The healthcare system will continue to undergo restructuring to reduce costs while meeting demands imposed on it by an aging population. This will lead to a need for other health professionals such as nurses, occupational therapists, pharmacists, and radiologists.

Demand will increase for specialties such as physiotherapy and plastic surgery that will help keep baby-boomers active and youthful-looking. Entrepreneurs will benefit from shifts in healthcare delivery by exploiting markets for sophisticated diagnostic technology and high-tech equipment that will keep people out of expensive hospital beds. Scientists such as biologists and physicists will benefit from R&D into commercial applications of biotechnology and pharmaceuticals.

### Leverage trends
*Take advantage of an aging population to find growth opportunities in many fields, including healthcare, travel, and recreation, esthetic services, and lifestyle housing.*

## Strategy 4: Market! Market! Market!

▶ *Are people you work with aware of your accomplishments, skills, and work experiences?* ▶ *Do you feel comfortable marketing yourself?* ▶ *Do you stay in touch with people to remind them of your skills and how you can add value?* ▶ *Are you keeping your network alive?* ▶ *Do you cultivate relationships with people outside your profession, employer, or industry?* ▶ *Do you feel comfortable networking, or do you see that as insincere?*

Today's workplace demands that you perform at a high level now while at the same time always marketing for the future—keeping one eye on the next work assignment and positioning yourself for it. This means being able to sell yourself.

### Overcome self-marketing malaise

"If I'm really good, why should I have to sell myself, constantly trumpeting my accomplishments? They should speak for themselves."

If you identify with this quote, you are suffering from what I call "self-marketing malaise," a discomfort with selling yourself. Instead of thinking of marketing yourself as endlessly parading your list of credentials and accomplishments to the world at large, think of it as letting key people know about your skills and how they add value. Think of it as information, not boasting.

Also remember, just because you once told someone something about your skills does not mean they will remember. Overstretched people have short memories. Keep potential clients informed of your significant accomplishments and how they can be applied to their needs. Talk about your skills and credentials matter of factly.

### Develop broad networks

Networking is one of the most important career-management skills. It is not only a powerful marketing vehicle, keeping you in the mind-space of decision-makers, but it also provides you with resources for carrying out your work at a high level.

**Sell yourself**
*Think of marketing yourself as keeping people informed of your skills, abilities, and accomplishments. You are not bragging; you are giving people information.*

*Do not equate the number of business cards you have handed out with effective networking.*

Network broadly and participate in multiple networks to gain access to new and unusual ideas and information. This will enhance your reputation for breadth. At the practical level, this will ensure that in the event of a downturn in the economy or in your profession or industry, you will not find yourself exclusively "schmoozing" people who are facing the same downturn as you.

Be thoughtful in your networking strategy. Think of yourself as building knowledge networks of people with ideas you can hook into. Do not equate the number of business cards you have handed out or collected at a conference or networking event with effective networking.

Good networkers are "wired." Their networks are broad, ranging well beyond their own professional boundaries. They cultivate relationships with people who know how to get things done. They know the right people to approach for information, referrals, or plum work assignments.

### Overcome networking angst

"Some people seem so comfortable passing out their business cards, calling up acquaintances, meeting people for lunch. But to me all this networking seems a little forced. I know I am supposed to be constantly marketing my skills, but at what point is enough enough?"

I hear this comment frequently. These people are suffering from networking angst. They avoid networking because they worry that they will be seen as using people, or else think it means acting phony. Instead of thinking of networking as using people, think of it as gathering and sharing ideas—in other words, as a knowledge resource. Other people are sources of potential new clients, new ideas, new opportunities, and information and knowledge for new ways of thinking about a problem, as you are to them.

Do not think purely in instrumental terms, evaluating the usefulness of a network member in terms of their ability to "pay off" by delivering a job lead or client contact. Think of yourself as developing mutually supportive relationships with interesting people.

# Dos and don'ts of networking

Many people today are tired of people who read a career book about networking and then robotically go through a series of canned questions or rigid networking strategies. Here are some Dos and Don'ts of networking:

## Do

- Network broadly. Include people from different disciplines
- Make it easy for someone to say yes to a meeting. Ask if they prefer phone or face to face.
- Maintain connections by following up on your contacts. Keep them abreast of how your career is developing. Send a thank-you note.
- Learn what the other person values. Can you meet their needs?
- Be engaging. Make the interaction interesting for your networkee. You are a human being, not an information machine.
- Think of every social interaction as an opportunity to learn something new, whether it is about human behavior or a cultural trend.
- Maintain and cultivate relationships in good times and bad.
- Make yourself valuable. Become a knowledge resource to others. Share information and contacts generously.

## Don't

- Equate endless lunches with effective networking.
- Confuse the level of the person you are networking with their ability to be helpful.
- Confine yourself to people just like you.
- Evaluate your activities in short-term instrumental terms.
- Ask for a face-to-face meeting.
- Promise lunch as a treat ("Can I take you out for lunch and talk to you about ...") Most people today are too busy to be motivated by the promise of a free lunch.
- Start a conversation with the promise, "I was wondering if we can get together to discuss something mutually beneficial," unless the other person really will benefit.
- Be a fair-weather networker.

# Career counsel

Develop alternative strategies to enhance your profile if you are uncomfortable with face-to-face networking. Become known as an expert in your field by writing articles for trade magazines, speaking at professional events, setting up your own web page, or chairing a professional conference.

Send an information brief—an article or reference that may be of interest. In today's hyper-kinetic business environment, being able to give busy potential clients hard information that they can use may be much more desirable than just "schmoozing" them.

### Sense of self

*Your work is not the centerpiece of your identity. Being rejected or failing does not make you a bad person. Maintain an independent sense of self.*

## Strategy 5: Be resilient

▶ *Do you feel better about yourself when you are accomplishing important things and getting recognition, and worse about yourself during slow periods with low recognition?* ▶ *Do you define yourself solely in terms of your accomplishments?* ▶ *Can you deal with your failures, learn from them, and bounce back?* ▶ *Can you demonstrate high levels of energy, stamina, and commitment to get the job done?* ▶ *Can you "depersonalize" rejection and the failure of others to respond to you, or do you become immobilized?*

The contemporary workplace is tough in many ways with its Darwinian atmosphere. You must withstand disappointment, juggle stressful situations, and handle pressure with aplomb. You need the resilience to deal with failures as well as successes. Rather than being immobilized by failure, learn from your setbacks and use them to your advantage. Successful people reflect honestly on something that does not go well, but they do not beat themselves up for it, endlessly revisiting events.

"No one ever returns my phone calls." "I worked so hard on that proposal and was sure I had the job. They went with someone else." Emotional resilience means being able to park your ego. You call someone, they do not call you back, you think they do not like you or want to talk to you. You wonder, "Should I call them again? Will they think I am bugging them?"

Chances are, they will not think anything about you, good or bad. They have probably simply forgotten. Everyone's overburdened schedules have led to short memories, short fuses, and a general erosion of manners. There is a pretty good chance that the unreturned call, for example, is not a reflection on you but on the other person's time commitments. Do not take it personally. Persist.

Learn to deal with rejection. It is a fact of life in our intensely competitive marketplace. Employers, for example, may interview several people several times before deciding you are not the right one.

## Strategy 6: Stay culturally current

▶ *Are you aware of broad-based social and cultural trends?* ▶ *Do you regularly read magazines and newspapers and visit Internet sites outside your business/professional area?* ▶ *When you think of work and your future, do you think of it locally, nationally, or internationally?* ▶ *What are the geographical boundaries of your work?*

It is amazing, given the complex economic, cultural, and demographic environment in which we operate, how culturally parochial many senior business and professional people are. Larger cultural trends have a direct impact on our work context, and on determining how we understand our work and carry it out. Here are some ways to stay culturally current:

- Read widely outside your professional milieu, everything from book reviews to international business magazines to nonfiction in areas related to general social trends.
- Get involved in on-line discussion groups.
- Stay in tune with pop culture and be engaged by viewpoints from different economic sectors and demographic groups.
- Glean from these sources important trends that will affect how your work is carried out; new potential applications, sources of competition; and customs. Never before has public opinion played such an important role in day-to-day political and business decision-making.

In a borderless work world, where the entire world is a potential market, the ability to speak other languages and be comfortable with other cultures will also be crucial. People who have learned a second language at their grandparents' knees will be valued commodities.

## Go global

Globalization means an expansion of work opportunities. It makes you less reliant on the local economy. People who move to work in other geographical locations have always gained special skills in self-management as they are forced into greater self-reliance.

**Stay connected**

*Read broadly outside of your professional area. Think about and carry out your work in creative and unconventional ways by building on cultural and demographic trends.*

# Career counsel

Hard-driving, achievement-oriented Type A behavior used to be the model for success, and indeed the focus, commitment, stamina, and task-orientation of Type As may make them better able than their more relaxed Type B counterparts to sustain today's intense productivity pressures.

However, the thankless, transitory nature of work today can be hard on Type As whose identity is so closely tied to their achievements. Their Type B brothers and sisters are better equipped to manage the frustrations and disappointments because their self-worth is not based solely on their work.

The trick often is to act like Type As but think like Type Bs, to feel good about yourself, both when you are producing and when you are not.

## Taking time out

If you want to quit your job and take a year off to travel, study, or spend more time with your family, will it look bad on your résumé? There used to be rigid ideas about what looked good or bad on a résumé—and periods of non-gainful employment were considered bad. In the new work environment, we have very different concepts about employment patterns.

Historically, people would go to school, then maybe "take a year off" to travel, and then get down to the serious business of earning a living, all in more or less linear fashion and in an expected and predictable linear professional progression. The path today is less straightforward. As we have seen, people will be constantly moving back and forth between different life domains, whether travel, work, family, or recreation.

So it no longer makes sense to see taking a year off as having no value. The payoff is career rejuvenation and heightened cultural sensitivity. You also have clearly displayed to employers your capacity for risk-taking, managing ambiguity, and self-management.

Consider living internationally to enrich your life and deepen your professional expertise. As organizations move into new international markets, they will look for individuals who can adapt to other cultures while interfacing with local management. Cultural and linguistic versatility will be a tremendous asset. Multicultural exposure that enables you to move between headquarters and global markets will improve your marketability, whether the exposure comes from an international tour of duty or backpacking through the Far East.

Be specific in your thinking about your own field and what is happening globally that will shape its future:

- Can you identify three trends that will have a significant impact on your industry in the next five years?
- Do you know what new technologies might shape your industry in the next five years?
- Do you know what the global threats are to your industry or profession?

## Strategy 7: Be a compelling communicator

▶ *Can you quickly capture your listener's attention and get your message across?* ▶ *Can you use words to paint a picture, tell a story, make information vivid?* ▶ *Can you write clearly, persuasively, and with impact?* ▶ *Can you quickly establish relationships and credibility with people you have never met?* ▶ *Do you have "tone-sensitivity"? Can you understand nuance and context?* ▶ *Can you decode nonverbal cues?*

Every time you talk to someone today, you are competing for their attention with a thousand other priorities. Can you get to the point quickly? Can you tell your story in a way that captures the listener's attention? Our hit-the-ground-running culture means that we must immediately establish credibility with co-workers, project members, and clients without the benefit of yesterday's stage of getting to know someone and exchanging pleasantries. The person you are communicating or working with today may also be halfway around the world and/or from a different discipline. Can you translate what you do in a way readily understandable to someone who does not share your professional expertise?

### Give yourself feedback/get feedback

I was perplexed when a young woman I had been mentoring said she wished I gave her more feedback. From my point of view there was very little I had not commented on, discussed, or documented short of the size of her belt loops. The real problem was that she did not understand that she was getting feedback until it was labeled as feedback. It was not enough for me to say, "You may want to consider…" I had to say, "Okay, I want to give you feedback on…"

Indeed, one of the most frequent complaints of overstretched managers is that they give their staff a lot of feedback that goes largely unheard. You may be getting more feedback than you realize. At the same time, take an activist stance and do not wait for your boss to give you feedback. Note to high-maintenance types: Managers can become quickly annoyed by "needy types."

**Stay focused**
*Get to the point quickly. Capture your audience's attention by tailoring your message. Do not drown your listener in irrelevant detail.*

## Strategy 8: Find a mentor/be a mentor

▶ *Do you have someone you can go to for direction and advice?*
▶ *Is there someone you can count on to give you honest feedback on your behavior and goals?* ▶ *Do you have an advocate: someone who cares enough about your career that they will advocate on your behalf, either by coaching you or lobbying for you?*

Your mentor may be your most important career-management resource. Your own manager is too busy to provide direction, and in any case, her perspective is limited to the job you are doing. A mentor can give you advice on how to deal with tricky situations and can help you understand the politics of the organization.

A mentor is a sounding board, someone who coaches you in effective behaviors and provides insight into everything from how to handle a tricky situation to how to pitch a client to how to handle corporate politics. Sometimes she may also open doors for you, set up contacts, and act as an advocate for you. Perhaps most crucially, a mentor gives you honest feedback and provides perspective.

Successful people almost always have had one or two mentors who have helped them along the way. Revealingly, in contrast to less successful workers, they have actively sought out their mentors.

### Find a mentor
Look for someone either inside or outside your organization with a more developed career intelligence than you.

Traditionally, a mentor was older than his or her protégé. In the classic mentoring relationship, a senior manager would take on a younger, high-potential version of himself or herself (although traditionally it was a "himself"). He would take the protégé under his wing and steer him into plum assignments. Today, an older worker may be able to benefit as much from mentoring by a young employee as vice versa. Where a younger worker may learn from an older worker about "how things

### Get mentored
*Savvy career managers seek out one or more mentors. They set realistic expectations, looking to their mentor for guidance. They do not expect them to be their personal talent agent.*

often get done around here" and who the key players are, the older worker may benefit from having their traditional beliefs about work challenged by younger, irreverent colleagues.

Your mentor may be your current manager but more commonly will be:

- A previous manager.
- A manager in another area of the organization (giving you access to other areas).
- An external consultant.
- Someone you worked with on a project team with whom you developed a rapport.
- A former teacher.
- Someone you met through volunteer work.
- A family friend.

Determine how you can benefit from someone else's know-how and expertise. Start with a self-assessment. Given your longer-term interests, what are your developmental needs? Who can help you develop in these areas? Find someone who is really good at what you are weaker in. Find more than one mentor. After all, given the multiple roles we play, many people are potential sources of support.

Traditionally, in finding a mentor, people thought about "chemistry." In fact, you may be better off with someone whose approach, style, and worldview are dramatically different from yours. Take advantage of new ways of thinking about things.

Many people do not avail themselves of the help of a potential mentor because they do not want to impose on the person. However, potential mentors, far from feeling imposed upon, appreciate the recognition that they have knowledge and wisdom to share.

What should you expect in terms of demands on your mentor's time? Typically, what works well is a face-to-face or telephone meeting every month or so. This can be combined with voice and email updates.

## Career counsel

Be realistic in your expectations.

Early in my career, after having a falling-out with my boss, I ran into my mentor's office expecting to be comforted. I thought she would immediately pick up the phone and intervene on my behalf. Instead, she responded with a cool, "I'm busy now. That's life."

Do not expect a mentor to act as your personal agent—not only guiding you but also promoting your interests and marketing you into new projects or positions.

**Be generous**
*Build from your own experience. Share what you wish you had known. Open doors. Provide practical advice. Reap the emotional benefits of contributing to someone else's development.*

## Be a mentor

Do you generously provide career-related advice and support to others? Do you have one or more people in your life who consider you an important sounding board and coach?

Every year I seek out one or two talented younger women to mentor. My mentoring work is very important to me. I am not alone. Many mid-career clients say that the mentoring work they do is a critical part of their career portfolio. They value the stimulation of exchanging ideas with protégés and are proud of contributing to someone else's development. A typical comment is, "I get as much or more out of this as the person I'm mentoring." In seeking a mentor, people are looking for more than just practical guidance. They want broader emotional and psychological support from someone who genuinely cares about them. Be generous in sharing your wisdom and know-how.

## What makes a good mentor?

If you are looking for a mentor, or want to be one, consider the following characteristics of good mentors:

- They take genuine pleasure in promoting others' interests.

- They have business savvy—understanding the politics, knowing how to maneuver in tricky situations, and most importantly, anticipating possible outcomes of different strategies.

- They are not threatened by the accomplishments of their protégés but are pleased by them, even when the protégés go on to surpass them.

- They are adept at reading people and situations.

- They sense intuitively what different types of work require in terms of personal characteristics, and where different work experiences can lead.

- They understand the business and can balance its needs against the needs of the individual.

- They are sensitive to individual differences in personality and values.

- They give advice based on the other person's needs, without imposing their values.

- They welcome the opportunity to give something back to their work or profession, and to make a difference in individuals' lives.

## SELF-ASSESSMENT     **What do you want** from a mentor?

Think about the areas in which you could benefit from career support and advice. Consider behaviors you need to develop.

*What I want from a mentor:*

..........................................................................................................................
..........................................................................................................................
..........................................................................................................................
..........................................................................................................................
..........................................................................................................................
..........................................................................................................................
..........................................................................................................................
..........................................................................................................................

Who could provide what you want? It may take more than one mentor. List one or more potential mentors and what you want from them.

| Potential mentor | What I want from them |
| --- | --- |
|  |  |
|  |  |
|  |  |
|  |  |
|  |  |
|  |  |

**Achieve career freedom**

*Do not allow your career choices to be driven by debt. Develop personal savings. Put aside 10 percent of your salary, as recommended by financial planners.*

## Strategy 9: Build financial independence

▶ *Do you save 10 percent of your salary?* ▶ *Are your most important career and life decisions driven by money?* ▶ *Are you "owned" by your debt?* ▶ *If you lost your income tomorrow, would you have sufficient savings to tide you over?*

The most important source of protection you can have is knowing that you are not owned by debt. Given the temporary nature of contemporary work, you cannot make any assumptions about employment continuity, nor can you make any assumptions about income continuity. Ensure that your finances are in order so that you can make career decisions based on your needs and desires, not on financial fear.

As financial planners are fond of saying, pay yourself first by putting aside 10 percent of your income before spending on necessities and pleasure. We can take a lesson here from many post-boomers. Having grown up in a period of economic instability, and with no illusions of ever having a guaranteed corporate or government pension plan, many of them already are aggressive savers.

We can no longer rely on all of our income coming from one source. Whether you are a full-time employee or an independent contractor, you should cultivate other sources of income as a fallback for difficult times.

### Rethink your relationship to money

He is the editor of a film magazine. Advertising revenues are down and he is worried about the magazine's future. His partner is a lawyer. On good days she tolerates her work. On bad days she hates it. They are about to undertake a major renovation to their house. Sound unrealistic? Perhaps, but this is one of the most common scenarios I hear of from otherwise intelligent clients. It is always a recipe for disaster, not only in terms of their work, but also for them as a couple.

We have been socialized since birth to believe we can be happy by owning stuff. In getting control over our finances, we could take a lesson from people in the Voluntary Simplicity movement who have decided to pursue a life outside the continual invectives of buy, spend, consume. Evaluate your purchases and "skinny down." Ask yourself: What do I really need? Will redoing the kitchen really make our life better? Do we really need a new car? Is a purchase worth two months of my life energy and sweat equity?

If you are reevaluating how you are living, recognize that there are no quick and easy bromides here. If there were, then philosophers, writers, and psychotherapists would not have been wrestling with these issues for so long. That said, there are some steps you can take to bring your life back into greater harmony with your most important values:

- Carefully review your personal values. Ask yourself, "What do I really care about?" For every financial undertaking or purchase, ask yourself, "Why am I doing this? Is this meeting important needs? Will it help me in my chosen role? Will I feel better about myself? Will it make my life any richer?"

- Be ruthless in evaluating how your current lifestyle meets your real needs for a satisfied life. For example, in making a purchase, ask, "How much of my life energy is this really worth? Will I feel better about myself if I do this? Am I trying to satisfy an emotional need for status or affection? Can I satisfy this need in another way?"

- Consider the costs of living the way you are living. What are you giving up to maintain this lifestyle? (*See* Overcome career challenges, *pages 280-289.*)

- Consider downshifting if you are making significant personal sacrifices to maintain a standard of living. People who downshift are surprised by how much they gain— and how little they miss what they have given up. Indeed, they feel liberated from living with "so much stuff."

## Career counsel

Often, financial independence is in the mind of the beholder. In working with artists I have often been struck by how many of them have developed an ability to design a life that feels "rich" to them despite their continuous financial challenges. As one dancer commented, "When I feel deprived relative to my financially successful friends, I look around my loft and see beautiful things made by friends or picked up at flea markets. I see a great wardrobe of beautiful vintage clothing. It's different from what they have or can afford, but ultimately it satisfies the same need."

**Outside the box**

*Effective people take their own counsel. They develop creative solutions by listening to the input of others while maintaining an independent stance.*

## Strategy 10: Think like an outsider

▶ *Do you avoid getting sucked into "groupthink"?* ▶ *Do you challenge conventional wisdom?* ▶ *Can you be an effective team player while maintaining an independent perspective?* ▶ *Do you evaluate the currency of your skills by external standards?*

There is a paradox in contemporary business. Organizations tell people to "think outside the box," but at the same time they encourage them to be good team players and to be sensitive to the organization's culture. They are saying "think outside the box but stay inside the box."

Managing your career and performing at a high level requires balancing different imperatives. You need to be able to work effectively in groups and be sensitive to your organization's culture, but you must also be able to work independently and evaluate your work from an external perspective, rising above "groupthink." Stay wired to external perspectives. Evaluate your work in terms of best practice, not the practice of "this is how we do things around here." Avoid knee-jerk assumptions about how things should be done.

If you routinely use jargon that only someone who works in your company or work team understands, you may be losing your capacity to think independently.

As a general rule, successful people get involved in teamwork judiciously. They recognize that teamwork is valuable where the combined talents of a group can deliver a better product than an individual working alone. They do not, however, regard this way of working as good for its own sake, nor do they value consensus achieved at any cost.

Being able to think independently will become even more important as people are increasingly forced to make quick decisions without the benefit of group input. People often become successful, in fact, because they do not know how things should be done. Without the benefit of building on accumulated wisdom, they invent their own solutions.

## Strategy 11: Decide whether to specialize

▶ *Do you want to grow and develop within your specialty?* ▶ *Do you prefer to broaden rather than deepen your skills and knowledge?*

"Should I be a specialist or a generalist to succeed in my work?"

The short answer is both. You need to have strong enough specialist skills to get you in the door—something that makes you unique and puts you in a position to add value to a client.

However, that is no longer enough. Can you use those specialist skills in high-pressure environments? Can you carry out your specialist skills in teams working with people from different disciplines? Here is the question you really should be asking: "Should I be *more* of a specialist or a generalist?"

For some people, there is very little to decide. They are clearly more interested in the technical content of their work. They enjoy thinking deeply about the kinds of problems associated with their specialty. Others have strong technical skills and broader career interests. Still others prefer to play a generalist role inside or outside their profession. Consider, for example, the difference between being a specialist in recruiting and being a generalist in HR responsible for recruitment, training, and compensation.

Because of their broader skills, generalists have more flexibility than specialists, which means they have more career options. Technical expertise narrows the potential market for your services. Choosing a career as a specialist is like putting your entire investment portfolio in one stock. What if the bottom falls out on your chosen profession?

And yet, this is an era in which expertise counts. Organizations need people with in-depth skills and knowledge who can apply their skills to respond to complex challenges. As a result, good specialists in in-demand professions are a scarce resource. Organizations compete to attract them and usually treat them better than people who are more easily interchangeable.

## Career counsel

Ask yourself what you like to think about. Problems associated with your technical specialty? Would you be unhappy making a career shift into a new area? Do you see yourself, in the future, as more of an individual contributor or a manager?

If you do think you want to specialize, here is the acid test: Your skills and talents are sufficiently deep and leading-edge for you to be able to complete a sentence that sounds something like this: "I am uniquely qualified for this because I am one of a handful of people who have the depth of knowledge to…"

### Assessing yourself

**Strategies for career success**

▶ What do you want from a mentor?
*page 317*

▶ Action plan to improve your career intelligence
*page 323*

## Nourish yourself

*Put yourself at the top of agenda. Celebrate your accomplishments. Take respite in areas that are personally and spiritually gratifying. Your soul deserves it.*

## Strategy 12: Be kind to yourself

▶ *Do you remind yourself of your successes, or do you beat yourself up for things that did not work out?* ▶ *Can you live comfortably with "less than perfect" in some domains of your life, or are you constantly struggling for everything to be 100 percent?* ▶ *Do you have a community of people—friends, colleagues, family members—who appreciate you?* ▶ *Do you take time for yourself?* ▶ *Do you recognize and reward your own successes?*

The ability to celebrate your successes and know you deserve to celebrate them may well be the most important skill of all.

Nurture your relationships. Surround yourself with people who delight in your accomplishments and support you in tough times. Develop a community of trustworthy, upbeat, and kind people for intellectual stimulation and emotional support.

Set realistic expectations of what is doable. Rather than focusing on what has not been completed to some idealized concept of perfection, think about what you have achieved.

Be ruthless in evaluating your time commitments. Get rid of the tasks that do not add to your sense of well-being. Ditto for people in your life who drain you of energy. It is extraordinary how life-rejuvenating it can be to fire so-called friends. For each commitment, ask yourself, "Is this contributing to my sense of well-being? By honoring this commitment, what am I giving up?" You are paying a price if you go out with that needy friend who sucks you emotionally dry. If you do not take time for yourself, you will have no emotional resources left to fulfill any of your commitments, much less derive any satisfaction. Give yourself time to play and reflect.

You are a complex human being. There are many roles you play that give you a sense of meaning and heightened satisfaction. Be vigilant and purposeful in making sure that you play out all those roles. Above all, celebrate your successes, and be kind to yourself.

## PORTFOLIO — **Action plan** to improve your career intelligence

How can you improve your career intelligence? Review the 12 new strategies for career success. What strategies are you currently not using? For each strategy, photocopy this questionnaire and make an action plan.

*Strategy*

...................................................................................................................

...................................................................................................................

*How I will act on this strategy:*
*I will start to:*

...................................................................................................................

...................................................................................................................

*I will stop:*

...................................................................................................................

...................................................................................................................

*I will do this by:*

...................................................................................................................

...................................................................................................................

*People who can help me:*

...................................................................................................................

...................................................................................................................

*I will look for opportunities to:*

...................................................................................................................

...................................................................................................................

*Be purposeful in pursuing your vision of how you want to live and work.*

# Epilogue

You have completed a critical stage in your life journey. You know who you are and what you need in your life to have a deep sense of purpose and personal fulfillment.

You understand how to make important career and life decisions, how to face significant challenges, when to push back, when it is time to move on. You are able to find or design work that speaks to your most important values and unique talents. You know how to ensure that your work expresses who you are and how to manage your career with intelligence.

What next? You will move through many chapters in your life. Each chapter will be shaped by your growth as a human being. New values and priorities will come to the fore as old ones recede and your life circumstances change.

Each chapter will provide its own special challenges, opportunities, and adventures. Time for professional engagement, artistic pursuits, and intellectual stimulation. Time for spiritual reflection, nurturing others, and contributing to society.

You will have good years, and years that are not as good. Not every day will provide you with a deep sense of accomplishment. You will, however, be able to bounce back from reversals and to heed signs that it is time to move on to your next life chapter.

As you move forward, be thoughtful about how you are spending your life. Seek out adventures. Be engaged. Make choices that resonate at a deep emotional and intellectual level. Be purposeful in pursuing your vision of how you want to live and work. Ask yourself, "Do I feel good about my life?" After all, that is what it is all about.

## Career directory

There are many excellent resources to support you in your work search and career development, including job boards, career associations, and sources of career-management and business start-up information. Here are some to get you started.

# Organizations

### US Department of Labor: Occupational Outlook Handbook

www.bls.gov/oco

*This guide, available online, provides information on different careers and occupations, including job profiles, training and education required, prospects, employment trends, etc. It is updated biannually.*

### America's Job Bank

www.ajb.dni.us

*Maintained by the US Public Employment Service, this site links state employment-service offices and offers mainly full-time jobs.*

### The Argus Clearinghouse: Employment

www.clearinghouse.net

*As well as job-search issues, this site also addresses work–life balance and temporary or part-time work.*

### Careerbuilder, LLC

333 Research Court
Suite 200
Norcross, GA 30092
Tel: (800) 891-8880

www.careerbuilder.com

*Advice on job-seeking or starting a business, plus expert advice and online job-search information for the US and Canada.*

### The Career Practitioners' Resource Store (USA): Career Research and Testing, Inc.

P.O. Box 611930
San Jose, CA 95161
Tel: (408) 441-9100
Fax: (408) 441-9101
www.careertrainer.com

### National Career Development Association (USA)

c/o Creative Management Alliance
10820 East 45th Street
Suite 210
Tulsa, OK 74146
Tel: (918) 663-7060
Fax: (918) 663-7058
Toll-free: (866) 367-6232
www.ncda.org

*Both the above cater to career counselors but sell a mix of materials, some of which is appropriate for individuals.*

### Career Resource Center

www.careers.org/index.html

*This site has over 7,500 links to jobs, employers, newspapers, Internet newsgroups, colleges, libraries, state employment offices, business, education, and career-service professionals on the web, plus other career resources around the world.*

## Edward Lowe Foundation

P.O. Box 8

Cassapolis, MI 49031

Tel: (800) 232-5693

www.lowe.org

*The Edward Lowe Foundation is a nonprofit organization providing services and peer-learning opportunities to would-be entrepreneurs, as well as a publishing and information program and a calendar of conferences and events.*

## US Department of Labor:
## Frances Perkins Building

200 Constitution Avenue, NW

Washington, DC 20210

Tel: (866) 4-USA-DOL

www.dol.gov

# Web sites

### Canadian Career Consortium—links for job seekers

www.hrdc.gc.ca/career  (many links)

### Canadian government help for job seekers

www.careerccc.org/nav/links_e.shtm#websites

## The Careers Organization

www.careers.org

*Web site with advice for job seekers and links to other sites.*

## Execunet: The Center for Executive Careers

www.execunet.com

*An interactive network and membership organization, focusing on the job-search and career-advancement needs of executives.*

## Fast Company

www.fastcompany.com

*This site offers information on subjects including career moves, starting a business, and salary surveys. It also includes a database of articles about many global companies.*

## Jobmart

www.jobmart.com

*This site advertises posted résumés according to their relevant field.*

## Job Hunt

www.job-hunt.org

*An index of online job-hunting resources. The site also rates the resources it lists in terms of usefulness.*

## Job Hunters Bible

www.jobhuntersbible.com

*This is the online supplement to the book by Richard Nelson Bolles,* What Color Is Your Parachute? A Practical Manual for Job-Hunters

### www.JobBankUSA.com

*This is one of the best-known online recruiting sites, providing services to over five million job seekers, hiring managers, recruiters, and human-resources professionals.*

### Monster

www.monster.com
*The Monster network is a worldwide online job source.*

### www.monster.ca

*Monster.ca is a career management portal for Canada.*

### The Riley Guide: Employment Opportunities and Job Resources on the Internet

www.rileyguide.com
*This is an online index of the job-hunting resources available on the Internet, with a summary of résumé databases, and job-search guides. It also includes information on a range of subjects from résumé-building to salary guides.*

### USA JOBS

www.usajobs.opm.gov
*USA JOBS is the US government's official source for federal jobs and employment information.*

### Wetfeet: helping you make smarter career decisions

www.wetfeet.com

*The Wetfeet Insider Guides and online guide offer a broad range of career advice and information as well as job listings.*

### Workopolis

www.workopolis.com
*Workopolis is a Canadian job-search site, offering more than 30,000 jobs daily.*

## Management organizations

### American Management Association (AMA)

1601 Broadway
New York, NY 100019
Tel: (212) 586-8100
Fax: (212) 903-8168
www.amanet.org
*Educational organization offering training in the Americas, the Pacific Rim, and East Asia.*

### National Management Association

2210 Arbor Boulevard
Dayton, OH 45439
Tel: (937) 294-0421
www.nmal.org
*The National Management Association encourages development through coaching, mentoring, and certification.*

### Canadian Institute of Management (CIM)

Toronto branch:
2175 Sheppard Avenue East
Suite 310
Toronto
ON, M2J 1W8

Tel: (416) 493-0155
Fax: (416) 491-1670
www.cim.ca
*Offers training and representation to management professionals.*

## Early careers advice

### College Grad
www.collegegrad.com
*An entry-level job resource for new or recent graduates that covers subjects from general preparation to writing a résumé and negotiating a salary.*

### www.jobpostings.ca
*A student job site for Canada.*

### www.jobpostings.net
*Jobs web site for US students.*

### www.studentjobs.gov
*US government job opportunities. This is a joint project between the US Office of Personnel Management (OPM) and the US Department of Education's Student Financial Assistance office.*

## Starting a business

### US Small Business Administration
Headquarters Office
409 3rd Street, SW
Washington, DC 20416
Tel: (800) U-ASK-SBA
www.sba.gov

*The US Small Business Administration provides financial, technical, and management assistance to help start, run, and grow businesses.*

### www.firstgov.gov/Business
*Online services for businesses provided by the US government.*

# Index

## Author's acknowledgments

I am privileged to have worked with people in many organizations and professional walks and have learned from them all. Space does not permit me to acknowledge each individually for their contributions.

Thank you to the following clients, colleagues, and friends for generously sharing your professional expertise and stories as human-resources leaders, transition specialists, and life coaches: Christine Barwell, Helen Bozinovski, Heather Campbell, Carolyn Clark, Heather Faire, Doug Goold, Margo Gordon, Lauri Hillis, Michele Johnston, Sharlene Kanhai, Susannah Kelly, Ruth Kemp, Karen Lambo, Doug Lawson, Jan Lowenthal, Pam MacIntyre, Margot McKinnon, Ian McCleod, Susan Montgomery, Bill Pallett, Wayne McFarlane, Lori Pearson, Brenda Tomini, Garth, Ann, and Mark Toombs, Leslee Wilson, Sharon Wingfelder.

I owe a special debt of gratitude for substantive comments on the manuscript and endless support to Oliver Blum, Jeff Davidson, Cindy Dachuk, Alexandra Hamilton, Jane Hutcheson, Tamara Weir-Bryan, and Margaret Wente. Thank you to business associates, national and international. Also, to my fine speakers' agents and the associations and organizations they represent, for linking me up with great audiences; my literary agent, Bruce Westwood; and my editors at *The Globe and Mail*. For their contributions to this beautiful book, I appreciate enormously the special contributions of my fine editor Don Bastian, researcher Laurel Hyatt, the DK editorial and design team, including Adèle Hayward, Corinne Asghar, May Corfield, and my fabulous publisher, Stephanie Jackson.

This book could not have been written without the extraordinary help and support of my husband, Andrew Weiner, the most insightful editor, and best partner, anyone could hope for.

---

**About the author and her firm**

Dr. Barbara Moses, best-selling author and organizational career-management consultant, is president of BBM Human Resource Consultants Inc. With its head office in Canada, BBM has worked with more than 2,000 organizations in every sector of the economy worldwide to implement career-management programs.

**BBM's services and products**

- *Keynote Speeches* by Barbara Moses, Ph.D., are praised for their personal impact and tell-it-like-it-is style. Subjects include managing and retaining the new worker; benefiting from workplace trends; managing across generations; understanding motivational types; achieving work–life balance; career-proofing children; and becoming a career activist.
- *The Career Planning Workbook* is a corporate best-seller that has helped over a million people worldwide plan and manage their careers. It has served as the cornerstone of career-management programs in over 2,000 organizations.
- *The Manager's Career Coaching Guide* prepares managers for developing staff.
- *Career Advisor* is an online, internet-based career-management resource for organizations to enable staff to respond to the most important issues facing them today.
- *Career Management Workshops* are tailored to different staff groups including executives, managers, trainers, and individual contributors.

For more information on Barbara and her firm, go to:
**http://www.bbmcareerdev.com**

## Publisher's acknowledgments

Dorling Kindersley would like to thank the following for their help in producing this book:

**Editorial** Corinne Asghar, Jude Garlick, Mary Lambert, Frank Ritter **Design and Layout** Isabel de Cordova, Tracy Miles, Jenisa Patel, Simon Wilder **Jacket editor** Beth Apple **Jacket designer** Nathalie Godwin **Picture Research** Samantha Nunn, Diana Morris, Juliet Duff **Proofreader** Jane Simmonds **Indexer** Margaret McCormack

## Picture credits

The publisher would like to thank the following for their kind permission to reproduce their photographs:

1: Taxi/Getty Images/Darren Robb; 2: Taxi/Getty Images/Darren Robb; 4: The Image Bank/Getty Images/Shaun Egan. 6-7: The Image Bank/Getty Images/Ray Massey;. 8-9: The Image Bank/Getty Images/Ray Massey; 10-11: The Image Bank/Getty Images/Ray Massey; 12: The Image Bank/Getty Images/Gary Vestal; 15: Corbis/Anthony Redpath; 17: Taxi/Getty Images/Adam Smith; 18: The Image Bank/Getty Images/ Jean Luis Batt; 21: Corbis/Ariel Skelley; 22: Taxi/Getty Images/Darren Robb; 26: Corbis/Chris Collins; 28: Taxi/Getty Images/Anne-Marie Weber; 29: Corbis/Owen Franken; 30: Taxi/Getty Images/David Lees; 32: Taxi/Getty Images/Jim Cummins; 34: Taxi/Getty Images/Photomondo; 36: Corbis/Jose Luis Pelaez, Inc.; 38: Taxi/Getty Images/Katzer; 40: Taxi/Getty Images/Karin Slade; 42: Corbis/Jon Feingersh; 44: Taxi/Getty Images/Bart Geerlings; 48: The Image Bank/Getty Images/Patrick J. LaCroix; 50: Corbis/Tom Stewart; 51: Taxi/Getty Images/Ron Chapple; 56: Corbis/Bryan F. Peterson; 58: Corbis/Jose Luis Pelaez, Inc; 60: Taxi/Getty Images/Phil Boorman; 80: Corbis/Joyce Choo; 86: The Image Bank/Getty Images/Malcolm Piers; 88: Stone/Getty Images/Chuck Keeler; 92: Taxi/Getty Images/David Lees; 93: Corbis/Jon Feingersh; 94: Taxi/Getty Images/Gary Buss; 95: Corbis/Peter Beck; 96: Corbis/Jed & Kaorn Share; 97: The Image Bank/Getty Images/Romilly Lockyear; 98: Corbis/Jon Feingersh; 100: The Image Bank/Getty Images/Adrian Weinbrecht; 102: Corbis/LWA-JDC; 103: Corbis/Ronnie Kaufman; 104: The Image Bank/Getty Images/Yellow Dog Productions; 106: The Image Bank/Getty Images/Ghislain and Marie David de Lossy; 110: Corbis/William Taufic; 114: EyeWire Collection/Getty Images; 116: Taxi/Getty Images/Phil Boorman; 122: Corbis/Jon Feingersh; 128: Corbis/David Turnley; 131: Corbis/Owen Franken; 132: Corbis/Gerhard Steiner; 136: Stone/Getty Images/ Kalnzny-Thatcher; 138: Stone/Getty Images/Andreas Pollok; 139: Taxi/Getty Images/Michel Bussy; 140: The Image Bank/Getty Images/Steve Murez; 143: Corbis/Chuck Savage; 146: Taxi/Getty Images/Stuart Hughes; 148: Taxi/Getty Images/Ryanstock; 150: The Image Bank/Getty Images/David Twood Pictures; 152: Taxi/Getty Images/Michael Malyszko; 156: Corbis/Bob Krist; 164: Taxi/Getty Images/Blow Up; 166: Corbis/ LWA-Dann Tardiff; 168: Taxi/Getty Images/Paul King; 173: Taxi/Getty Images/Chabruken; 175: Superstock Ltd/Francisco Cruz; 178: Superstock Ltd/Banana Stock; 184: Corbis/Paul Barton; 186: Corbis/Rob Levine; 188: Corbis/Larry Williams; 195: Taxi/Getty Images/Rob Lang; 200: Stone/Getty Images/Frank Herholdt. 202: Corbis/LWA-Stephen Welstead; 205: Stone/Getty Images/Alexander Walter; 207: Corbis/Jose Luis Pelaez, Inc.; 208: The Image Bank/Getty Images/Stephen Darr; 210: Corbis/Rob Levine; 213: Photonica/Johner; 217: Taxi/Getty Images/V.C.L.; 222: Taxi/Getty Images/Michael Krasowitz; 224: Corbis/Jon Feingersh; 186: Corbis/Rob Levine; 208: The Image Bank/Getty Images/Stephen Darr; 230: Stone/Getty Images/Shaun Egan; 233: Stone/Getty Images/Christopher Bissell; 234: Photodisc/Getty Images/David Buffington; 236: Taxi/Getty Images/Kate Powers; 238: Photonica/David Brookover; 240: Corbis/Ronnie Kaufman. 244: Corbis/Ronnie Kaufman; 249: Corbis/Charles Gupton; 251: Taxi/Getty Images/Mel Yates; 252: Taxi/Getty Images/Denis Boissary; 254: Taxi/Getty Images/Phil Boorman; 257: Stone/Getty Images/Andreas Pollok; 259: Corbis/Jon Feingersh; 262: Corbis/Jose Luis Pelaez, Inc.; 264: Taxi/Getty Images/Charly Franklin; 266: Taxi/Getty Images/Alexander Walter; 269: The Image Bank/Getty Images/Juan Silva; 270: Corbis/Jon Feingersh; 271: Stone/Getty Images/Christopher Bissell; 272: The Image Bank/Getty Images/Marc Romanelli; : 275: The Image Bank/Getty Images/Marc Romanelli; 278: Stone/Getty Images/Howard Kingsnorth; 280: Stone/Getty Images/Zigy Kalnzny; 282: Stone/Getty Images/Andrew Errington; 286: Taxi/Getty Images/Benelux Press; 290: The Image Bank/Getty Images/Joseph Szkodzinski; 293: Corbis/George Simian; 294: Stone/Getty Images/Adrian Weinbrecht; 298: Taxi/Getty Images/Barry Rosenthal Studios; 300: Corbis/Jon Feingersh; 301: Corbis/Chuck Savage; 302: The Image Bank/Getty Images/Color Day Production. 304: The Image Bank/Getty Images/Romilly Lockyer; 305: Taxi/Getty Images/ Adam Smith; 306: The Image Bank/Getty Images/Barros & Barros; 307: Stone/Getty Images/Peter Correz; 310: Taxi/Getty Images/Chris Ryan; 311: Corbis/LWA-Dann Tarditt; 313: Powerstock Photolibrary/Zefa/Photex/Miles; 314: Corbis/Jim Cummins; 316: Stone/Getty Images/Jim Brown; 318: Robert Harding Picture Library; 320: EyeWire Collection/Getty Images; 322: The Image Bank/Getty Images/John Kelly; 324: The Image Bank/Getty Images/Shaun Egan.